Attitudes, Conflict, and Social Change

Contributors

ROBERT P. ABELSON

DAVID G. BOWERS

GEORGE M. GUTHRIE

ROBERT HELMREICH

BERT T. KING

RENSIS LIKERT

ELLIOTT McGINNIES

MARTIN T. ORNE

THOMAS F. PETTIGREW

ROBERT T. RILEY

HARRY C. TRIANDIS

WALTER WEISS

RALPH K. WHITE

PHILIP G. ZIMBARDO

Attitudes, Conflict, and Social Change

Edited by

BERT T. KING

Group Psychology Programs
Office of Naval Research
Arlington, Virginia

ELLIOTT McGINNIES

Department of Psychology
The American University
Washington, D.C.

ACADEMIC PRESS   New York and London   1972

ACADEMIC PRESS, INC.
111 Fifth Avenue, New York, New York 10003

United Kingdom Edition published by
ACADEMIC PRESS, INC. (LONDON) LTD.
24/28 Oval Road, London NW1 7DD

LIBRARY OF CONGRESS CATALOG CARD NUMBER: 73-190107

PRINTED IN THE UNITED STATES OF AMERICA

To Peggy and Amy

Contents

11.   The Pro-Us Illusion and the Black-Top Image
       Ralph K. White

List of Contributors

Numbers in parentheses indicate the pages on which the authors' contributions begin.

ROBERT P. ABELSON, Department of Psychology, Yale University, New Haven, Connecticut (19)

DAVID G. BOWERS, The Institute for Social Research, The University of Michigan, Ann Arbor, Michigan (101)

GEORGE M. GUTHRIE, The Pennsylvania State University, University Park, Pennsylvania (191)

ROBERT HELMREICH, Department of Psychology, The University of Texas at Austin, Austin, Texas (33)

BERT T. KING, Group Psychology Programs, Office of Naval Research, Arlington, Virginia (1)

RENSIS LIKERT, The Institute for Social Research, The University of Michigan, Ann Arbor, Michigan (101)

ELLIOTT McGINNIES, Department of Psychology, The American University, Washington, D.C. (1, 55)

MARTIN T. ORNE, Institute of the Pennsylvania Hospital and University of Pennsylvania, Philadelphia, Pennsylvania (55)

THOMAS F. PETTIGREW, Harvard University, Cambridge, Massachusetts (155)

ROBERT T. RILEY, Harvard University, Cambridge, Massachusetts (155)

HARRY C. TRIANDIS, Department of Psychology, University of Illinois, Champaign, Illinois (127)

WALTER WEISS, City University of New York, Hunter College, New York, New York (137)

RALPH K. WHITE, George Washington University, Washington, D.C. (211)

PHILIP G. ZIMBARDO, Department of Psychology, Stanford University, Stanford, California (211)

Acknowledgments

The editors wish to thank the following for their cooperation and assistance: The Office of Naval Research for support of the University of Maryland contract which provided for the "Symposium on Attitudes, Conflict, and Social Change" held at the University of Maryland, May 15-16, 1970; The University of Maryland, its Center for Continuing Education, and its Psychology Department for sponsorship of that symposium; the contributors who made oral presentations at the attitude symposium and who prepared the papers herein for publication; Professor Charles D. Ward for assistance in planning that symposium and for chairing one of its sessions; Drs. Glenn L. Bryan and John A. Nagay for sage counsel with respect to administrative and technical problems and (in the case of Dr. Nagay) for providing "Welcoming Remarks" for the symposium participants; Mr. Michael Daniels for helping to organize the symposium and this volume; Miss Dresda Lambert, Miss Cathy Alexander, and Mrs. Eunice Burton for secretarial assistance.

1

Overview: Social Contexts and Issues for Contemporary Attitude Change Research

Bert T. King
Office of Naval Research

and

Elliott McGinnies
The American University

By coincidence, our symposium on attitudes, social change, and intergroup conflict was conducted on the University of Maryland campus at the height of the college student upheavals following the Cambodian incursion. Some of our symposium participants had difficulty gaining access to the campus by taxi because of demonstrations along U.S. Route 1 in College Park, and all of us probably wondered whether the campus disorders would cause a premature termination of the meetings. While we fortunately completed our sessions without disruption, news bulletins provided an unexpected (but relevant?) atmosphere of tension for our scholarly scientific transactions dealing with social change, intergroup conflict, and attitude change.

In editing this volume, as in organizing the symposium on which it is based, we focused on the following interrelated topics and issues:

1. The concepts of "attitude" and "attitude change" as they are used in psychological, sociological, and political science research.
2. How people change their attitudes and behavior in response to technological change and broad social currents as well as to specific persuasive communications delivered via the mass media or within an organization or a small group.
3. The role of attitudes and their modification in social change.
4. The role of attitudes in the genesis, the processes, and the outcomes of intergroup conflict at the level of the organization, at different societal levels, and at the international level.
5. The perplexing problems involved in determining how attitudes and overt behavior relate to each other.
6. Relationships between theories of attitude change and action programs designed to change attitudes in various social, cultural, ethnic, and national groups.

7. Relationships between laboratory experiments and field research involving attitude change.
8. The directions that future attitude research might take in order to be most productive with respect to both theory development and applications.

Naturally, any single volume can hardly do full justice to such a range of topics. Nevertheless, we feel that it is important to make an effort here to trace some of the relationships among these areas. We begin, accordingly, by commenting briefly on those aspects of the current world scene which seem to have special significance for the attitude change researcher. Next, we try to identify some of the current main streams in the various disciplines that study social attitudes. Finally, we discuss some of the theoretical issues that inevitably arise either to stimulate or to plague the researcher in these areas.

THE CURRENT WORLD SCENE

Social change and social conflict may well constitute the *leitmotivs* of the 20th century. Sociologists tell us that our present rate of social change exceeds anything experienced in human history and, rather alarmingly, the rate seems to be accelerating (Moore, 1963). Regardless of what happens to the *future* rate of change, we are obviously surrounded now, if not inundated, by social change, social problems, social conflict, and drastic shifts in attitudes, opinions, and values throughout the world. Much of this social ferment stems from scientific advances and the related technological changes that have characterized the industrial revolution. The present "Second Industrial Revolution," with its emphasis on new interactions between man and machine, man and computer, and man and information systems can be expected to generate additional changes—and problems.

MODERNIZATION

The social and psychological consequences of these scientific and technological changes constitute a worldwide trend that involves the phenomenon of "modernization." The importance of modernization, in our present context, is that it encompasses pervasive changes in attitudes, opinions, values, and behavior. As an underdeveloped nation modernizes, for example, drastic changes occur in the attitudes of its citizens toward the developing nation itself as well as toward former colonial powers. Attitudes toward education, attitudes toward authority, and the prospects for an improved quality or life also become matters of prime concern.

One of the most prominent cognitive aspects of modernization is commonly labeled "the revolution of rising expectations." This rubric refers to changes not only in expectations but also in favorable or unfavorable attitudes toward the government, hopeful or pessimistic attitudes toward the future, positive or negative attitudes toward those institutions (church, state, family, and others) which are perceived as either facilitating or blocking social progress.

ATTITUDES TOWARD WORK AND LEISURE

Attitudes toward work, employers, and leisure are changing rapidly not only in the United States but abroad as well. In this country we presently see widespread questioning of the traditional "Protestant ethic," with its insistence on industrious work habits and individual responsibility. Abroad, we find pervasive questioning of the fatalistic attitude that one must perform, without complaint, whatever labor is demanded by his role or his social status. These attitude changes accompany changes in life style, such as those characterizing "beats," "hippies," and other social groups which deny (or at least deemphasize) the need for conventionally valued types of work. Other relevant behavioral and attitudinal changes involving work (in a broad sense) underlie the ferment, riots, strikes, and protests burgeoning in colleges and universities throughout the world. Here many youthful advocates of institutional change, or even revolution, justify their actions by questioning both the intellectual relevance and social utility of the "work" assigned to them by the academic organization.

Other relevant phenomena involve not a drastic social change but a culture lag consisting of the perpetuation of traditional attitudes which seem increasingly less appropriate as time passes. Many observers, for example, have pointed out the reluctance of educated elite groups in various parts of the underdeveloped world to enter vocations involving any manual tasks. In many areas where agronomists, engineers, and architects are urgently needed, we may find an inordinate proportion of college and university students majoring in the humanities or other specialties which offer little immediate prospect of employment.

Sociologist Daniel Lerner and anthropologist Stillman Bradfield, for example, have both reported reactions abroad to modern, urban, industrial forms of employment that conflict with traditional, agragrian (rural) attitudes and values. Bradfield has studied the reactions of Peruvian Indians, who migrate to urban areas where they may choose to work for only short periods of time. Having earned enough money for their immediate needs, many fail to report to work again until they have no money left.

In the United States, many prophets foresee an imminent condition in which our technological accomplishments will permit a drastically reduced work week. If this does come about, concomitant drastic changes in many of our own attitudes toward work and leisure may become necessary. In any event, an important focus of research on attitudes and attitude change will be the organizational and social setting in which work occurs. Here we need to look not only at the individual's attitudes toward work and leisure, but also at the collective attitudes of management and labor toward each other (for example, scientific and technical managers versus fiscal and accounting managers, blue-collar workers versus white-collar workers, white workers versus black workers). Among the chapters in the present volume, those by Guthrie and by Likert and Bowers both describe research programs focused on attitudes toward work within a framework of traditional behavioral patterns, organizational matrices, and social arrangements. Likert and Bowers describe primarily domestic organi-zational research (with some international implications). Guthrie describes atti-tudinal, perceptual, and behavioral responses overseas which involve a cultural lag. In this case, we find a persistence of certain attitudes and behavior which may be more appropriate to a rural economy based on scarcity than to a developing nation which needs to stress achievement and entrepreneurial risk-taking behavior.

INTERNATIONAL ATTITUDES AND BEHAVIOR

In the area of international relations, a number of psychologists have pointed out the importance of attitudes, opinions, images, and perceptions. Both Bron-fenbrenner (1961) and White (1965), for example, have stressed the mirror images of each other that national adversaries may develop. Bryant Wedge, a social psychiatrist, has published extensively on the ways that attitudes, expecta-tions, values, and related variables may influence relationships among nations (1965). Much of this type of material is conveniently summarized in Kelman's volume, *International Behavior* (1965). Published works like these testify to the importance of studying public opinion and attitudes in order to attain a fuller understanding of the forces that determine the level of international agreement or disagreement at any given point in time.

Two chapters in the present volume represent the current research being conducted by social and behavioral scientists in this area. White's chapter deals with the way that attitudes, threat perception, and images of each other relate to the behavior of international adversaries. Guthrie analyzes some of the changes in traditional attitudes, values, and behavior that form an important part of the national development process currently underway in many countries.

STUDENT ATTITUDES AND UNREST

While every generation must to some extent engage in "conflict" with its predecessor in order to gain appropriate privileges and influence, the current spate of intergenerational conflict seems unusually pervasive and rancorous. If the degree of this conflict has actually reached new levels, we might attribute this, in part, to the increasing rate of social change. In a period of rapid technological development, widespread education, and instantaneous worldwide transmission of news and information, younger individuals may well be better informed in some technical areas than older people. Many youths—as well as some older social scientists—have concluded that not only are youths better informed technically, but they are actually wiser than their elders when it comes to general issues of values, ethics, and social choice. In fact, many students now criticize the academic curriculum as "irrelevant" and take the position that those who know best (that is, youths) must bring about—through violence, if necessary—social changes that are drastic to the point of revolution. In one of the chapters, Martin Orne and Elliott McGinnies offer some interpretations of the phenomena of student unrest that have recently drawn so much attention. In his chapter, Philip Zimbardo views the effectiveness of "radical" persuasion from the viewpoint of the activist student and the political organizations he may join.

RACIAL CONFLICT, ATTITUDES, AND ECONOMIC OPPORTUNITY

The racial conflict now so prominent both in this country and abroad may well have increased in frequency as a result of both social change and legal evolution. In recent years, we have witnessed the effects of massive population changes in the United States as Negroes have increasingly moved from rural areas to urban settings. We have also observed marches, demonstrations, and riots by both blacks and white that testify vividly to the depth of intensity of the attitudes involved.

In the present volume we have included some coverage of attitudes and opinions toward minority groups as well as those attitudes manifested by the minority group members toward themselves, toward the rate of social change, and toward the prospect of future civil violence. Two of these chapters provide descriptions of research programs which have focused on the relationships between racial attitudes and racial behavior. Both of them make reference to a combination of sociological and psychological variables. Thus, Harry Triandis invokes the more sociological concepts of norms and values in order to explain interracial phenomena. Thomas Pettigrew and Robert Riley examine both attitudes and voting behavior as predictors of the course of desegregation in the South.

Problems involved in providing economic opportunity and social welfare obviously involve not just blacks and whites, but various other subcultures: Indians, Chicanos, the Appalachian poor, and urban poor people in general. Vocational-skill training apparently will not suffice for such groups. Rather, those preparing for better economic opportunities probably must acquire certain kinds of attitudes, values, and expectations if they are really to advance economically and socially. Hence, we need to know more about the relative importance for such advancement of strictly vocational skills (for example, typing, running a lathe, operating a computer) as opposed to those attitudes that relate to work. How important is it that a worker have favorable attitudes toward his supervisory personnel? What happens when the economically deprived worker develops job skills but lacks the social skills and attitudinal dispositions that typically determine social acceptance or rejection? If such attitudes and social skills are critically necessary, how can they best be inculcated and how fast can we expect this learning process to occur? How do the black person's attitudes toward himself and toward his race affect his performance *vis-à-vis* whites in the job or organizational context? Should we wait for the deprived individual to alter these attitudes and self-images more or less spontaneously, or can we facilitate this process by suitable education and training? These, of course, are just a few of the kinds of questions we must answer with the help of future research on attitudes and ethnic conflict. The chapters by Guthrie, Triandis, and Weiss describe some current research developments that point in the direction of future progress in this area.

DIFFERENCES AMONG DISCIPLINES

The disciplines of psychology, sociology, and political science have attacked problems involving attitudes and opinions in characteristically different manners. They diverge in their focus (for example, "attitudes" in the case of psychology, versus "opinions," which are emphasized more within sociology and political science), in their methodology (for example, field studies versus laboratory experiments), and in the relative degree of interest they show in building general theories and discovering the general principles of attitude change as opposed to study of the determinants of particular attitudes, opinions, and social issues.

Certainly social psychologists have awarded a central position to the concepts of attitude and attitude change. In the *Psychological Abstracts* each year, for example, we find hundreds of entries under "attitude" and related headings. McGuire (1969) states: "The growing interest in attitudes over the past 15 years has by now made it the most popular area of social psychological research [p. 138]."

In psychological treatments of attitudes and attitude change, we discern a common denominator of preoccupation with: (*a*) principles, laws, and theories, and (*b*) psychological processes and variables that are inside the subject's skull and not directly observable. In this respect, the typical psychological investigation of attitudes and opinions has varied, in predictable ways, from that conducted in the other social and behavioral sciences. Sociology and political science, in particular, tend to turn away from processes inside the head and focus on socially relevant, observable behavior (for example, buying a product, voting in an election, or engaging in social relationships with members of minority groups).

Sociologists seem to devote less attention to attitude and attitude change *per se* than do psychologists. The *Handbook of Modern Sociology*, a comprehensive survey of current sociological activities by Faris (1964), contains no chapter heading at all which includes the word "attitude" or even "opinion." (It does, however, contain chapters on "mass communication" and on "race and ethnic relations," which touch on attitudes and opinions.) This contrasts with the *Handbook of Social Psychology* by Lindzey & Aronson (1968), which contains two chapters whose titles include the words "attitude" or "attitude change."

The field of political science presents a situation more like that in sociology than in psychology. Here, too, we find relatively little evidence of concern with "attitudes" or "attitude change" *per se*, although we do find a good deal of interest in public opinion and in survey research on opinions, preferences, expectations, and even values. When political scientists do study opinion, it is usually "public opinion" and is typified by a concern with large groups or masses of people. Political science also tends to concern itself with the relationships between public opinion, on the one hand, and other variables pertinent to political structure and political processes, on the other.

As a case in point, consider the research currently being conducted by the political scientist H. Bradford Westerfield.[1] One of his major current interests is analyzing the domestic and international influences shaping the foreign policy decision-making process in Australia, especially those affecting Australia's relationships with the United States and with the United Kingdom. In order to better understand such decision-making, Westerfield studies both public opinion (as manifested in available Australian public opinion surveys) and elite opinion. The latter he measures by means of content analysis of Australian parliamentary debates and periodicals. These opinion measures are being considered, however, not in isolation but in conjunction with data on political parties, interest groups, and religious and ethnic groups. A crucial part of Westerfield's analyses involves the attempt to discover what causal relationships exist between the opinion data and both national and international political events. Furthermore, he concerns himself with temporal relationships between the opinion data and social, economic, and political developments—do opinions lead (or precede) political events or do they lag behind them?

[1] Personal communication.

What we want to stress here is Westerfield's emphasis on relating opinion (or attitude) data to objective aspects of the social environment, or to what many would refer to as "behavior." This emphasis (which we believe characterizes much sociological and political science research on attitudes and opinion) contrasts with the apparent emphasis in much psychological research on opinions and attitudes as sufficiently interesting in themselves. Certainly this is a defensible decision on the part of the psychologist. However, we might raise the question as to whether much psychological research on attitudes and opinions could not benefit from a greater concern with the relationships between these theoretical dispositions and those behavioral events in the natural environment to which they are related.

The chapters by Abelson and by Helmreich bear particularly on these points. Abelson considers relationships between attitudes (an internal predisposition) and observable behavior and asks whether we really need the seemingly mentalistic concept of "attitude." Helmreich points up some of the implications of a researcher's choice of either laboratory experiments or field-oriented studies for the social relevance of his scientific labors.

SOME THEORETICAL CONSIDERATIONS

While the current scene in social psychology reveals a great deal of empirical agreement, it also reflects divergences among theories of attitudes. At base, the theoretical controversies stem from how one conceptualizes an attitude. Traditionally, attitudes have been viewed as predispositions to behave in a characteristic manner with respect to specified social objects or classes of such objects. Ultimately, as Berscheid and Walster (1969) have commented, a "predisposition to act" refers to the kinds of predictions that we make about someone's behavior. Such predictions, of course, are based on whatever information we have about his past behavior. For example, individuals have been described as having negative attitudes toward Mexicans or Irishmen, or favorable attitudes towards "mother," "the home," or "the flag." In order to so describe a person, we must have observed his verbal or nonverbal behavior in the presence of these social entities or their symbolic representations.

A serious problem with this view has been that the persons so described do not always behave consistently toward the objects of their attitudes. In many instances, the behavioral discrepancies consist of those responses that the individual makes on an attitude scale or inventory, on the one hand, and the behaviors that he manifests in the actual presence of those social objects toward which his verbal attitudes are presumably directed, on the other. For example, a person who replies to the items on an attitude questionnaire in a manner reflective of prejudice toward the members of a minority ethnic group may actually behave quite civilly toward individuals from that group when he encounters them personally. Or, he may not shrink from social contact with certain individuals, although he would deny them the right to vote. Such apparent inconsistencies and even contradictions between a person's attitudes and his behavior in specific situations has led some social theorists to define an attitude simply as a class of performances that is under the control of a specified social referent—much as any other learned behavior (McGinnies, 1970). Situational control rather than cognitive mediation is stressed in this behavioral concept of attitude. (We should note that at least one of the contributors to the present volume, Abelson, disagrees with this view.)

Another feature of attitudes that has often been accepted with little question is their function not only to direct but to *energize* behavior. Attitudes thus have been given a dynamic as well as a structural function. The problem here is essentially the one that confronts any theorist who deals with the concept of motivation, namely, that of effectively giving scientific credibility to a state of the organism that is inferred rather than observed. Relatively few psychologists have maintained that attitudes have drive or motivational force; most have been content to assign attitudes a directive function.

Even if one considers an attitude to be in the nature of an intervening variable, having a purely directive function in behavior, it is still necessary to anchor it to observable antecedent and consequent conditions. The antecedents, of course, would include those features of the individual's history that have led to the disposition in question, as well as those immediate features of the environment that have prompted its expression. Thus, an attitude toward Negroes has its genesis in the family and other early social contacts, and its manifestation is prompted by actual Negroes or by references to Negroes. One assumes that the disposition toward Negroes (or any other social referent) is latent in the individual's behavioral repertoire until aroused by some relevant stimulus. In the final analysis, however, an attitude, as McGuire (1969) concedes, is operationally defined in terms of observable responses.

The observable responses from which we infer the existence of an attitude are, for the most part, reactions to items on a questionnaire or attitude scale. Whether or not such verbal responses to verbal stimuli correlate with nonverbal performance of the same general class (that is, approach or avoidance, acceptance or rejection) is often a moot question. A number of investigators have reported examples of discrepancies between what an individual *says* and what he *does* with respect to an attitudinal object. For example, while traveling about the country with a Chinese couple in 1934, the sociologist LaPiere was refused service only once during hundreds of stops. When contacted later by mail, however, over 90% of those proprietors who replied alleged that they would be unwilling to serve Chinese patrons (LaPiere, 1934). Similarly, Kutner, Wilkins, and Yarrow (1952) found that not one of eleven restaurants in a northeastern city would make reservations for a mixed party of whites and Negroes, although the very same establishments had earlier served without delay or unpleasantness two white women and a Negro companion. The white members of a labor union that had a record of promoting job equality for Negroes were reported by Lohman and Reitzes (1954) to have organized themselves to prevent Negroes from purchasing property in their neighborhood. Thus, a discrepancy between *verbal* and *action* attitudes, as Green (1954) has termed them, commonly occurs.

Such inconsistencies call into question the validity of paper-and-pencil devices for measuring attitudes. More specifically, they suggest that the attitudes, either verbal or nonverbal, that may be measured under laboratory or testing conditions will not necessarily be emitted under less artificial and contrived circumstances. The behaviors that we measure so carefully in the setting of a social psychological experiment frequently become evanescent in the outside world, where the social consequences of revealing a particular disposition are considerably more profound.

Research in a "field" setting, of course, presents fewer social artificialities than those ordinarily found in laboratory studies. But what is gained in realism or relevance is frequently lost through inadequate control of the variables under investigation. It is simply not possible in most instances to manipulate with precision outside of the laboratory those factors that determine social outcomes. Some recent and encouraging steps in this direction have been taken recently, however. Brock (1965), for example, performed an experiment in a retail paint department, and Miller and Levy (1967) manipulated an insult "inadvertently" delivered to women in shopping plazas. Still other investigators (see Piliavin, Rodin, & Piliavin, 1969) have studied altruistic, or "helping," behavior on subway trains in New York City. Such attempts as these to manipulate the independent variables of social psychological research in naturalistic settings strengthens the *external validity* of our generalizations.

To a great extent, as Karlins and Abelson (1970) have observed, we have studied the handy college student. They conclude:

> Too frequently, our experiments are conducted within the environs of a psychology department or within the confines of an academic classroom where associations with the intellect, grades, and other aspects of the student-teacher relationship are paramount. We think that the time is past due for corroborating findings on sophomores with findings on other segments of the public [p. 159].

The problems that beset the social psychologist in his interactions with student subjects have become painfully obvious in recent years. It is now clear that the investigator no longer can approach his subjects as if they were passive objects of his experimental manipulations. In fact, they seem to actively generate hypotheses about the purposes of the experiment and to react accordingly. The mere fact that students know they are in an experiment, as Martin Orne has emphasized, disposes them to cooperate in tasks that they would not for a moment consider doing otherwise (for example, doing pushups, sorting meaningless scraps of paper). They frequently react in terms of what Orne has termed the "demand characteristics" of the situation, that is, in response to what they have told themselves about the probable goals of the experimenter. They may also suffer from what Rosenberg has called "evaluation apprehension," or the suspicion that the experimenter's procedures are designed to ferret out something about their hidden personality characteristics. Finally, in addition to these uncontrolled sources of variance, there is the subtle interaction between experimenter and subject that yields what Rosenthal has termed an "experimenter effect," whereby subjects often behave in the way that the experimenter predicted they would behave.

Nowhere do these several considerations appear more painfully evident than in research on persuasion and attitude change. Hundreds of articles have appeared in recent years dealing with certain "nonobvious" predictions based on the assumption that an "insufficient reward" for compliance with the experimenter's request to engage in behavior inconsistent with one's attitudes results in greater attitude change than would occur under conditions of ample reward. This manipulation of the magnitude of an incentive offered for compliance in a disagreeable task has been alleged by Festinger (1957) and his colleagues to influence the amount of "cognitive dissonance" aroused by the compliant behavior. Presumably, the greater the aroused dissonance, the greater will be the amount of attitude change that occurs as a vehicle of dissonance reduction. According to this line of reasoning, a small incentive provides less justification to the individual for engaging in counterattitudinal behavior, particularly if he believes that he has chosen freely to comply. Thus, by inducing greater dissonance, a small incentive generates more attitude change than would be prompted by a larger incentive. Not surprisingly, this logic runs counter to what one would predict on the basis of reinforcement theory, where magnitude of reward for a particular behavior has generally been found to increase the frequency of that behavior.

We cannot undertake here to do more than take note of this area of research and controversy which is described in detail in several chapters of *Handbook of Social Psychology* (Lindzey & Aronson, 1968). We simply wish to point out that a great deal of experimental skill and sophistication have been unleashed in pursuit of empirical answers to the many questions and issues that have been raised. In fact, this is one instance in which the complexities of the experimental manipulations may have been counterproductive, at least as far as providing a basis for replication in other laboratories is concerned. Zajonc (1968) has commented provocatively on this matter as follows:

> The conceptual bravado of dissonance psychologists has been accompanied by an appropriately cavalier approach to experimentation. Experiments on dissonance have almost without exception been extremely imaginative and engaging; so much so in fact, that one simply finds it difficult to resist their implications or to ignore their results. But researchers on dissonance have not exactly been compulsive about following standard procedures. Experiments in the area of counterattitudinal behavior, for example, are all extremely complicated, and their replications and extensions are never faithful in reproducing previous conditions. Each experiment uses different attitude issues, different attitude measures, and different means to induce subjects to make counterattitudinal statements. Many of these experimental manipulations involve the resources of a minor theatrical production. There are no two postdecision experiments that involve decisions between the same sets of alternatives. These observations apply equally to research that favors the theory of dissonance and to research that attacks it [p. 390].

The present volume, and the symposium on which it is based, respond to what appears to be a rather severe set of limitations inherent in the type of attitude research ordinarily conducted in a university laboratory. Of course, careful, controlled study of the variables that underlie attitude formation and change should continue under laboratory conditions, but these efforts can quite usefully be supplemented by exploratory investigation under "field" conditions. The advantages of field studies and critical analysis of social phenomena that cannot readily be brought under experimental control in the laboratory are several: for one thing, they point out the directions that precise, controlled laboratory investigations might fruitfully pursue; for another, they sharpen our awareness of the gap still to be bridged between behavior theory and its effective application to the enrichment of human life. Recent history should have convinced us that the distinction between pure and applied research is largely semantic. Research findings that have any relevance to the human condition eventually and inevitably are implemented for political or other purposes. The social psychologist should be the last to shrink from this realization and the first to view his own domain from the perspective of its actual or potential relevance in the world beyond his laboratory windows. We hope that the contents of this volume, in small measure, will advance this viewpoint.

REFERENCES

Berscheid, E., & Walster, E. Attitude change. In J. Mills (Ed.), *Experimental social psychology*. Toronto: Collier-Macmillan, 1969.

Brock, T. C. Communicator-recipient similarity and decision-change. *Journal of Personality and Social Psychology*, 1965, 1, 650-653.

Bronfenbrenner, U. The mirror image in Soviet-American relations: A social psychologist's report. *Journal of Social Issues*, 1961, 17, 45-56.

Faris, R. E. L. (Ed.) *Handbook of modern sociology*. Chicago: Rand McNally, 1964.

Festinger, L. *A theory of cognitive dissonance*. New York: Harper, 1957.

Green, B. F. Attitude measurement. In G. Lindzey (Ed.), *Handbook of social psychology*, Vol. I. Reading, Massachusetts: Addison-Wesley, 1954, pp. 335-369.

Karlins, M., & Abelson, H. I. *How opinions and attitudes are changed*. New York: Springer Publ., 1970.

Kelman, H. C. (Ed.). *International behavior*. New York: Holt, 1965.

Kutner, B., Wilkins, C., & Yarrow P. R. Verbal attitudes and overt behavior involving racial prejudice. *Journal of Abnormal and Social Psychology*, 1952, 47, 649-652.

La Piere, R. T. Attitudes vs. actions. *Social Forces*, 1934, 13, 230-237.

Lindzey, G., & Aronson, E. (Eds.), *Handbook of social psychology*. Reading, Massachusetts: Addison-Wesley, 1968.

Lohman, J. D., & Reitzes, D. C. Deliberately organized groups and radical behavior. *American Sociological Review*, 1954, 19, 342-344.

McGinnies, E. *Social behavior: A functional analysis*, Boston: Houghton-Mifflin, 1970.

McGuire, W. J. The nature of attitudes and attitude change. In G. Lindzey & E. Aronson (Eds.), *Handbook of social psychology*. Vol. III. Reading, Massachusetts: Addison-Wesley, 1969.

Miller, N., & Levy, B. H. Defaming and agreeing with the communicator as a function of emotional arousal, communicator extremity, and evaluation set. *Sociometry*, 1967, 30, 158-175.

Moore, E. *Social change*. Englewood Cliffs, New Jersey: Prentice-Hall, 1963.

Piliavin, I. M., Rodin, J., & Piliavin, J. A. Good samaritanism: An underground phenomenon? *Journal of Personality and Social Psychology*, 1969, 13, 289-299.

Wedge, B., & Muromcew, C. Psychological factors in Soviet disarmament negoti-
ation. *Journal of Conflict Resolution*, March 1965, 9, No. 1, 18-36.

White, R. K. Images in the context of international conflict: Soviet perceptions
of the U.S. and the USSR. In H. C. Kelman (Ed.), *International Behavior*.
New York: Holt, 1965.

Zajonc, R. B. Cognitive theories in social psychology. In G. Lindzey & E.
Aronson (Eds.), *The handbook of social psychology*, Vol. 1, Reading,
Massachusetts: Addison-Wesley, 1968, pp. 320-411.

Part One
The Concept
and Role
of Attitudes

In the next chapter, Abelson confronts insightfully the relationship between attitudes and behavior. It is his contention that the concept of attitude is not adequately handled by assigning it to a subprovince of learning theory. He points out that no systematic relationship has been established between how much a person learns from a persuasive communication and how much his related attitudes are found to change. Moreover, the correlation that one would expect between behavior and professed attitudes is frequently low or absent. Instead of supporting a position of reductionism, in which our attention would be directed exclusively toward behavior, Abelson prefers to think of attitudes and behavior as being separate conceptual entities, each deserving scrutiny. One is reminded here of the "psychophysical parallelism" of Leibniz, where "mind" and "body" were conceived as occupying different tracks but going in the same direction; except that in the case of attitudes and behavior the tracks do not always seem to be parallel.

In effect, Abelson presents a compelling argument for reexamining the essentially phenomenological aspects of attitude. He argues that people "know how they feel," that they moderate their feelings on the basis of new information, and that their attitudes, so modified, serve as guides to behavior. When he argues that situations must strongly encourage the attitude-behavior relationship, however, he comes very close to suggesting that attitudinal behavior is, in fact, situationally determined—that anticipated consequences of a performance determine its occurrence or nonoccurrence. The reader may decide for himself whether such an interpretation is best approached from a cognitive or a behavioral standpoint. Certainly the often perplexing juxtaposition of the verbal and nonverbal components of attitudinal behavior compels one to distinguish at least between the overt and covert manifestations of an attitude. As Abelson puts it (see page 25), "We are very well trained and very good at finding reasons for what we do, but not very good at doing what we find reasons for." He concludes his analysis with the suggestion that the impact of information on attitudes be reexamined. The problem of "selective exposure" enters here, with the evidence for preference of supportive over nonsupportive information being equivocal, at best. Nearly everyone assumes that attitudes can be changed (certainly politicians and advertisers believe so), but we actually know relatively little about how relevant information or simply sheer exposure operate to effect such change. Attitudes probably are necessary—at least they are an integral part of our psychological glossary—but their status in behavior theory remains a problem. Abelson's discussion highlights this problem and offers proposals for its resolution.

Concern with the definition and conceptual status of attitudes, however, has not deterred psychologists from embarking on extensive programs of research into the factors that are involved in attitude change. The chapter by Helmreich is concerned primarily with the impact of stress on an individual's reactions to persuasion. It is generally conceded that attitudes are characterized by cognitive (verbal), emotional (autonomic), and behavioral (performance) components. Probably more research has been directed toward the cognitive and behavioral aspects than toward the emotional dimension. As Helmreich points out, the research dealing with attitude change under the impact of fear-arousing communications has not always yielded consistent findings. Some investigators have suggested that the relationship between fear arousal and attitude change takes the form of an inverted U, with maximum influence being exerted by communications that are only moderately threatening. Others, including Helmreich himself, have found a generally positive relationship between level of fear arousal and acceptance of a persuasive argument—even one unrelated to the source of threat.

Helmreich's specific concern in this chapter is with the interactive effects of emotional arousal, feelings of self-esteem, and credibility of a communicator on attitude change. Previous studies had shown that individuals under stress are more than normally disposed to accept suggestions made by authority figures. But it turns out that this generalization must be qualified according to the *degree* of stress imposed upon the subject. Somewhat surprisingly, Helmreich and his colleagues discovered that, while the usual relationship between communicator credibility and persuasiveness holds under conditions of low stress, the induction of high stress leads to greater attitude change in response to a communicator of ostensibly lower credibility, or prestige. He postulates that these relationships may be understood in terms of a lowering of self-esteem that occurs in individuals under stress. This, as he elaborates in this chapter, involves an appeal to social comparison theory. "Agreeing with a peer," he states, "may bolster the self-concept by decreasing feelings of difference and augmenting feelings of being part of a 'normal' group" (page 41).

Helmreich concludes his discussion by suggesting that the traditional laboratory approach to certain social psychological problems may have severe limitations of both an ethical and a practical nature. His portrayal of "the college freshman reluctantly participating in a psychology experiment for credit" strikes a resonant note with many of us who have imposed our research requirements upon just such a captive population. His arguments for extending research on social behavior into the natural environment are being echoed by an increasing number of social psychologists.

2

Are Attitudes Necessary?

Robert P. Abelson
Yale University

In the social psychological laboratory there have recently emerged a number of phenomena which cast considerable doubt upon the role which attitudes are typically assumed to play in human social behavior. Furthermore, a number of older laboratory and field results which have long been puzzling and embarrassing can be better understood if we adopt a new skepticism.

Before launching into any kind of assault on the usual conception of attitudes, I should first explain what I take this conception to be, and I should also promise that I will try to compensate for any damage done to this comfortable old friendly conception by supplying new ideas for reconstructing it. The work to be discussed is drawn from many sources, partly from my own research and experience, but mainly from students, colleagues and social psychologists at large. My involvement in this topic represents the culmination of a crisis of discrepancy between what I always thought I believed about attitudes and what the facts seem to be trying to say.

Historically, attitude definitions have covered a great deal of conceptual territory, ranging from Allport's (1935) mentalistic "... state of readiness ... exerting a dynamic influence upon the individual's response to all objects and situations to which it is related [p. 810]" to Campbell's (1950) behavioristic "consistency in response to social objects." Haggling over the most appropriate definition seems to have died out, but there presently exists a consequential theoretical bipolarity. Some psychologists would like to regard the attitude field as a special case potentially subsumed by learning theory. Thus, attitudes toward Swedish girls, spinach, Negroes, air pollution, or Richard Nixon would be seen basically as approach or avoidance tendencies—as learned response habits to stimulus classes, subject to well-known laws of conditioning and reinforcement. In this view, slight theoretical extension (but only slight) would be required to handle the fact that experience with the stimulus classes is often symbolic rather than direct.

This reductionist point of view has some currency in the psychological literature (Staats, 1968; Lott & Lott, 1968; Weiss, 1968), but is not the general theoretical position of social psychologists. The learning theory concept of attitude may well be essentially correct in certain cases, but these are the least interesting from the social psychologist's standpoint. The subtleties of racial attitudes and behaviors—for example, the common tendency for whites to display exaggerated politeness to individual blacks in mundane social contacts— seem hardly explicable on the basis of simple approach or avoidance tendencies. Also, linguistic and cognitive factors are of intrinsic interest.

The more mainstream social psychological view of attitudes (McGuire, 1968a) is one which recognizes closely interrelated affective, cognitive, and conative components, and which interests itself deeply with the details of cognitive structure and persuasive communication—that is, with attitude as a mediating construct with a complicated life of its own. The componential, mediational view is central not only for most social psychologists, but also for the colloquial view of attitudes: you knowingly feel a certain way about something, and this determines how you act about that something when you get the opportunity.

Alongside the notion that attitudes mediate behavior, there is the companion notion that information modulates attitudes: that the direction of the attitude is determined by the information, old and new, available to us about the properties of the object. Thus, a commonly accepted strategy for changing an attitude is to present the individual with new information with value implications tending to reverse the direction of the original attitude. It is well realized that this informational strategy does not always work, especially when the original attitude is strongly held, but that information typically guides and regulates attitudes is hardly ever questioned (except perhaps in a simple conditioning model approach which abolishes the cognitive aspect of the attitude construct altogether).

We are ready now to begin a querulous review of some peculiar findings in the attitude literature. One of the most aggravating peculiarities is one of the oldest. In many of the early studies of the Yale Attitude Change Program it was standard procedure to give brief information retention tests to experimental subjects following exposure to informative persuasive communications, along with measures of attitude change. It was the supposition of the Yale group that while learning the content of the communication would not guarantee that it would be accepted, one ought to find that individuals who did not absorb or remember the information in the communication would tend to be far less persuaded by it. Thus, one would expect a positive correlation between information retention and attitude change. No such positive correlation was typically found across experimental conditions, however; instead, the correlation was essentially zero in several studies (Hovland, Janis, & Kelley, 1953, pp. 37, 38,

231). This failure was, and still is, rationalized as due to the restriction on range of intelligence among the usual collegiate samples of subjects. It is assumed that almost everyone in a homogeneously bright group adequately comprehends the persuasive message (retention failures being essentially minor and capricious), and therefore degree of information absorption exerts no leverage on the degree of persuasion. Still, this zero correlation remains annoying, and it has been obtained repeatedly in more recent studies by Greenwald (1968), by Watts and McGuire (1964), and others.

Another more well-publicized experimental failure pertaining to the attitudinal role of information concerns the so-called "selective avoidance principle." It is assumed in Festinger's (1957) cognitive dissonance theory that opinion disagreement with other individuals is dissonance-arousing and that individuals will act so as to avoid dissonance arousal; therefore, it should follow that individuals will avoid exposure to viewpoints that they know in advance are contrary to their own. There should be a motivated "tuning out" of the other side of the argument even before it begins, says dissonance theory. In fact, the experimental evidence for the existence of this effect is abysmally poor. In study after study, no selective avoidance result has been found, and in their review of the literature, Freedman and Sears (1965) conclude that there is no empirical evidence indicating a general psychological preference for exposure to supportive over nonsupportive information. Various explanations have been offered for this failure, chiefly that certain positive aspects of anticipated contrary information such as utility, novelty, or challenge may override its negative role as potential enemy of personal attitudes (Berscheid & Walster, 1969, pp. 129-142). Also, it is generally agreed by critics and supporters of the selective avoidance postulate alike that in the world of mass media there does exist some tendency toward greater exposure to supportive than nonsupportive information. The audience that hears a message tends already to agree with it. However, this is apparently (Sears, 1968) a sociological, rather than a psychological, phenomenon, having to do with the largely accidental mechanisms by which audiences are recruited. That is, the potentially agreeable audience has a much greater opportunity to be exposed due to better advance notice and more subcultural pressure than the disagreeable audience. With equal opportunity, it is probable that there would be equal exposure. McGuire (1968b) has summed up the state of affairs in this area by commenting: "In view of the paucity of supportive findings, it is rather touching to witness the tenacity with which the selective avoidance 'principle' has been asserted early and late by many behavioral scientists [p. 797]."

I suspect that what may be fundamentally wrong with the selective avoidance postulate is the hidden assumption that information may virtually compel an unwanted change of attitude following exposure to it, rather like contracting the Hong Kong flu. One wonders whether information is ordinarily so powerful a change agent. Indeed, if information absorbtion did not typically mediate attitude change, then there would be no reason for people who would rather not change attitudes to avoid exposure to contrary information. It might be amusing to hear the other side of an argument, or permit one to work up a hearty good sweat of indignation, but hardly so threatening as to be necessary to avoid it.

An unpublished survey study Michael Kahn and I conducted on commuter trains a few years ago enforces my growing conviction that individuals are capable of being marvelously impervious to contrary argumentation. During the 1963 New York City newspaper strike, an anomaly occurred by which the liberal *New York Post* was for several weeks the only regular newspaper on the news stands. All the afternoon commuting bankers and businessmen accustomed to reading the conservative *New York World Telegram and Sun* or the very conservative *Journal American* (remember?) were first deprived of their usual fare and then offered the presumably offensive substitute of the nauseatingly liberal *New York Post*. In fact, the *New Yorker* had a cartoon of a carload of portly, vested types all reading the New York Post, with one disgruntled gentleman indignantly proclaiming, "Who the hell *is* this Max Lerner?"

During and also following this period, we had a survey organization distribute questionnaires to a sample from this beleagured commuter population. We wanted to know whether the group newly reading the Post was more liberal than their colleagues choosing not to read the *Post*, and second, whether the enforced *Post* readers would become more liberal afterwards. The answers were reasonably clear. There was virtually no political difference between *Post* adopters and nonadopters. People deciding to read the *Post* were generally those who claimed that they missed a newspaper more, that they had a reading habit to be served. Thus, as many analysts of mass media have known for a long time, it is the utility and entertainment value of the media rather than informational or ideological content that determines exposure (see Stephenson, 1967). Also, those who did temporarily adopt the *Post* displayed no change toward greater liberalism on attitude questions asked of them following the end of the newspaper strike. The exposure had no apparent ideological effect.

I would like now to turn to the attitude-behavior relationship by briefly reviewing an assortment of studies which cast grave doubt on the straightforwardness of the connection between attitude and behavior.

First, there are several catchy studies in which people are found to behave in ways that they themselves find surprisingly contrary to their own assumed values. In the classic Asch (1956) study, many people conform to the false group consensus which belies their own senses. In the classic Milgram (1963) study, a majority of subjects deliver apparently very dangerous electric shocks to an apparently vulnerable victim on the bland instruction of the experimenter. In recent studies of "bystander effects" by Latane and Darley (1970), subjects are found with great frequency to be unable to bring themselves to help victims in ambiguous distress situations, despite strong internal feelings that perhaps they ought to.

Turning to another area, a great number of studies have shown that behavior and professed attitudes toward Negroes are often quite discrepant. Incidentally, this is more than a matter of deception of interviewers—self-deception seems involved too. In a fairly recent study by Linn (1965), many women were quite surprised and agitated when they found they were unable to behave as liberally as they thought they should.

Recent studies in behavior therapy, where the therapist tries to relieve the patient of simple phobias, suggest that there may be two quite disparate modes of relief. Reassuring practice sessions with the imagined phobic objects (such as snakes, spiders, or swimming pools) result in a lessening of anxiety in imagination, but not with the real objects. Only reassuring behavior toward the real objects improves the ability to approach them. The behavioral and imaginal systems seem to work independently (Sherman, 1969). I have in mind here a series of studies on so-called misattribution therapy. Valins and Ray (1967) produced decreased avoidance of snakes among snake phobics without changes in reported fear of snakes; Davison and Valins (1969) produced increased shock tolerance without changes in reported painfulness of the shocks; Storms and Nisbett (1970) produced reported earlier sleep onset in insomniacs without differences in subjective reports of suffering; and so on.

If we look at studies of behavior change as a predicted consequence of attitude change, there is a rash of disconcerting studies. Experiments by Janis and Feshbach (1953), Leventhal and Niles (1964), and many others on fear appeals concerning dental hygiene, smoking, and other health-related topics have typically turned up different patterns of results for change of attitude toward the health danger than for change in actual preventive behavior. Some people are apparently persuaded, but do nothing about it. Others do something about the danger even though they do not seem persuaded. A similar mishmash has turned up in separate persuasion studies concerning toilet training practices (Maccoby, Maccoby, Romney, & Adams, 1961, as amplified by Festinger, 1964), breast feeding and rooming in with the newborn baby (Mazen & Leventhal, in press), the ostracism of an experimentally obnoxious fellow Jew (Iwao, 1963), and many other issues.

We have now arrived at the valley of theoretical despond, the most depressing place in the narrative. I have severely questioned whether information has any effect upon attitudes and whether attitudes have any effects upon behavior. This conceptually morbid theme, however entertaining it may be, is, of course, not original with the present author. In a perceptive analysis a decade ago, Campbell (1961) pointed out that unsophisticated conceptualizations of attitudes and behaviors have led us to expect more consistency than is either observed or is reasonable to observe. In his parting message before leaving the field of social psychology, Festinger (1964) explored the meaning of the dismal correlation between attitude change and behavior change. Recently, Smith (1969) has said:

> Currently stylish social-psychological theory makes much of a presumed strain toward consistency among a person's beliefs and feelings, or between his attitudes and behavior. But it would be naive to count very much on such a tendency . . .to bring people's behavior into line with their moral principles. The whole history of human frailty scores against such a result [p. 400].

Thus, a number of social psychologists have sounded appropriate warnings, but until recently, such cautionary communications seem not to have been generally persuasive. Now perhaps the trend will be for complacency on the attitude-behavior issue to be supplanted by panic. The unsettling question of my title, "Are attitudes necessary?," has its skeptical parallel in the personality field (Mischel, 1968) where one might almost ask, "Is personality necessary?"

But surely we are not ready to give up. We feel that somewhere in social psychology, to say nothing of life, there must be a place for human beings who know how they feel, who moderate their feelings on the basis of what they newly learn, and who guide intentional action on the basis of the resulting attitudes. In fact, I do believe that attitude is a useful concept and that it can be brought in touch with reality. But if such a model exists, where is it hiding?

Let us look at the matter this way. The naive view of the relationship between attitudes and behavior is that attitudes *make ready* certain behaviors, so that the appropriate situation or situations will simply elicit the relevant actions. An alternative should be considered—namely, that the attitude to behavior connection is tenuous and uncertain, and that situations must strongly *encourage this connection* in order for action to occur.

Why should the attitude to behavior connection be tenuous and uncertain? To make a long and dimly understood story short, it is in my judgment because this connection is difficult to learn and exercise, and most people (in American culture, at any rate) do not receive much training or practice in doing what they believe. It is hard enough to learn behaviors appropriate to social expectation in a variety of complex situations, and it is even more difficult to try to guide one's behavior with an internal program that may often run at cross purposes to social expectations. In many cases, one simply does not obtain the necessary experience. As Ehrlich (1969) has remarked in a pertinent article:

> The major determinant of attitude-discrepant behavior may be that an actor has not learned how to express his attitude in action competently.

One determinant of the adequacy of such learning may be the level of direct or vicarious experience of the actor, if any, in such behavior situations. Under this condition of no or poor learning, inaction, inappropriate behavior and sometimes ineffective behavior are defined by the observer as inconsistent acts. Certainly, learning how to behave in a manner consistent with one's attitudes is a primary objective of socialization at all stages of the life cycle [p. 32].

As one poignant example, consider the bystander called upon to help an accident victim when a peer in the situation appears quite unconcerned. The tendency to avoid looking or seeming foolish or presumptuous is apparently the most basic element of the situation. To give help, the person must act despite discomfort about looking foolish, and this is much harder than doing nothing, especially if the actor has never done anything of the required nature before. Of course, to do nothing may involve feelings of discomfort about the welfare of the victim. But people in laboratory and real bystander situations display easy native ingenuity inventing reasons justifying inactivity. One observer of the famous Kitty Genovese murder (38 bystanders) is reported to have remarked, "I thought it was just a lovers' quarrel."

We are very well trained and very good at finding reasons for what we do, but not very good at doing what we find reasons for. Such an asymmetry has been emphasized by the dissonance theory tradition in social psychology. When behavior is situationally elicited by the manipulation of independent variables and attitude ratings are the dependent variables, it is quite easy to show that behavior can influence attitude. People readily justify what they have done by accommodating their attitude statements accordingly. The reverse connection has proved more refractory.

There are two general ways in which the connection between attitudes and behavior might be strengthened. The first occurs through the formation of bonds through practice. Here the simple-minded notion is: if an individual is thinking favorable or unfavorable thoughts about an object at the same time that he is behaving favorably or unfavorably toward the object, then the next time he thinks thoughts in the presence of the object, he is a little bit more likely to behave appropriately toward it rather than doing nothing. An eerie version of this "practice model" is followed by the Communist Chinese with their endless rehearsals of Chairman Mao's quotations, which intrude upon every imaginable area of daily behavior. For Communist ideologies in general, thought and action are so closely linked that thinking bad thoughts is as serious a deviation as doing bad things. But our culture is much more tolerant of minor (and sometimes major) hypocrisies. Despite our ambivalence as to whether hypocrisy is a good thing or not, it is clear that children are often well trained in its usefulness.

The second set of ways for strengthening the connection between attitudes and behavior works through "encouragement cues," that is, situational or contextual factors which will lead the individual to express his attitudes behaviorally.

There are, I believe, a rather large number of types of encouragement cues, and experimental work on them has barely begun. I will content myself with a brief review of a few possibilities, grouped under the three headings: (a) social modeling, (b) self-perception as a "doer", and (c) unusual emotional investment.

First, let us consider social modeling. In recent years there have been a large number of laboratory and field studies showing a substantial facilitating effect on behavior. This has been shown for such diverse activities as volunteering for an experiment (Rosenbaum, 1956), putting money in a Salvation Army kettle, or helping a damsel in distress change a flat tire (Bryan & Test, 1967), disobeying traffic signals or other signs (Freed, Chandler, Mouton & Blake, 1955), refusing to conform to the demands of an authoritarian experimenter (Milgram, 1966, p. 258), accepting a free chocolate chip cookie from a hippie (Regan, unpublished), staring from the street at an upper-story window (Milgram, Bickman & Berkowitz, 1969), returning a lost wallet (Hornstein, 1970), and so on. The modeling effect is apparently so primitive in its psychic origins that it is difficult to explain exactly how it works in detail. Nevertheless, it is clearly a powerful independent variable, increasing the incidence of otherwise infrequent behavior by 50 up to several hundred percent.

Somewhat less obvious is the second notion that a person can be influenced to express his attitudes in behavior by planting the idea with him that perhaps he is the sort of person who admirably and forcefully acts on what he believes, leaving enough doubt about it so that he is motivated to prove to you that he really is this sort of person. In a recent study by McArthur, Kiesler and Cook (1969), the experimental subject is told after a bogus personality test that he will be paid a great deal to come back for a later study simply because he is that rare kind of individual who is a "doer"—who translates feeling into action. Each such subject later is exposed in an apparently fortuitous way to a request for help from the graduate student who wants to pass out antipollution leaflets. The experimental subjects as a group were vastly more likely to agree to help than were subjects in either of two control groups who got the leaflet request but not the "hard sell" about being rewarded for their activist personalities. In an earlier study by Freedman and Fraser (1966), housewives who agreed to participate in a consumer survey by telephone later were much more likely than others to agree to an extensive and rather bothersome home product inventory. This finding, dubbed the "foot-in-the-door effect," quite possibly comes about because the housewives see themselves as active, helpful people as a result of participation in the first activity. Individuals who seek activist experiences may in general be products of very different early backgrounds from those (with equivalent ideology) who tend to avoid personal activism (Cowdry & Keniston, 1970).

My third category concerns unusual emotional investment. I have in mind here that often when individuals do not act as they believe, it is due to a sense of restraint or a fear of looking foolish, or because of other uncertainties in the behavioral decision situation. However, if these restraints or uncertainties can be flooded out with strong feelings consistent with a particular behavior, then the behavior may be free to emerge. For example, a sense of irreparable grievance, as is currently the fashion with student radicals, justifies the performance of otherwise suppressed behaviors. Strong fear or anger can often release hostile behaviors toward disliked outgroups. Perhaps exuberant joy can have the effect of freeing cooperative behaviors from embarrassment, as in the Woodstock phenomenon. Of course, there have been frequent overt advertising appeals to a variety of primeval motives, and sometimes these do well when the product can be convincingly related to the motive. The implicit theory behind this very common style of advertising presumably goes beyond the obvious notion that the motivational appeal will increase the salience of the ad, and therefore its attitude-change potential. Probably the skillful copy writer would also believe (if he thought about it) that favorable attitude toward Brand X will convert into favorable *behavior* toward Brand X because the insidious motive (to be beautiful, rich, powerful, virile, and so on) may happen to be aroused at a later time in contiguity with a purchasing opportunity.

If I may venture a further speculative detour, it is interesting to note that certain forms of activism, for example, campus activism, combine all three of the above types of encouragement cues. Typically, the campus activist has at least a vague ideology that pictures the student as aggrieved, and provides both social support and self-images as doers to the participants in the group. A great deal of the zest and excitement accompanying the activities of student radicals, whether or not such activities are misplaced, thus may be due to the satisfaction provided the participants in uniting a set of attitudes with a set of behaviors. One interpretation of the modern malaise of youth (if not of adults) is indeed the underlying recognition that meaningful attitudes are not held; but if held, then not sensible; and if held and sensible, then not expressed. It is very gratifying to an individual, I think, to fulfill a lost legend: that subjectively sensible attitudes may be held and expressed; that values are indeed necessary to govern behavior, both personally and nationally.

As a final theme, let me return briefly to the relation between information and attitude. I think that the empirical failures in this area stem from an oversophisticated view of the typical individual. In fact, most people do not use information very well, probably because they do not know how, just as they do not know how to express their attitudes in behavior. Teaching people how to use information intelligently is, of course, the mythological purpose of a liberal education, but it would be very naive to suppose that this purpose is widely realized, either in intent or in execution. There are too many temptations in using information superficially for most people to bother to try using it well. The advertising fraternity has long had a much more accurate instinct on how to reach the public with "information" than has the academic fraternity—keep things simple, don't be heavy handed, tie the message into something of central concern to the individual, and rely on repetition. Recently Zajonc (1968) has marshalled a good deal of psychological evidence that repetitive exposure to a stimulus produces substantial increments in liking for it, presumably because a sense of unfamiliarity mediates mild conflict and discomfort. Thus, there are signs of a new research interest in the homely and important problem of simple repetition, and perhaps a larger reexamination of information-attitude linkages will ensue.

It is in the area of attitude-behavior relationships that we have all been badly out of touch with reality, however, and where the most promising new developments must come if we are to correct our past naivete. It is not my purpose in this brief contribution to try to develop a new theoretical synthesis, but I cannot resist leaving a tantalizing hint on the direction such theorizing might lead me in future efforts. The key attitude concept is the "disposition to place oneself into appreciated episodes of interaction with a class of objects." "Appreciated episodes," or "parables" or "scripts" would be symbolic organizations of the self in relation to an environment, serving the function of response programs which an individual could run off whenever the situation compellingly activated one or another particularly appropriate such organization. The notion of the parable or script would be related to the popular theoretical concept of role (Sarbin & Allen, 1968) and to the computer program metaphor of the "plan" (Miller, Galanter, & Pribram, 1960), except that it would be more occasional, more flexible, and more impulsive in its execution than role or plan, and more potentially exposed in its formation to affective and "ideological" influences. Perhaps the notion is closer to what Berne (1964) calls a "game," though without the artificiality of connotation of that term. I have in other writings (Abelson, 1968a, b; Abelson & Reich, 1969) dropped previous hints, using the term "molecule" to refer to cognitive organizations of attitude, but without comment on behavioral implications. Clearly social psychologists have an important work agenda in this theoretical area.

REFERENCES

Abelson, R. P. Computers, polls, and public opinion. *Transaction*, September 1968, 20-27.   (a)

Abelson, R. P. Psychological implication. In R. P. Abelson, E. Aronson, W. J. McGuire, T. M. Newcomb, M. J. Rosenberg, & P. H. Tannenbaum (Eds.),

Theories of cognitive consistency: A sourcebook. Chicago: Rand McNally, 1968. (b)

Abelson, R. P., & Reich, C. Implicational molecules: A method for extracting meaning from input sentences. *Proceedings of the International Joint Conference on Artificial Intelligence*, 1969, 641-648.

Allport, G. W. Attitudes. In C. Murchison (Ed.), *Handbook of social psychology.* Worcester, Massachusetts: Clark University Press, 1935. pp. 798-884.

Asch, S. E. Studies of independence and conformity: I. A minority of one against a unanimous majority. *Psychological Monographs, 1956,* **70**(9), Whole No. 416.

Berne, E. *Games people play: The psychology of human relationships.* New York: Grove Press, 1964.

Berscheid, E., & Walster, E. Attitude change. In J. Mills (Ed.), *Experimental social psychology.* Toronto: Collier-Macmillan, 1969.

Bryan, J. H., & Test, M. A. Models and helping: Naturalistic studies in aiding behavior. *Journal of Personality and Social Psychology*, 1967, **6**, 400-407.

Campbell, D. T. The indirect assessment of social attitudes. *Psychological Bulletin,* 1950, **47**, 15-38.

Campbell, D. T. Social attitudes and other acquired behavioral dispositions. In S. Koch (Ed.), *Psychology: A study of a science,* Vol. 6. New York: McGraw-Hill, 1961.

Cowdry, R. W., & Keniston, K. The war and military obligation: Private attitudes and public actions. *Journal of Personality*, 1970, **32**, 1-13.

Davidson, G. & Valins, S. Maintenance of self-attributed and drug-attributed behavior change. *Journal of Personality and Social Psychology*, 1969, **11**, 25-33.

Ehrlich, H. J. Attitudes, behavior, and the intervening variables. *American Sociologist*, 1969, **4**, 29-34.

Festinger, L. Behavioral support for opinion change. *Public Opinion Quarterly*, 1964, **28**, 404-417.

Festinger, L. *A theory of cognitive dissonance.* Stanford, California: Stanford University Press, 1957.

Freed, A., Chandler, P. J., Mouton, J. S., & Blake, R. R. Stimulus and background factors in sign violation. *Journal of Personality,* 1955, **23**, 499.

Freedman, J. L., & Fraser, S. C. Compliance without pressure: The foot-in-the-door technique. *Journal of Personality and Social Psychology*, 1966, **4**, 195-202.

Freedman, J. L., & Sears, D. O. Selective exposure. *Advances in experimental social psychology*, 1965, **2**, pp. 57-97.

Greenwald, A. G. Cognitive learning, cognitive response to persuasion, and attitude change. In A. G. Greenwald, T. C. Brock, & T. M. Ostrom (Eds.), *Psychological foundations of attitudes.* New York: Academic Press, 1968.

Hornstein, H. A. The influence of social models on helping. In J. Macaulay & L. Berkowitz (Eds.) *Altruism and helping behavior.* New York: Academic Press, 1970.

Hovland, C. I., Janis, I. L. & Kelley, H. H. *Communication and persuasion.* New Haven: Yale University Press, 1953.

Iwao, S. Internal vs. external criticism of group standards. *Sociometry*, 1963, **26**, 410-421.

Janis, I. L., & Feshbach, S. Effects of fear-arousing communications. *Journal of Abnormal and Social Psychology*, 1953, **48**, 78-92.

Latane, B., & Darley, J. M. Social determinants of bystander intervention in emergencies. In J. Macaulay & L. Berkowitz (Eds.), *Altruism and helping behavior.* New York: Academic Press, 1970.

Leventhal, H., & Niles, P. A field experiment on fear arousal with data on the validity of questionnaire measures. *Journal of Personality,* 1964, **32**, 459-479.

Linn, L. S. Verbal attitudes and overt behavior: A study of racial discrimination. *Social Forces,* 1965, **43**, 353-364.

Lott, A. J., & Lott, B. E. A learning theory approach to interpersonal attitudes. In A. G. Greenwald, T. C. Brock, & T. M. Ostrom (Eds.), *Psychological foundations of attitudes.* New York: Academic Press, 1968.

McArthur, L. A., Kiesler, C. A., & Cook, B. P. Acting on an attitude as a function of self-percept and inequity. *Journal of Personality and Social Psychology,* 1969, **12**, 295-302.

Maccoby, E. E., Maccoby, N., Romney, A. K., & Adams, J. S. Social reinforcement in attitude change. *Journal of Abnormal and Social Psychology,* 1961, **63**, 109-115.

McGuire, W. J. The nature of attitudes and attitude change. In G. Lindzey & E. Aronson (Eds.), *Handbook of social psychology*, Vol. III. Reading, Massachusetts: Addison-Wesley, 1968.   (a)

McGuire, W. J. Selective exposure: A summing up. In R. P. Abelson, E. Aronson, W. J. McGuire, T. M. Newcomb, M. J. Rosenberg, & P. H. Tannenbaum

(Eds.), *Theories of cognitive consistency: A sourcebook.* Chicago: Rand McNally, 1968. (b)

Mazen, R., & Leventhal, H. The influence of communicator similarity upon the beliefs and behavior of pregnant women. *Journal of Personality and Social Psychology,* in press.

Milgram, S. Behavioral study of obedience. *Journal of Abnormal and Social Psychology,* 1963, **67**, 371-378.

Milgram, S. Some conditions of obedience and disobedience to authority. In I. D. Steiner & M. Fishbein (Eds.), *Current studies in social psychology.* New York: Holt, 1966. pp. 243-262.

Milgram, S., Bickman, L., & Berkowitz, L. Note on the drawing power of crowds of different size. *Journal of Personality and Social Psychology,* 1969, **13**, 79-82.

Miller, G. A., Galanter, E., & Pribram, K. H. *Plans and the structure of behavior.* New York: Holt, 1960.

Mischel, W. *Personality and assessment.* New York: Wiley, 1968.

Rosenbaum, M. E. The effects of stimulus and background factors on the volunteering response. *Journal of Abnormal and Social Psychology,* 1956, **53**, 118-121.

Sarbin, T. R., & Allen, V. L. Role theory. In E. Aronson & G. Lindzey (Eds.), *Handbook of social psychology,* Vol. I. Reading, Massachusetts: Addison-Wesley, 1968.

Sears, D. O. The paradox of *de facto* selective exposure without preferences for supportive information. In R. P. Abelson, E. Aronson, W. J. McGuire, T. M. Newcomb, M. J. Rosenberg, & P. H. Tannenbaum (Eds.), *Theories of cognitive consistency: A sourcebook.* Chicago: Rand McNally, 1968.

Sherman, A. R. Therapeutic factors in the behavioral treatment of anxiety. Unpublished doctoral dissertation, Yale University, 1969.

Smith, M. B. Some thoughts on the legitimation of evil. *Social psychology and human values.* Chicago: Aldine, 1969.

Staats, A. W. Social behaviorism and human motivation: Principles of the attitude-reinforcer-discriminative system. In A. G. Greenwald, T. C. Brock, & T. M. Ostrom (Eds.), *Psychological foundations of attitudes.* New York: Academic Press, 1968.

Stephenson, W. *The play theory of mass communication.* Chicago: University of Chicago Press, 1967.

Storms, M. D., & Nisbett, R. E. Insomnia and the attribution process. *Journal of Personality and Social Psychology*, 1970, 16, 319-328.

Valins, S., & Ray, A. Effects of cognitive desensitization on avoidance behavior. *Journal of Personality and Social Psychology,* 1967, 7, 345-350.

Watts, W. A., & McGuire, W. J. Persistence of induced opinion change and retention of the inducing message contents, *Journal of Abnormal and Social Psychology,* 1964, 68, 233-241.

Weiss, R. F. An extension of Hullian learning theory to persuasive communication. In A. G. Greenwald, T. C. Brock, & T. M. Ostrom (Eds.), *Psychological foundations of attitudes.* New York: Academic Press, 1968.

Zajonc, R. B. Attitudinal effects of mere exposure. *Journal of Personality and Social Psychology Monograph Supplement,* Part 2, 1968, 9, 1-27.

3
Stress, Self-Esteem, and Attitudes[1]

Robert Helmreich
The University of Texas at Austin

Possible relationships between stress, self-esteem, and aspects of attitude change will be explored in this discussion. The focus will be on speculation rather than on a summation of the state of the research area. Tangentially, problems of research strategy will also be considered, and an appeal will be made for more naturalistic approaches to data collection.

PSYCHOLOGICAL STRESS

Psychologists have yet to provide a generally accepted definition of psychological stress. The wide range of definitions proposed can be seen in reviews of the literature of stress such as those by Janis and Leventhal (1968), Appley and Trumbull (1967), and Lazarus (1966). For the purposes of this discussion, however, stressful situations will be defined, using Scott's (1949) terminology, as "situations in which adjustment is difficult or impossible but in which motivation is very strong [p. 61]," and stress will be defined as the state resulting from exposure to a stressful situation.

Both field and laboratory investigations have specified a number of environmental factors which interfere with adjustment and are generally accepted as being stressful. These factors include physical danger (threat of injury or death), isolation, solitude, crowding, noise, heat, cold, exotic breathing gases, lack of privacy, monotony, and personality incompatibilities.

In few, if any, of the studies in the literature is only a single stress factor

[1] The author's research reported in the paper was supported by a contract with the Office of Naval Research, Group Psychology Branch. I am grateful to Dr. John Nagay and Dr. Bert King whose support and encouragement have been invaluable. I particularly wish to express my gratitude to Dr. Roland Radloff of the Naval Medical Research Institute whose collaboration over the last five years has been both stimulating and rewarding.

33

present. Even in controlled laboratory situations, a combination of environmental stresses typically acts on the subject while field environments usually contain a multiplicity of stressors.

Although some exceptions can be noted, it is a safe generalization to assert that a high intensity of or prolonged exposure to any of the conditions noted above will lead to difficulty in adjustment and decrements in performance. Although it has been proposed that moderate levels of arousal from stress (particularly physical threat) may lead to facilitation of performance, the degradation of performance under extreme or prolonged stress is not questioned (see Janis & Leventhal, 1968, for a discussion of this inverted U function hypothesis).

Stress researchers have had few successes in developing equations to predict individual reactions to environmental stresses (Janis & Leventhal, 1968; Radloff & Helmreich, 1968). Relationships found in one population or stress situation fail to generalize to other settings. The result is a paucity of quantified relationships pertaining to stress effects.

Similarly, Radloff and Helmreich (1968) have noted that examining the results of laboratory and simulation studies of stress, confinement and isolation leads to conclusions about man's capacity for tolerating stress very different from those reached through examination of field studies of exposure to stressful environments. In laboratory studies where conditions are typically less extreme than those in real-life settings, investigators note high frequencies of failure to complete the study because of excessive emotional strain, large decrements in performance, and profound interpersonal conflict (Fraser, 1966; Haythorn & Altman, 1967). In contrast, successful confrontations with extreme stress have been noted in combat (Stouffer, Suchman, Devinney, Star, & Williams, 1949), exploration parties (Lester, 1964; Nordhoff & Hall, 1934), paratroop training (Basowitz, Persky, Korchin, & Grinker, 1955) and saturation diving (Radloff & Helmreich, 1968). In other words, a projection from laboratory and simulation studies of environmental stress would lead to the patently false prediction that humans could not successfully tolerate the high stress found in many natural settings.

SELF-ESTEEM AND STRESS

For the purpose of this discussion, self-esteem will be defined as the evaluation an individual typically reaches and maintains regarding his personal worth. This self-definition expresses a judgment of approval or disapproval and is a global personal conclusion about overall ability, and worthiness. Self-esteem so defined is a subjective appraisal by the individual of his own value as a human being. More extensive and theoretical discussions of the nature of the self-concept can be found in monographs by Wylie (1961, 1968) and Coopersmith (1967).

Most research dealing with self-esteem has dealt with it as a chronic or enduring individual characteristic; that is, a person is seen as acquiring a pervasive conception of his self worth during socialization which later influences his reactions to a wide variety of social and environmental stimuli. Level of self-esteem is usually assessed by means of a paper-and-pencil test and the results of the test related to social or performance variables. Representative studies have found that chronic self-esteem influences persuasibility, interpersonal attraction, morality, academic performance, sociometric choices, leadership, affiliation, and compliance (see Wylie, 1961, 1968; Janis & Field, 1956; Abelson & Lesser, 1959; Zimbardo & Formica, 1963; Coopersmith, 1967; Berkowitz & Lundy, 1957; Nel, Helmreich, & Aronson, 1969; Helmreich, Aronson, & LeFan, 1970).

Another less extensively pursued line of research consists of manipulating the self-esteem of the subject, usually by giving him false feedback about the results of psychological tests, the feedback designed to *raise* or *lower* the individual's feelings of personal competence (see Aronson & Mettee, 1968; McMillen, 1968; McMillen & Helmreich, 1969; McMillen & Reynolds, 1969; Freedman & Doob, 1969). The results of such studies indicate that although self-esteem appears to be one of the more enduring individual characteristics, it can be manipulated successfully by relatively weak laboratory techniques, and these manipulations can significantly influence social behavior.

The theoretical importance of the self-concept for the consideration of adjustment and performance under stress lies not only in the effects of chronic self-esteem on stress reactions but also in the possibility that exposure to environmental stress may in itself manipulate (lower) self-esteem. This has been proposed by several clinical observers of reactions to stress induced by threat of physical damage to the self. Grinker and Spiegel (1945) reported that a basic effect of combat was *a loss of self-confidence* concerning personal invulnerability. Wolfenstein (1957) reported the same effect among survivors of natural disasters; while Schmideberg (1942) found a corresponding increase in feelings of vulnerability among victims of bombing raids.

Although the above formulations deal with reactions to the threat of physical injury, Janis (1969) proposes that the same basic attitude change

may develop if a highly stressful and frustrating life situation continues for a long time. The relentless accumulation of stresses day after day lowers the person's stress tolerance to the point where he begins to react to every minor stress as though it were a serious threat [p. 71].

It is our proposal that continued exposure to environmental stresses such as those noted earlier serves to lower an individual's self-esteem by reducing his feelings of *competence* [in White's (1959) sense of the word] in dealing with his physical and social environment.

If environmental stress does indeed lower an individual's self-esteem or sense of competence, then assessments of probable reactions to a stressful environment should take into account behavior associated with low (or lowered) self-esteem—particularly greater dependency on both peers and leaders, heightened persuasibility, and impaired performance. Indeed, consistency theorists (Aronson, 1968, 1969; Aronson & Mettee, 1968; Nel, Helmreich, & Aronson, 1969) have suggested and demonstrated that an individual with low or lowered self-esteem may (because of needs for cognitive consistency) behave in maladaptive and self-defeating ways because such behavior is most consistent with his low self-evaluation. Aronson and Mettee (1968) found that those with experimentally lowered self-concepts were more likely to cheat when given an opportunity while Aronson and Carlsmith (1962) reported that those convinced of their lack of ability at a task would tend to change their reported performance to make it consistent with their assumed incompetence. These findings suggest that a major goal of those exposing individuals to environmental stresses should be to explore and devise means to aid in the maintenance of a stable and high self-concept (Helmreich & Radloff, 1969).

STRESS AND ATTITUDE CHANGE

Research on stress and attitude change has generated a large literature composed of frequently contradictory results (see McGuire, 1966; Janis & Leventhal, 1968). Most investigators have shared a common experimental paradigm: subjects are presented with a communication designed to arouse fear about some form of behavior (such as smoking) and are given recommendations for alleviating the perceived threat induced by the message (such as giving up smoking). Differential levels of stress are usually produced by varying the amount or nature of fear-arousing material in the communication, while dependent variables may be paper-and-pencil measures of acceptance of the communication or behavioral indices such as changes in the number of cigarettes smoked daily.

In a pioneering study on the effectiveness of fear arousing communications, Janis and Feshbach (1953) found greatest acceptance of recommendations for dental hygiene with a minimal fear appeal and decreased acceptance with moderate and high fear appeals. Other investigators (Haefner, 1956; Nunnally & Bobren, 1959; Janis & Terwilliger, 1962) also have found that strong threat appeals produce more resistance to change than less arousing communications. To account for this decreased effectiveness of high threat appeals Janis and Feshbach (1954) proposed a "defensive avoidance" hypothesis. They suggested that when a high level of fear is aroused and is not fully relieved by recommendations or reassurances in the communication, the recipient of the message will be motivated to deny or ignore the threat.

On the other hand, many investigators have found a positive linear relationship between fear arousal and attitude change (see Berkowitz & Cottingham, 1960; Niles, 1964; Leventhal, Singer, & Jones, 1965; Leventhal & Singer, 1966; Dabbs & Leventhal, 1966).

Janis (1969, 1967) hypothesizes a curvilinear (inverted U) relationship between the level of fear arousal and acceptance of a communication with acceptance increasing with higher fear until the individual's point of maximum stress tolerance is reached and then decreasing sharply with any further increase in stress. He argues further that many of the studies which found a positive relationship between fear arousal and attitude change may not have induced stress levels above the postulated level of maximum stress tolerance and that personality and other predispositional factors may interact with fear communications to influence stress tolerance and acceptance.

While Janis' interpretation of the effects of fear arousing communications on attitude change may be correct, it involves many *ex post facto* interpretations of data and will be difficult to evaluate except through a large series of parametric studies varying all factors which may influence stress response and acceptance. In addition, there are methodological factors in the use of fear arousing communications which may confound the results obtained.

A difficulty with most studies using fear communications is that the communication differs across experimental conditions. That is, in the same study the communication designed to arouse high fear will differ from that aimed at inducing moderate or low fear. Typically, this will involve presenting varying amounts of information about the topic. Thus, it is often difficult to conclude that differential attitude change between stress conditions, in fact, is due to differing fear arousal and not due to differential information transmittal. For example, in the study by Janis and Feshbach (1953) on oral hygiene, the strong fear-appeal condition emphasized the threat of pain and disease and included color slides of festering gums and rotting teeth. In the minimal-fear condition, on the other hand, unpleasant consequences of improper dental hygiene were merely alluded to and diagrams instead of color photographs were used.

Another factor, suggested by Dabbs and Leventhal (1966), which may affect both the level of stress induced and the acceptance of a communication is the nature of recommendations made for coping with the threat posed in the message. Some recommendations may elicit avoidance because they are difficult to follow or, themselves, may induce stress differentially.

The results certainly indicate that the effects of fear-arousing communications on attitude change are highly complex. This line of research also casts little light on a broader question—whether there is a systematic relationship between a general state of arousal due to stress and attitude change. It should add to our understanding of the processes of attitude change to investigate the relationship between fear arousal and persuasion where there is a minimal connection between the source of fear and the communication.

A simple paradigm can be employed for studying the general effects of stress on attitude change. Individuals under conditions of high or low threat can be presented with the *same* persuasive communication on a topic unrelated to the source of threat. In the laboratory, we have used minor variations on the following procedure (Helmreich & Hamilton, 1968; Sigall & Helmreich, 1969; Helmreich, unpublished research). Subjects volunteer to participate in a study of the effects of stimulation. In high-stress conditions they expect to receive painful stimulation such as high levels of electric shock and withdrawal of blood samples; in low-stress conditions they anticipate only mild or subliminal stimulation. After the stress induction, during a "waiting period" while physiological equipment is readied, subjects take part in a "communication survey" run under entirely different sponsorship. In this supposedly unrelated study, subjects can be exposed to persuasive communications and their attitudes assessed. Using this procedure, it is also possible to gather data on the physiological arousal induced by the stress manipulation as part of the "physiological study."

The same procedure can be used in field research where groups exposed to varying amounts of naturally occurring stress can be presented with persuasive communications. Going into the field under relatively controlled conditions gives the investigator the opportunity to examine the effects of stress levels greater than any which could be ethically induced in a laboratory setting. For example, in one field study (Helmreich, Kuiken, & Collins, 1968), we presented communications to Navy recruits who were waiting to undergo training on exposure to tear gas—an experience all felt to be highly stressful.

Using this paradigm, which might be described as measuring the effects of irrelevant stress, both field and laboratory results to date show a general, positive relationship between level of arousal and acceptance of a persuasive communication unrelated to the source of threat. That is, greater attitude change is elicited under conditions of high stress than under low stress, using anticipation of exposure to tear gas, electric shock, and withdrawal of blood samples as stressors. The relationship is corroborated by significant, positive correlations between attitude change and both a physiological measure of arousal (the Palmar Sweat Index, Helmreich & Hamilton, 1968) and self-report measures of fear obtained by a mood adjective check list (Helmreich *et al.*, 1968; Helmreich & Hamilton, 1968).

In related research, Mills (Mintz & Mills, 1971) has studied the effects of nonspecific arousal on attitude change produced by a persuasive communication. Mills based his research on Schachter's (1964) formulation that an emotional state is a function of a state of physiological arousal and a cognition appropriate to the state of arousal. Schachter argues that cognitions arising from the ongoing situation provide the framework for understanding and labeling feelings.

Mintz and Mills extend this reasoning to the case of attitudes:

> When a person interprets his arousal as an emotion resulting from something positive or negative affecting the object of an attitude, he may infer that the greater the degree of emotion, the stronger his attitude toward the object. If the degree of emotion experienced is increased by an increase in physiological arousal, then a stronger attitude may be inferred. When the source of the arousal is not known there may be a greater increase in the degree of emotion and thus in the attitude change produced, than when the source of arousal is known.

In a test of this formulation, Mintz and Mills found that subjects aroused by caffein showed more attitude change than those receiving a placebo (in each case describing the drug as an analgesic). In support of the Schachter hypothesis that cognitive labeling influences reactions to arousal, the authors found that more attitude change was produced by caffein arousal when the caffein was described as an analgesic than when it was described as a stimulant.

Further clarification of the specific effects of arousal on attitude structure and change should have high priority as a research goal. Precise delineation of attitude change as a function of arousal should add considerably to our understanding of the overall process of attitude modification. The remainder of this discussion, however, will be limited to a consideration of probable interactions between stress-produced arousal, self-esteem, and communicator effects on attitude change.

COMMUNICATOR CREDIBILITY

Since the pioneering research of Hovland and his associates (Hovland, Janis, & Kelley, 1953), the positive relationship between communicator credibility and attitude change has been one of the most stable and replicable effects in social psychology. The same communication produces more attitude change when attributed to a highly credible, authoritative source than when it is alleged to come from a less knowledgeable and trustworthy communicator. The high-credibility communicator presumably has more extensive and valid information than the recipient who cannot refute an honest and authoritative source of influence. Although later research has clarified considerably the concept of communicator credibility along such dimensions as perceived intent (Walster & Festinger, 1962), personal characteristics of the communicator (Aronson & Golden, 1962), and relevance of expertise to the message (Sigall & Helmreich, 1969), the basic finding that high-prestige sources induce more attitude change has remained.

Since one general finding of stress research has been that high stress causes increases in dependency needs and in reliance on authority figures (Janis, 1963; Helmreich & Collins, 1967; Radloff & Helmreich, 1968), an early hypothesis in our research was that communicator credibility effects would be enhanced by external threat.

The results to date have been consistently different from that plausible outcome. The normal pattern of credibility effects, obtained under low stress, is eliminated or reversed under conditions of high stress. Navy recruits in the high-stress condition of a field experiment (anticipating tear gas) were more persuaded by the same communication when it was attributed to a student or fellow recruit than when it was attributed to an admiral (Helmreich *et al.*, 1968). College students awaiting electric shock were more persuaded by a videotaped communication about drugs when the speaker was introduced as a postal clerk than when he was introduced as a distinguished researcher in the field of drug effects: under low stress, the opposite effect was obtained—the high-credibility scientist produced significantly more attitude change than the low-credibility postal clerk. Another recent laboratory study (Helmreich, unpublished research) has produced a similar pattern of results with a crossover interaction. Predictably, under low stress, a videotaped message on the effects of television violence produced more attitude change when the speaker was introduced as a Ph.D. media expert than the identical message with the speaker introduced as a fellow student. Under high stress, though, the peer elicited more change than the expert. This stress-induced change in the usual effect of communicator credibility seems to be stable across a variety of experimental settings and communication issues.

As mentioned earlier, exposure to stress can be pictured as a temporary manipulation of the individual's self-concept—a situational *lowering* of self-esteem. If this assumption concerning the effects of stress is correct, the stress-credibility interaction may become more understandable in the light of self-esteem and social comparison phenomena (Festinger, 1954). Schachter's (1959) research and subsequent investigations of affiliative preference under stress have demonstrated sharp increases in desire to associate with similar peers under conditions of high threat. Janis (1963), Radloff and Helmreich (1968), and others have also noted great increases in peer group influence under field conditions of high stress. In other relevant research, Zimbardo and Formica (1963) found that subjects with low measured self-esteem showed more affiliative behavior under stress than did high scorers on the same self-esteem measure. In attitude research, Berkowitz and Lundy (1957) have found that subjects with low self-esteem are less influenced by high- than by low-status communicators, while Freedman and Doob (1969) report that subjects manipulated to feel deviant from peers (on psychological tests) are more influenced by a communication from a peer than from an authoritative source.

The greater social dependence of low-self-esteem individuals noted through-out the literature probably results from a lack of confidence in the validity of their personal judgment. The individual with low self-esteem counts on others to provide him with normative data on the correct and acceptable response to novel situations and ideas. The individual whose self-esteem is temporarily lowered by situational factors is likely to perceive himself as different or deviant from his peers and should be highly motivated to enhance his self-concept, to return to his normal state of perceived competence. Indeed, the individual who has received a temporary blow to his self-esteem should be much more strongly motivated to gain a sense of acceptance and normality than the person with chronic feelings of unworthiness. This desire to restore self-esteem should be reflected in strong needs for social comparison with peers who can provide information on normative behavior and attitudes. As social comparison theorists have indicated (see Festinger, 1954; Schachter, 1959; Radloff, 1968), persons close to the individual in emotional state or ability can provide the best models for social comparison. Thus, individuals with social comparison needs aroused by a stress-produced feeling of low self-esteem should have the strongest desire to emulate the behavior and attitudes of peers.

From this line of reasoning, it is possible to propose a tentative explanation for the enhanced effectiveness of low credibility communicators under con-ditions of lowered self-esteem (or high stress). In this situation, the individual's need to minimize his perceived noncomparability with or deviation from others of "normal" or average competence should cause him to see the "normative" response as being that of a peer or other low status individual. Agreeing with a peer may bolster the self-concept by decreasing feelings of difference and augmenting feelings of being part of a "normal" group. Agreeing with an authority may be irrelevant to the individual's need to feel "typical" or may indeed increase feelings of deviance if the authority is seen as holding views divergent from a peer reference group.

A general hypothesis is that when self-esteem is lowered or threatened by stress, one's dominant need becomes to react in the same way that he assumes his peers will respond. Under such conditions, even an authority towards whom one displays great dependency may be a less potent referent for determination of attitudes than a peer or status equal who can define a "normative" response. Perception of a reference group reaction may be a strong enough influence to outweigh all other considerations in determining the effectiveness of attempts at persuasion. In a conflict between loyalty to the group and loyalty to the leader under stress, it is probable that group loyalty will dominate.

The arguments set forth in this contribution represent an attempt to tie together several disparate approaches to the study of attitude change. The central assumption is that psychologically stressful situations threaten an indi-vidual's self-esteem. This assumption and those derivative from it are based primarily on circumstantial evidence. Although the line of reasoning followed may turn out to be either partly or wholly erroneous, such speculations would still have a desirable outcome if they provoked research aimed specifically at clarifying interactions between stress, arousal, self-esteem, and attitude change. Primary emphasis should be placed on isolating relationships between stress and self-esteem. More direct tests of self-esteem-communicator credibility interactions under differing levels of stress should also be performed. Additionally, the effects of nonspecific arousal on communicator credibility need to be assessed.[2]

A NOTE ON RESEARCH STRATEGY

A comprehensive examination of stress and attitude change will involve a program of both field and laboratory studies. Laboratory experimental studies are needed because controlled manipulations which give precise information on causal relationships are essential for the development of theoretical models. In many areas, however, particularly the study of stress effects, laboratory research can provide only limited data. In the case of stress, for example, ethical and practical considerations make it impossible to investigate the effects of really severe stress or of prolonged stress (that is, no laboratory manipulation could approximate the levels or duration of stress found in many natural situations such as combat). The investigator concerned with testing the generality and validity of laboratory derived theoretical formulations will be forced into naturalistic research using ongoing social situations.

In the area of research design, it is possible that social psychologists have overemphasized the traditional laboratory, deception study—perhaps in the interest of ensuring precise control over relevant variables and making valid causal inferences, perhaps also to demonstrate "scientific" respectability to skeptical audiences of "real" scientists.

The standard laboratory deception study has become the object of serious criticism on ethical grounds with opponents contending that we are not justified in deceiving subjects and forcing them to endure even momentary discomfort in

---

[2]The question of what effect nonspecific arousal may have on communicator credibility raises several interesting issues for research. One question is whether nonspecific arousal (produced as in the Mintz and Mills research design) increases needs for social comparison and concomitantly enhances the effectiveness of low credibility communicators. If nonspecific arousal does change credibility effects, the question is whether this effect is mediated through a lowering of self-esteem. It is possible that a state of ambiguous arousal may cause a decrease in self-perception of competence. Research along these lines should prove fruitful.

the interests of research (see Ring, 1967; McGuire, 1967; Kelman, 1967; Radloff & Helmreich, 1968, for discussion of some of these arguments). A second line of criticism would argue that the laboratory social psychology experiment too frequently deals with trivial issues, uses pallid manipulations which in no way approximate the nature of things in the "real world" thus leaving only a social psychology of the college freshman reluctantly participating in a psychology experiment for credit. A separate but related line of reasoning would lead to the conclusion that ethical constraints leave the experimenter with no choice but to use weak manipulations dealing with issues peripheral to the subject's most basic concerns.

Aronson and Carlsmith (1968) have eloquently defended the laboratory deception study as the best technique for the pursuit of social psychological studies. Their arguments in support of laboratory experimentation are certainly valid and need not be repeated here. It is probably also true, however, that social psychologists have been seriously remiss in failing to validate theories in naturalistic settings. It is too often assumed that laboratory findings are directly applicable to the "real world," or that it is somehow demeaning to forsake theoretical pursuits to explore the applicability and generality of laboratory based formulations.

At a time when ever-increasing demands are heard for relevance and when support for research is greatly diminished, it is not surprising that social psychologists are asked to justify their work in terms of its relationship to real social processes. Far from being an encroachment upon academic and intellectual freedom, these pressures may force us to refine our theories, to explore their parameters, and to discard many untenable concepts. If we test our hypotheses not only in the laboratory but also under naturalistic conditions, we will be able both to make precise statements about causal relationships and to specify the relative strength and generality of obtained effects. The imaginative experimenter willing to forsake the laboratory seems to have little difficulty in finding controlled natural settings for research (see Willems & Raush, 1969, for a comprehensive discussion of naturalistic approaches). An encouraging number of recent studies have employed either field settings or a combination of field and laboratory techniques (see Wrightsman, 1969; Ellsworth & Carlsmith, 1968; Varella, 1969; Doob, Carlsmith, Freedman, Landauer, & Tom, 1969; Milgram, Bickman, & Berkowitz, 1969; Nisbett & Kanouse, 1969; Goldman, Jaffa, & Schachter, 1968). The current resurgence of interest in naturalistic research (aided by more sophisticated techniques of data collection and data processing) may lead us happily back to the investigation of problems which were once considered basic concerns of social psychology. If social psychologists do acquire a broader and more flexible orientation towards research design, both the theoretical scope and the social relevance of the field should increase dramatically.

REFERENCES

Abelson, R., & Lesser, G. S. The measurement of persuasibility in children. In I. L. Janis & C. K. Hovland (Eds.), *Personality and persuasibility.* New Haven, Connecticut: Yale University Press, 1959.

Appley, M., & Trumbull, R. *Psychological stress.* New York: Appleton, 1967.

Aronson, E. Dissonance theory: Progress and problems. In R. Abelson, E. Aronson, W. McGuire, T. Newcomb, M. Rosenberg, & P. Tannenbaum (Eds.), *Theories of cognitive consistency: A sourcebook.* Chicago: Rand McNally, 1968.

Aronson, E. The theory of cognitive dissonance: A current perspective. In L. Berkowitz (Ed.), *Advances in experimental social psychology.* New York: Academic Press, 1969.

Aronson, E., & Carlsmith, J. M. Performance expectancy as a determinant of actual performance. *Journal of Abnormal and Social Psychology*, 1962, **65**, 178-182.

Aronson, E., & Carlsmith, J. M. Experimentation in social psychology. In Lindzey, G., & Aronson, E., *Handbook of social psychology*, Vol. II. Reading, Massachusetts: Addison-Wesley, 1968. pp. 1-79.

Aronson, E., & Golden, B. W. The effect of relevant and irrelevant aspects of communicator credibility on attitude change. *Journal of Personality,* 1962, **30**, 135-146.

Aronson, E., & Mettee, D. Dishonest behavior as a function of differential levels of induced self-esteem. *Journal of Personality and Social Psychology,* 1968, **9**, 121-127.

Basowitz, H., Persky, H., Korchin, S., & Grinker, R. *Anxiety and stress.* New York: McGraw-Hill, 1955.

Berkowitz, L., & Cottingham, D. R. The interest value and relevance of fear arousing communications. *Journal of Abnormal and Social Psychology,* 1960, **60**, 37-43.

Berkowitz, L., & Lundy, R. M. Personality characteristics related to susceptibility to influence by peers or authority figures. *Journal of Personality*, 1957, **25**, 306-316.

Coopersmith, S. *The antecedents of self-esteem.* San Francisco: Freeman, 1967.

Dabbs, J. M., Jr., & Leventhal, H. Effects of varying the recommendations in a fear-arousing communication. *Journal of Personality and Social Psychology,* 1966, **4**, 525-531.

Doob, A. N., Carlsmith, J. M., Freedman, J. L., Landauer, T. K. and Tom, S. Effect of initial selling price on later sales. *Journal of Personality and Social Psychology*, 1969, **11**, 345-350.

Ellsworth, P. C. and Carlsmith, J. M. Effects of eye contact and verbal content on affective response to a dyadic interaction. *Journal of Personality and Social Psychology*, 1968, **10**, 15-20.

Festinger, L. A theory of social comparison processes. *Human Relations*, 1954, **7**, 117-140.

Fraser, T. M. The effects of confinement as a factor in manned space flight. NASA Contractor Report #511, Washington, D. C., 1966.

Freedman, J., & Doob, A. N. *Deviancy*. New York: Academic Press, 1969.

Goldman, R., Jaffa, M., & Schachter, S. Yom Kippur, Air France, dormitory food and the eating behavior of obese and normal persons. *Journal of Personality and Social Psychology*, 1968, **10**, 117-123.

Grinker, R. R., & Spiegel, J. P. *Men under stress.* New York: McGraw-Hill, 1945.

Haefner, D. Some effects of guilt-arousing and fear-arousing persuasive communications on opinion change. Technical Report No. 1, Office of Naval Research, Contract No. Nonr 668 (12), 1956.

Haythorn, W., & Altman, I. Personality factors in isolated environments. In M. Appley & R. Trumbull (Eds.), *Psychological stress.* New York: Appleton, 1967.

Helmreich, R., & Collins, B. Situational determinants of affiliative preference under stress. *Journal of Personality and Social Psychology*, 1967, **6**, 79-85.

Helmreich, R., & Hamilton, J. Effects of stress, communication relevance and birth order on opinion change. *Psychonomic Science*, 1968, **11**, 297-298.

Helmreich, R., & Radloff, R. *Environmental stress and the maintenance of self-esteem. Technical Report* #13, Office of Naval Research, December, 1969, 16 pp.

Helmreich, R., Kuiken, D., & Collins, B. Effects of stress and birth order on attitude change. *Journal of Personality,* 1968, **36**, 466-473.

Helmreich, R. Aronson, E., & LeFan, J. To err is humanizing—sometimes: Effects of self-esteem, competence and a pratfall on interpersonal attraction. *Journal of Personality and Social Psychology*, 1970, 16, 259-264.

Hovland, C. I., Janis, I. L., & Kelley, H. H. *Communication and persuasion.* New Haven, Connecticut: Yale University Press, 1953.

Janis, I. L. Group Identification under conditions of external danger. *British Journal of Medical Psychology,* 1963, **36,** 227-238.

Janis, I. L. Effects of fear arousal on attitude change: Recent developments in theory and experimental research. In L. Berkowitz (Ed.), *Advances in Experimental Social Psychology,* 2, New York: Academic Press, 1967.

Janis, I. L. Stress and frustration. In Janis, I. L. (Ed.), *Personality: Dynamics, development and assessment.* New York: Harcourt, 1969.

Janis, I. L., & Feshbach, S. Effects of fear arousing communications. *Journal of Abnormal and Social Psychology,* 1953, **48,** 78-92.

Janis, I. L., & Feshbach, S. Personality differences associated with responsiveness to fear-arousing communications. *Journal of Personality,* 1954, **23,** 154-166.

Janis, I. L., & Field, A. Behavioral assessment of persuasibility: Consistency of individual differences. *Sociometry,* 1956, **19,** 241-259.

Janis, I. L., & Leventhal, H. Human reactions to stress. In E. Borgatta and W. Lambert (Eds.), *Handbook of personality theory and research.* Chicago: Rand-McNally, 1968.

Janis, I. L., & Terwilliger, R. An experimental study of psychological resistances to fear-arousing communications. *Journal of Abnormal and Social Psychology,* 1962, **65,** 403-410.

Kelman, H. C. Human use of human subjects: The problem of deception in social psychological experiments. *Psychological Bulletin,* 1967, **67** 1, 11.

Lazarus, R. S. *Psychological stress and the coping process.* New York: McGraw-Hill, 1966.

Lester, J. T., Jr. Behavioral research during the 1963 American Mt. Everest expedition. ONR Contract Nonr-3930(00) NR 171-257, Final Report, September, 1964.

Leventhal, H. and Singer, R. P. Order of affect arousal and recommendations as determinants of attitude change. *Journal of Social and Personality Psychology,* 1966, **4,** 137-146.

Leventhal, H., Singer, R., & Jones, S. Effects of fear and specificity of recommendation upon attitude and behavior. *Journal of Personality and Social Psychology,* 1965, **2,** 20-29.

McGuire, W. J. Attitudes and opinions. In P. R. Farnsworth (Ed.), *Annual Review of Psychology.* Palo Alto, California: Annual Reviews, 1966.

McGuire, W. J. Some impending reorientations in social psychology! Some thoughts provoked by Kenneth Ring. *Journal of Experimental Social Psychology,* 1967, **3,** 124-139.

McMillen, D. Application of the gain-loss model of interpersonal attraction to responses to ingratiating behavior following an argument. Unpublished doctoral dissertation, The University of Texas at Austin, 1968.

McMillen, D., and Helmreich, R. The effectiveness of several types of ingratiation techniques following an argument. *Psychonomic Science,* 1969, **15,** 207-208.

McMillen, D., and Reynolds, J. E. Self-esteem and the effectiveness of reconciliation techniques following an argument. *Psychonomic Science,* 1969, **17,** 208-209.

Milgram, S., Bickman, L., & Berkowitz, L. Note on the drawing power of crowds of different size. *Journal of Personality and Social Psychology,* 1969, **13,** 79-82.

Mintz, P., & Mills, J. Effects of arousal and information about its source upon attitude change. *Journal of Experimental Social Psychology,* 1971 (In press).

Nel, E., Helmreich, R., & Aronson, E. Opinion change in the advocate as a function of the persuasibility of his audience: A clarification of the meaning of dissonance. *Journal of Personality and Social Psychology,* 1969, **12,** 117-124.

Niles, (Kafes), P. The relationship of susceptibility and anxiety to acceptance of fear-arousing communications. Unpublished doctoral dissertation, Yale University, 1964.

Nisbett, R. E., & Kanouse, D. E. Obesity, food deprivation and supermarket shopping behavior. *Journal of Personality and Social Psychology,* 1969, **12,** 289-294.

Nordhoff, C. B., & Hall, J. N. *The Bounty Trilogy.* Boston: Little, Brown, 1934.

Nunnally, J. D., & Bobren, H. M. Variables governing the willingness to receive communications on mental health. *Journal of Personality,* 1959, **27,** 38-46.

Radloff, R. Opinion evaluation and affiliation. In D. Cartwright and D. Zander (Eds.), *Group Dynamics.* New York: Harper, 1968.

Radloff, R., & Helmreich, R. *Groups under stress: Psychological research in SEALAB II.* New York: Appleton, 1968.

Ring, K. Experimental social psychology: Some sober questions about some frivolous values. *Journal of Experimental Social Psychology,* 1967, **3,** 113-123.

Schachter, S. *The psychology of affiliation.* Stanford, California: Stanford University Press, 1959.

Schachter, S. The interaction of cognitive and physiological determinants of emotional states. In L. Berkowitz (Ed.), *Advances in experimental social psychology*. 1, New York: Academic Press, 1964.

Schmideberg, M. Some observations on individual reactions to air raids. *International Journal of Psychoanalysis,* 1942, **23**, 146-176.

Scott, J. P. Relative importance of social and hereditary factors in life adjustment during periods of stress in laboratory animals. *Life stress and bodily disease*. New York: Association for Research in Nervous Mental Disease, 1949. pp. 48-60.

Sigall, H., & Helmreich, R. Opinion change as a function of stress and communicator credibility. *Journal of Experimental Social Psychology,* 1969, **5**, 70-78.

Stouffer, S., Suchman, E., Devinney, L., Star, S. A., & Williams, R. *The american soldier. Vol. 1. Adjustment during army life.* Princeton, New Jersey: Princeton University Press, 1949.

Varella, J. Research cited in P. Zimbardo and E. Ebbesen, *Influencing attitudes and changing behavior.* Reading, Massachusetts: Addison-Wesley, 1969. Pp. 114-121.

Walster, E., & Festinger, L. The effectiveness of "overheard" persuasive communications. *Journal of Abnormal and Social Psychology,* 1962, **65**, 395-402.

White, R. W. Motivation reconsidered: The concept of competence. *Psychological Review,* 1959, **66**, 297-333.

Willems, E. P., & Raush, H. L. *Naturalistic viewpoints in psychological research.* New York: Holt, 1969.

Wolfenstein, M. *Disaster.* New York: Free Press, 1957.

Wrightsman, L. Wallace supporters and adherence to Law and Order. *Journal of Personality and Social Psychology,* 1969, **13**, 17-22.

Wylie, R. *The self-concept.* Lincoln, Nebraska: University of Nebraska Press, 1961.

Wylie, R. Present status of self theory. In E. F. Borgatta & W. W. Lambert (Eds.), *Handbook of personality theory and research.* Chicago: Rand McNally, 1968.

Zimbardo, P. G., & Formica, R. Emotional comparison and self-esteem as determinants of affiliation. *Journal of Personality,* 1963, **31**, 141-162.

Part Two
Conformity and Conflict in Organizational Contexts

Student dissent, activism, riots, and violence have frequently occupied newspaper front pages in recent years. Since much of this disaffection has been directed at academic organizations and their administrators, we find it useful to consider here student attitudes and behavior in an organizational context. The organizations that seem particularly pertinent here are, of course, academic organizations and also political organizations—those composed largely of students and those (like national political organizations) which include more widely representative members.

A number of fascinating questions or issues here involve matters of attitude *per se*, as well as organizational factors. What is the incidence of student dissent in colleges and universities? What is the relationship between students' attitudes and the attitudes and behavior of other groups composing the academic organization: teaching assistants, untenured faculty, tenured faculty, administrators, and clerical and service personnel? Do academic organizations which are large, urban, or liberal arts oriented manifest a greater incidence of student dissent than the average? What personnel selection and recruitment factors are involved in determining the extent to which the student body and the faculty at a given academic organization will manifest attitudinal conformity or attitudinal dissent? One can pursue this matter further and ask not only what are the relative amounts of attitudinal conformity and dissent in the academic community as a whole, but also in the smaller groups and organizations composing it (departments, schools, and the like). Obviously, individuals who vociferously voice dissent on the policies of the college or university as a whole may manifest lock-step conformity to the norms, attitudes, and values of a particular subgroup within the academic organization. What characteristics of the academic administration help determine whether attitudinal dissent will be directed against the academic organization itself or against some element of local, state or federal government? What role do national foreign and domestic policies play in the genesis of student riots? How do national governmental decisions and actions combine with the decisions of the academic administrators, the composition of the student body, and local campus issues to determine whether student dissent will be expressed constructively or destructively, peacefully or violently, episodically or chronically?

In this section, we approach problems and issues in this area from several different vantage points. Orne and McGinnies in their chapter examine the phenomena of student dissent, speculate about some etiological factors, and propose some organizational and social changes that could reduce the level of campus conflict and violence. Zimbardo considers organized political canvassing activity by students as an alternative to more violent, revolutionary paths toward their goals of social change. Likert and Bowers describe various organizational strategies for managing conflict which are relevant to campus disruptions, as well as organizational conflict in general, and even to international conflict.

Orne and McGinnies have chosen to highlight selected findings on student dissent and violence and to speculate on their origins and on possible means of reducing undesirable extremes of such behavior. Such an emphasis on social change properly leads to an attempt to place modern student outbursts in the United States in context by considering analogous current behavior abroad as well as historical trends. The comparative approach comes naturally for these authors since both have participated in international or cross-cultural research programs and both have a personal interest in other cultures as well.

In common with other contributors to this volume, Orne and McGinnies stress the fruitfulness of a learning approach to attitudinal and behavioral conformity/dissent. Thus, we find their attention directed toward both specific learning experiments or principles that can explain behavioral rigidity or fixation, as well as broad parental and social influences that determine the psychological growth and adaptation of young people. Coupled with these comparative and learning emphases, stress is placed on the organizational environment in which student attitudes and behavior occur. All in all, in this chapter a far-ranging set of hypotheses and speculations is given which attempts to integrate our keynotes to this volume: attitudes, conflict, social change.

The issue of implicit versus explicit attitudes and behavior also appears here, as it does throughout the volume, in the guise of what might lie under the overt behavior of protesting students. The authors raise an important question as to whether the apparent dissent may stem from covert, chronic anxiety and distress connected with other pervasive factors such as alienation, low self-esteem, perceived lack of any useful social role, rather than from deep-felt concern with the manifest content of their specific protests.

Turning now to Zimbardo, we regard two characteristics of his research as particularly relevant in the present context: first, his concern with what functioning in large bureaucratic organizations, and in even larger social matrices, does to the perceptions, attitudes and behavior of the individual; second, his high degree of interest in utilizing psychological research findings in real-life settings. He has manifested concern with such research utilization in several of his recent publications. Zimbardo (1969), for example, deals at length with the phenomenon of deindividuation and how it is manifested in, or can help explain, acts involving a loss of control over emotional and impulsive behavior, resulting in suicide, homicide, drug abuse, violence, and destruction of property. In *Canvassing for Peace* (1970) he and Abelson attempt to combine available social psychological knowledge on persuasion and attitude change with the wisdom of practical politics and street "savvy." In this manual they help orient prospective canvassers by looking at the following:

1. The psychological situations they will encounter in canvassing.
2. Detailed alternative strategies which can be effective in vote getting.
3. Specific election issues and arguments.
4. Social psychological principles to be used in organizing groups of volunteers.

Zimbardo's contribution to this volume, "The Ethics and Tactics of Persuasion," provides tactical guidance and raises some of the ethical issues involved in any sales, political, or even educational program or campaign designed to influence attitudes and behavior. He provides what is, in effect, a "how-to-do-it" manual for the would-be communicator whether he intends to "sell" soap, salvation, peace, a particular political candidate or party, or entry into, or retention in, an organization like the police or the armed forces.

One can conceive of this kind of persuasion campaign by students as *one* possible remedy, as it were, for student distress. Zimbardo states that where students—or any other group— are unalterably opposed to the goals of their society, the two alternatives are either revolution or persuasion campaigns designed to change these goals.

Available evidence, both from opinion polls and from more intensive research with students, indicates that confirmed activists on the campus constitute only a small—and statistically unrepresentative—minority of all students (Trent & Craise, 1967). Since this is the case, it is interesting to speculate as to what results would ensue from political persuasion campaigns like those envisaged by Zimbardo. In the long run, how will the majority of students react to such a minority effort? How will academic administrators, the boards of trustees and regents, and philanthropists (who supply funds for academia) react? Will voters outside the campus be influenced positively or negatively by students acting in a highly partisan and even Machievellian manner, the tactics for which are outlined by Zimbardo?

We are currently ignorant of the practical impact of such campaigns. Hopefully, scientific studies of the effects of student political activities like those that occurred in the fall of 1970 will soon reduce that state of ignorance.

However, we do see some signs that student dissent may be decreasing or at least changing its manner of expression. Several recent journalistic accounts indicate that since the 1970 elections, campuses seem calmer. If so, is this due to the fact that students are more satisfied, or because they despair of bringing about change through force, or what? Certainly, we need much more research on topics like these.

The chapter by Likert and Bowers grows out of an extremely influential program of research on work organizations conducted for more than two decades at the Institute of Social Research of the University of Michigan. While it focuses on organizations and their management systems, the authors indicate in their last section that these ideas apply not only to attitudes and conflict within industrial organizations but also to conflict in colleges and universities, racial conflict, and conflict at the international level.

The reader will note in the Likert-Bowers chapter an emphasis on field situations and field testing of the usefulness of theoretical models. Much of the research upon which this chapter is based was conducted in business organizations—where relatively precise measurements of job performance and costs can be obtained—but this long-term research program has also included studies in government agencies, hospitals, and other nonbusiness organizations. We might note in passing that field orientation has characterized much of the past research on organizations conducted by social and behavioral scientists, although laboratory research and simulation efforts are becoming more prominent now.

With respect to the topic of this section of the volume—student dissent and organizational conflict—the contribution by Likert and Bowers stimulates thoughts on organizational and leadership factors that may be involved in the genesis and the hoped-for amelioration of student violence. One wonders, for example, about the role of the particular leadership pattern shown in a given academic organization. Some colleges and universities exhibit what amounts to a benevolent despotism in which the faculty and administration reserve almost all major decision-making for themselves and allow little opportunity for participative decision-making by students, graduate assistants, clerical and service personnel, or even junior faculty members. Can we conclude from the frequent demands by students (and other members of the academic community) for more participation in decision-making that this is a major "cause" of student dissent, of student violence? If so, why does this demand appear at this particular point in time with such relatively high frequency? Whatever the causes, Likert and Bowers imply that the adoption of different leadership patterns in such cases should result in a decrement in the amount of student distress, disruptions, and violence.

Such implications could, and should be checked in academic organizations. For example, one could measure "effectiveness" and job satisfaction in academic organizations after a change in administration that replaces a Systems 1 administration with a Systems 4 administration. The seemingly high turnover rate of academic administrators should provide many opportunities for such research comparisons.

Taking all three of these contributions together, we gain a well-balanced perspective on student distress and disruptions in particular, as well as organizational effectiveness in general. The picture emerging here is a complex one that points to some sources of student disaffection in social change, other sources in the systems of leadership and governance that prevail in the academic environment, and even some sources that reside at the level of government—national and international decision-making and policies that impinge on students' lives and social consciences.

Is there anything we can add to this composite viewpoint? One thing that might well deserve more emphasis is a set of variables ordinarily treated under the rubrics of imitation, identification, and modeling. That is, we may speculate that socially and politically activist students are displaying attitudes, values, and actions that correspond in crucial respects to those that characterize—or those which the students perceive as characteristic of—their parents and certain categories of faculty members that they admire and emulate.

Such students may predominantly stem from home backgrounds that are affluent and that stress intellectualization, social justice, and individualistic standards of judgment more than they do conformity to the norms of conventional organizations and middle-class society. Such individuals might be expected to identify disproportionately with selected academic standards such as those prevailing in the humanities and the social and behavioral sciences rather than those typifying the natural and biological sciences, administration, and engineering. In organizational terms, then, we would expect that different segments of the academic organization would recruit differentially in terms of attitudes, values, and the like, and that once "recruited" the students selected by a given faculty or academic subculture would be reinforced, or punished (typically in fairly subtle ways) to the extent that their behavior and attitudinal expressions conform to those of the reinforcing group.

To the extent that this is true, we would have to reject the notion that student disaffection represents *only* a failure to conform. Rather, it actually may involve a high degree of conformity to the norms of specific groups and subcultures, while involving at the same time a rejection of some of the norms of the larger society surrounding them.

What we could be seeing here, then, is a manifestation of a sort of elite attitude which emphasizes intelligence, aesthetic sensibility, social justice, participatory democracy, and autonomy, not those values which may be more typical historically—wealth and family. Such attitudes, of course, are not totally absent in schools or departments involving social and behavioral science or the humanities.

If there is such a fit between what some students have learned at home and what they find in their preferred part of the campus, what can we say about the vaunted generation gap? That "gap' may not, in fact, account (in large degree, at least) for activism and dissent.

All such speculation needs to be checked against more extensive data than those which seem to be available now. We need additional studies of the organizational and social factors involved in occupational choice, recruitment, and "socialization," including those that determine choice of a particular *alma mater*, a specific broad field of study (law, medicine, social science), and a specific major within such broad fields (for example, psychiatry, English literature, or electrical engineering).

Certainly, we also need more research on the degree to which specific leadership approaches and organizational climates of opinion can affect student behavior, given the putative influence of factors like these mentioned above. To what extent, for instance, would Likert's Systems 4 approach "work" with different categories of students, different kinds of campuses, or different parts of a given campus? To what extent does political activism of the kind described by Zimbardo appeal to different types of students (and faculty members), and to what extent can it be expected to reduce tensions within and between different parts of the academic body? Let us hope that current research will soon provide some of the answers we urgently need in this area.

REFERENCES

Abelson, R. P., & Zimbardo, P. G. *Canvassing for peace: A manual for volunteers.* Ann Arbor, Michigan: Society for the Psychological Study of Social Issues, 1970.

Trent, J. W., & Craise, J. L. Commitment and conformity in the American college. *Journal of Social Issues, 1967,* **23**, No. 3, 34-51.

Zimbardo, P. G. The human choice: Individuation, reason, and order versus deindividuation, impulse, and chaos. In W. J. Arnold & D. Levine (Eds.), *Nebraska Symposium on Motivation.* Lincoln, Nebraska: University of Nebraska Press, 1969.

4

Conflict and Change in the Universities

Martin T. Orne
Institute of the Pennsylvania Hospital
and University of Pennsylvania

and

Elliott McGinnies
The American University

To those of us whose lives center around a university, the changing attitudes and social concerns of students have assumed even greater significance in recent years. Although the violent upheavals at the turn of the decade have given way in the early 1970s to an atmosphere more characteristic of the placid 1950s, the seeds of unrest remain. How these will affect the future of universities will depend on a variety of occurrences, not the least of which involves the role that academicians themselves choose to play in this process of social change. Regardless of the direction taken by students in their quest for meaning and purpose in life, it seems certain that they will not be the same pliable, acquiescent individuals whom we had come to accept as fixtures in the academic community. The disaffection of youth in general with many of the traditional values of American society seems unlikely to reverse itself. Certain changes are here to stay. Stringfellow Barr (1970) writes:

> The young sneer at the C.I.A., the F.B.I., and General Hershey. They do not feel disgraced by jail. As sons of that Man in the Gray Flannel Suit, they are prepared to go barefoot, unshaven and unshorn, and to burn not only their draft cards but a flag or two. Many of them believe that the political process is as rotten as the rigged price system and that it should not be reformed but sabotaged. Hence riots and guerrilla tactics in the cities, and sufficient noise to drown out candidates at the hustings [p. 70].

Shoben (1970) summarized students' disenchantment in his observation that overpopulation, nuclear weapons, and Vietnam are symptoms of a "cultural system gone amok [p. 690]." Certainly it has been tempting to ascribe students' behavior as a response to the more pressing social problems of the day. At a meeting of the American Psychiatric Association a few years ago, a panel concerned itself with student unrest and the participants generally agreed that

55

the stress of the unpopular Vietnam war and racial discrimination were the roots of the current tensions. A French psychiatrist, Leon Chertok, pointed out, however, that his country no longer had a Vietnamese problem, and that even its Algerian difficulties were now over; further, it had a long history of racial tolerance, yet, nonetheless. France had recently experienced the worst student riots in its history. Similarly, it can be pointed out that Japan has neither a war nor a racial problem, yet Japanese students behaved so riotously as to force the virtual shutdown of many Japanese universities for nearly a year.

The social issues that correlate with student unrest are obviously different from one country to another, and it seems unwise to search for a simple explanation of the demonstrations that we have recently witnessed in American universities. There is no doubt that the bulk of the concrete issues raised by students here and abroad are intrinsically important and relevant. At the same time, some aspects of these events resemble a contagion that has swept campuses throughout the world.

Never has the "generation gap" appeared wider or more unbridgeable, and the breach extends not just between age groups, but also between those who attend colleges and universities and those who do not. For example, the *Washington Post* (November, 1970) reported the results of a Harris Poll in which 74% of the adult population registered their view that unrest on the college campuses is due to activity by "radical militant student groups." No more than 26% agreed with the observation of the Scranton Commission that a "lack of willingness on the part of the Nixon administration to listen to what students think" had contributed to restiveness on the nation's campuses. Only 24% felt that unrest stemmed from "politicians, such as Vice President Agnew, who have tried to get votes by attacking student protestors."

According to Harris (1970), these findings portray an impression by the American people of a university environment heavily infiltrated with radical, militant, and irresponsible students bent on causing trouble and professors and administrators who either actively encourage disorder or are too permissive to prevent it. The "town and gown" confrontation seems to have been revived with a vengeance. This is a situation which has the direst implications, because it threatens to split the nation into opposing camps of intellectuals and "know-nothings" (as H. L. Mencken was wont to call them). The nation can and should expect its leaders to be drawn principally from the ranks of college graduates. Yet, how can college graduates "lead" if they find themselves estranged from many of their noncollegiate countrymen who, for a variety of reasons, fail either to understand or to sympathize with their actions?

Although the causes of these breakdowns in the orderly processes of our universities are numerous and complex, let us first summarize some of those that have seemed most obvious to a number of observers.

CURRENT ANALYSES OF STUDENT UNREST

Alienation or estrangement from the adult community and its values.   As described by Keniston (1965), this involves feelings of withdrawal, distrust, pessimism, apathy, and anxiety. The surges of intense activism that have been witnessed recently among college students may represent, among other things, escape from alienation. For the first time in their lives, many students have experienced a sense of commitment, of excitement, and of importance (Sampson, 1967). In a word, they suddenly achieved an *identity* that they have not enjoyed previously. That students have often resorted to violence and disruption is attributable at least in part to the rigidity and autocracy that has characterized too many of our university administrations. In this regard, Williams (1970) has commented incisively,

> A conservative, highly-structured institution, such as the American university, . . . tends to resist change, and meets demands for change most often after situations have reached crisis status and after strident voices of dissent have inundated the calmer tones of mediators and temporizers. Such highly-structured institutions . . . must necessarily break down in a turbulent society. The alternatives to chaos are repression or decisive and rapid change [p. 16].

Little wonder that the feelings of alienation of the college freshman are fueled afresh by his experiences in the impersonal "multiversity."

The retreat into noninvolvement, apathy, and indifference may be partially dispelled through periods of intense activity—some of it constructive, such as that on Earth Day, and some of it destructive and counterproductive, as that at the University of Wisconsin in Madison. All of us are inclined at times to feel that our lives are governed by remote and impersonal forces over which we exercise little or no control—except at election time, we participate scarcely at all in the economic and political decisions that affect us. Most university students are even more susceptible to feelings of helplessness. Even within their own institutions, their fates are controlled by an administrative hierarchy of faculty members, deans, vice-presidents, presidents, and boards of trustees, all of which are often unreachable and unresponsive.

Even so, responsible student and faculty leadership must conclude sooner or later that *social action,* not campus disruption, is the means by which student helplessness can be converted into student influence. Students by themselves, however, as Peterson (1968) has pointed out, cannot by their own efforts effect major social changes. They must ally themselves with other radical and liberal elements, whether these be church people, intellectuals, Negroes, the poor, or those trade unionists who are sympathetic to their goals. To the extent to which they can persuade the public that the social changes they advocate are indeed desirable, they will succeed in influencing not only the universities, but society at large.

Disillusionment with higher education.   Teaching methods in our universities have changed little in the past 50 years. The lecture method still prevails, and its effectiveness is frequently diluted by the large size of many classes. Students often feel, with justification, that they are simply numbers. They lack the opportunity to ask questions in class or carry on a meaningful dialogue with their instructors or with their fellow students. In the larger universities, the energies of the faculty are frequently directed more toward graduate than undergraduate teaching. Course content, even in the humanities and social science, often seems to be unrelated to the pressing social problems of our time. We can hope, with Wierzynski (1970), that "The day may soon come when U.S. campuses stop using teaching methods that were popular at the University of Bologna during the Renaissance [p. 40]."

Despite these shortcomings of our system of higher education, it is important to note, as Keniston (1967) has done, that protest demonstrations have tended to occur at the *better* rather than the inferior institutions. In other words, despite the frequently cited factors of largeness and impersonality that would seem logically to underlie student discontent, in fact, student activists are often found in the programs that provide them with a great deal of personal attention, that is, honors programs, advanced seminars, and individual tutorial. Keniston (1967) comments: "they probably receive relatively *more* individual attention and a *higher* calibre of instruction than do non-protestors [p. 123]." Sheer size, then, is not the critical element in student dissatisfaction. The small, elite, private institutions have their share of political demonstrations (Lipset, 1970).

We agree with Bundy (1970) that: "People should enroll in a university because they want to learn there and they should stay only as they continue to want that [p. 557]." This may involve, as Bundy points out, a nice discrimination between the freedom to choose a way of learning and the lack of freedom to neglect the work learning demands. Here, of course, is where the professor plays a critical role, since it is he who must arrange an environment in which learning can take place without coercion and yet with responsibility. This is probably where the issue of "relevance" is likely to have its greatest significance. One can always ask, "Relevance for what?" It is becoming increasingly apparent that nearly any course of study can be organized, at least in part, in terms of its relevance to the broader spectrum of human activities, which is probably all that students ask or require; surely it is not too much to achieve. As students increasingly become involved in the day-to-day administrative functions of the university, they themselves will begin to define what is relevant and what is irrelevant to their particular penchants and goals. Perhaps we have not sufficiently recognized several rather obvious and different functions of teaching. As summarized by Morison (1970), these include (*a*) training for particular professions, (*b*) preparation for citizenship in general, and (*c*) the cultivation of the individual for his own purposes. Different pedagogical methods are indicated in each instance, and the development of appropriate environments for these different types of learning remains a challenging goal for both the educator and the student. Neither can shunt the task off on the other.

Concern with international problems. Today's students are probably neither more nor less idealistic than those of the 1940s, who willingly, for the most part, went off to defend their country against totalitarianism. But today's villains are not so readily identified; to some they are represented by international Communism, to others by an incipient Fascism that lurks in the background of all societies and was not interred with the ashes of Nazi defeat in World War II. However, it is difficult to forcus one's hostilities on such amorphous targets. Vietnam, and later Cambodia and Laos, of course, have been focal points of student militancy. But the villain is not the enemy in these countries; it is ourselves. We have allowed ourselves to become trapped in a war that few any longer feel is justified. Yet, a practical manner of exit is not easily accomplished. Thus, the patriotic zeal of the 1940s was transformed into the searing self-criticism and ideological fratricide of the 1960s.

Concern with domestic problems. A distinguishing feature of student activism during the 1960s, as contrasted with that of earlier years, is the integration of student concerns with political issues of wider currency (Skolnick, 1969). In rough chronological order, the domestic events that seem to have captured student attention during this decade were (*a*) segregation policies at public facilities adjacent to campuses, (*b*) nuclear arms testing by the government, (*c*) the plight of the poor and other minority groups, (*d*) denial to students of the right to use campus facilities in support of off-campus political activities (the "free speech" movement), (*e*) policies of the Johnson Administration in Vietnam (the march on Washington), (*f*) the use of grades to determine draft eligibility, (*g*) the use of campus facilities for recruiting purposes by the military and certain defense industries, and (*h*) the relative lack of involvement by students in decision-making processes of the universities. As Skolnick (1969) has pointed out, these years were characterized by " . . . a precipitous decline in the degree to which active participants in the student movement attributed legitimacy to national authority and to the university [p. 99]." A similar observation has been made by Lipset (1968). He notes that historically one should expect student unrest in societies where social and political values are being questioned and where there are obvious failures in national policy. Under these conditions, students, as well as youth in general, may come to question the legitimacy of constituted authority.

A number of more diffuse issues and social concerns also seem to have

playcd a role in arousing student disaffection with the Establishment—overpopulation, environmental pollution, littering and disfigurement of the landscape, and
the indiscriminate destruction of animal life. To the sensitive and concerned
student, these seem to be a monstrous series of swindles perpetrated by past
generations of heedless profiteers and exploiters. In short, today's youths feel
that they are faced with the mess and the waste of their elders, and that the task
of cleaning up the mess falls largely upon them, who obviously are not responsible for it. It is significant that Earth Day was observed primarily by the youths
of the country, and that preservation of the natural environment has become
one of their rallying points.

Even more important to many is the failure of older generations to provide
equal justice and opportunity for minority ethnic groups. For example, despite
misunderstandings and failures of effective communication, many white college
students have joined their black counterparts in a struggle to right prejudicial
wrongs of 300-years' standing. The relatively few resources that have been
allocated to these pressing domestic social problems contrast vividly with the
vast expenditures on wars.

Prospects after graduation.   Impressed as many students are by what they
frequently perceive as the misplaced values and mindless materialism of the adult
society around them, they often contemplate the postgraduation future with less
than exhilaration. Students envision themselves as being absorbed by an increasingly impersonal and corporate economic structure that will turn them into
carbon copies of the very adults who have failed to inspire them with either trust
or admiration. In developing countries, as Skolnick (1969) points out, this
mistrust takes the form of questioning the relevance of traditional, religious,
prescientific, authoritarian values. In advanced nations, however, students are
more apt to perceive the " . . . irrelevance of commercial, acquisitive, materialistic, and nationalistic values in a world that stresses human rights and social
equality and requires collective planning" (Skolnick, 1969, p. 85). Sampson
(1967) has captured the spirit of this disaffection as follows:

Today's university campus has become for many students the last
point in their lives in which they see any hope for exercising significant
influence. The activist youth have seen the bureaucratized world make
older voices whisper thin. The campus seems the last stronghold for testing
ways of influencing their world. They are afraid that when they leave the
university, get a job, marry and raise a family, the weight of responsibilities will weaken their impetus for change. Those over thirty are not to be
trusted, because of their increasing investment in the system as it exists
[p. 21].

Student unrest in other places.   A certain amount of imitation cannot be discounted as contributing to the spread of campus disorders. Students have become, in a sense, a worldwide fraternity. Riots on campuses in most countries are quickly publicized through the media of radio and television. Students in universities on opposite sides of the country are in immediate communication with one another, and a "contagion" of unrest occurs in which a certain amount of prestige and status is conferred on those who are in the forefront of demonstrations. Some have admitted of an urge to live up to the image of them created by the mass media. In addition, a sense of brotherhood, often lacking on a large campus, quickly develops among students who are active in a common cause. The experience of "togetherness" in a time of crisis, such as that precipitated by the tragedy at Kent State, provides surcease from the feelings of alienation and apathy that all too commonly prevail among the majority of students.

A lack of older and experienced leadership.   The students of today have too few heroes to whom they can look for goals and purposes and whose behavior they can emulate. One suspects that neither the country in general, nor youth in particular, had recovered by 1970 from the assassinations of a president, a senator, and a civil rights leader with whom both liberals and young people could identify. The liberals temporarily lost their most effective leaders, and those that had the ability and charisma to assume a leadership role squandered their energies in internecine political struggles. The leaders that arose among youths themselves—such as Rennie Davis, Jerry Rubin, and Bobby Seale—could not, by virtue of their self-generated estrangement from the mainstream of American culture, provide the type of leadership necessary to channel the energies of college students into activities that would effectively bring about the social changes they wanted. Youth needs adult leadership from someone already within the power structure; when such leadership is lacking, their energies tend to dissipate in fruitless demonstrations of protest.

Lack of factual information about the relevant issues.   To aggravate their sense of alienation and helplessness further, all too many students fail to seek out factual information on the issues that have moved them to dissent. They often are surprisingly naive about both the history and current status of problems that have captured their attention. Their very disdain for conventional approaches to problems and methods of analysis has blinded students to a great deal of relevant information. Thus, students lack the practical tools with which to combat the reactionary forces that they feel threaten them. Trent and Craise (1967), for example, point out that student activists, those who provide leadership to large-scale student demonstrations, are actually a small, select group. The percentage of students actively engaged in fomenting protest movements is variously found to range from 3 to 9%. These authors conclude from their research on a sample of nearly 10,000 high school graduates that of those graduates who entered and remained in college over a four-year period, "... very few were concerned with any of the current political, social, or educational issues that might disturb student activists" (Trent & Craise, 1967, p. 36). As a matter of fact, Lipset (1970) has argued: "The principal predisposing factors which determine who among the students will become activists exist before they enter the university [p. 685]." The following remarks are based upon his assumption, and we have singled out what we feel to be a critical element in such a predisposition.

TOWARD A HEURISTIC ANALYSIS OF STUDENT UNREST

The legitimacy and importance of many specific student grievances cannot be overemphasized. We recognize that student attitudes and behavior are highly responsive to conflicting currents within the society at large and usually exemplify positive and idealistic components albeit in exaggerated form. Since this has been discussed at length by a number of authors, the focus of our discussion will be on some of the significant background factors which have, in our view, not received the attention they deserve. The overall behavior of students seems to reflect a basic dissatisfaction that characterizes students in general no matter what their country or origin. These cannot be explained simply by local or idiosyncratic factors. In short, an important aspect of the phenomenon of student unrest may best be understood not as a set of reasons for behavior but, rather, as behavior looking for reasons. Without denying the importance of concrete issues that often trigger student riots, it would seem profitable to examine the changing nature of the student's role as he sees himself interacting with his peers and society at large. This should facilitate an understanding of why this segment of the population responds as it does to environmental pressures.

The following analysis is an attempt to formulate a plausible set of heuristic hypotheses about student unrest which may help explain some aspects of the phenomenon which have received relatively little attention. We recognize that these views have not been tested, but feel that they lead to testable hypotheses. In view of the current interest in these issues, we take the liberty of putting forth these views without adequate evidence in the hope that they may stimulate empirical work.

In one sense, of course, there is nothing novel about student involvement in civil disturbances. As Halsey and Marks (1968) have noted: "Histories of the medieval universities in Europe abound with records of violence [p. 116]." In his review of the history of student unrest throughout the world, Lipset (1968) observed that students—unlike other elements of society such as trade unions— have *remained* a source of both radical leadership and mass support for such leadership. In the same vein, Scott (1968) notes that during the past several years nearly every country in Latin America has experienced some sort of organized student protest that not only disrupted the process of higher education but disturbed the residents of the surrounding community. In some regards, students and student unrest have shared certain common features through the ages. In others, we are currently dealing with new and different phenomena.

Historically, students, especially those in higher education, have always been members of the privileged group: the sons of middle-class, upper-middle-class, and upper-class parents, typically with few, if any, demands made upon them. The students (predominantly male until relatively recently) were for the first time in their lives away from parental control and in the envious situation of having little actual responsibility, while enjoying relatively good social status and material circumstances. It should not be surprising that groups of young people, confronted for the first time with many aspects of life from which they had previously been protected in the parental home, attempting to find themselves, searching for life goals, and fired by enthusiasm and idealism, should occasionally be captured by appeals to radical solutions. In a group, such individuals tend to like excitement and can be mobilized relatively easily toward any kind of activity that seems, at the moment, interesting. For the most part, societies have tended to be tolerant toward the exuberance characterizing the student population—in large part owing to the fact that the individuals involved were the sons of the elite. In fairly stable, class-oriented societies where the individual's status and role are largely determined by accident of birth, the role of student is one of the few in which the individual is permitted a certain degree of autonomy and freedom. It is a role of transition, of standing somewhat outside of the structure of the society in which the individual will ultimately be required to join.

In earlier times, knowledge and education were available exclusively to the privileged class whose style of life was largely assured, regardless of the substantive knowledge they might obtain in school and college. The purpose of education was more to identify oneself as a member of the group than to prepare one with specific skills needed to be economically successful. Upper-class Englishmen went to public school and university for much the same reason that their sisters attended finishing school and learned to play the harpsichord. This divorcing of relevant knowledge from formal education is underscored by the fact that it was quite possible for individuals to become physicians or lawyers without attending a university; they simply sought appropriate apprenticeships in the professions. The fact that an occasional individual actually became interested in the sciences or the humanities and contributed to them in a meaningful way was quite coincidental and, in fact, had no significant impact on either his status in the community or his economic well-being.

This situation contrasts vividly with the role of higher education in the United States. Although the analysis here will focus largely on what has been happening in the university campuses throughout this country, we suspect that similar mechanisms are involved in student unrest throughout the world. The present situation on the campuses appears particularly startling when we compare it with the behavior of students over the past 30 years. Comments often have been made about the American student's docility, his lack of political commitment and involvement, his callousness concerning social problems which were not directly related to him, and his willingness to accept with little questioning the importance of whatever course of study was prescribed for him. Such past behavior seems totally out of character in today's students. What basis is there for the present change? What does it mean? Where might we anticipate it is going?

The role of higher education in the United States is highly germane to our discussion. While America has never been a truly classless society, it was relatively easy to be upwardly mobile, and such mobility was seen as an obtainable ideal. The two principal ways by which mobility was achieved were acquiring wealth and obtaining an education. Although the importance of wealth in this process has received much attention, education emerges as the real key to middle-class society. That education should have become so prized is remarkable, considering the agrarian, pioneering, and business character of the developing United States. The proliferation of colleges and universities in Europe was made possible by the tendency of the merchant princes of the 19th century to endow such institutions. In this country, on the other hand, religious organizations and state governments (including even the poorer ones) all chose to found and support institutions of learning. It should be emphasized that the function of these colleges and universities was to provide education for a far greater proportion of our population than that of any other country. First a high school diploma, and later a college education, became the goal and ambition of parents for their children and of the children for themselves.

Since the turn of the century, the United States has not only created much new wealth but has also been remarkably successful in distributing wealth to a very large segment of the population. During this same period, education for the masses has become a reality. It is well to remember, however, that education was first conceived as an instrumental act—as the way of assuring an individual's social and economic success. During World War I, for example, practically all college graduates became officers when they enlisted in the services. The development of ROTC programs in colleges and universities was seen as a perfectly appropriate and natural means of creating an officer corps from among those individuals who had qualified for middle-class status by virtue of attending college. Even during World War II, college graduates who had not taken ROTC could directly enter Officers Candidate School to become "90-day wonders." Society seemed convinced that possession of a college degree automatically qualified the owner for a position of leadership.

Many of these attitudes toward a college education have persisted to the present day. Guidance teachers in high schools are fond of quoting the statistics which indicate that college graduates earn far more during their lifetime than high school graduates, who, in turn, earn far more than those individuals who do not complete high school. They seldom mention the statistics indicating that graduates from Ivy League schools who later earn doctorates tend to earn less on the average than graduates who do not. (Incidentally, it is probable that there is a relatively limited causal relationship between income and education as such, and more probable that the ability to complete school covaries with the kinds of skills necessary to succeed in other fields. This correlation is further boosted by the effects of inherited wealth.) Whatever the "true" causal relationship, it has been assumed by a large segment of our population that a college education leads to economic success.

The children of the middle class, of course, were expected to acquire an education. Children who were not born into the middle class but who acquired an education were assumed to have the opportunity to become members of the middle class. Whereas in Europe education had often been conceived as the process of maturing, of becoming a whole person, and of developing intellectual resources, in this country it has tended more to be seen as a means of acquiring those skills necessary to succeed in a variety of occupations. As long as a college degree assured a modicum of success in some managerial capacity, the relevance of the training was assumed and not subject to serious question. However, such an invariant relationship between education and vocational success is no longer assured. With the instrumentality of education called into question, the issue of its relevance has become suddenly important.

In considering the nature and causes of student unrest, it is important to note that such unrest typically involves students from middle- and upper-class homes who, while not necessarily affluent, are at least comfortable (Flacks, 1967).[1] Not only are the individual students who engage in various movements and radical behavior on the whole economically secure, but student unrest, as

---

[1] We do not consider the very real revolts of the intelligentsia in India, for example, as characteristic of student unrest, because the situation there involved actual deprivation and hardship for a highly educated group which could not find employment. In most countries, student unrest has typically involved concerns not immediately relevant to economic security. Since this has not been the case in the Indian riots, our analysis is not considered germane to them. The bases for student riots in Japan are also probably unique, involving among other things the dramatic social changes that have occurred in that country since World War II (McGinnies, 1965).

such, occurs during prosperous times and in the absence of major external threats to the integrity of the country. During World War II not only was student unrest as we know it today absent, but even the college pranks and fraternity activities characteristic of the 1930s were curtailed. By the same token, student unrest has been considerable in the United States, Japan, and parts of Western Europe and notably absent in Israel, where problems of national survival are endemic.

In order to understand the present campus scene, it seems helpful to consider the student's situation over the past 50 years and why disturbances did not occur previously in the same manner. Between World Wars I and II, as we have indicated, the importance of a college education as a means of upward social mobility was particularly pronounced. During this period, however, there were proportionally far fewer students than today. Those individuals who attended college either belonged to the middle and upper class and enjoyed an assured future, or they belonged to a relatively small percentage who were on scholarship or who worked their way through school. Although many changes were taking place in the structure of American society during this period, the value system was reasonably stable for much of the middle class. Immediately after World War I, a major economic boom occurred in the United States and a considerable number of parents were able to send their children to college. Furthermore, opportunities existed for the poor but determined student to obtain either a scholarship or part-time work. The depression, by creating serious financial difficulties for a large segment of society, made a college education more difficult to obtain and, consequently, more desired and valued. It was certainly not a period when one would have anticipated student unrest, since many students were preoccupied with the economic problems of the day. Those students from relatively affluent backgrounds tended to avoid confronting the grim realities which faced the bulk of the population. A great many others, however, became involved in leftist causes. (The same students today would probably be involved with the New Left and similar movements.) While involving students and some faculty as individuals, radical causes during the 1920s and 1930s were not principal concerns of the academic community.

A dramatic expansion of educational opportunities occurred at the conclusion of World War II with the inauguration of the G.I. bill of rights. This led to an explosion of the educational establishment which drastically altered the character of education. For the first time it was possible for individuals from poor families to obtain college and even graduate school training without serious hardship to themselves or to their families. As a result, colleges and universities from the mid-1940s on enrolled a large number of veterans, many of whom came from backgrounds where they were the first to have such an opportunity. These students were not in a mood to rebel. They were eager to take advantage of the educational opportunities newly available to them. As long as economic conditions remained favorable, and there were no external threats, the population of students was liberally sprinkled with, and often dominated by, individuals coming from lower-middle-class backgrounds who perceived the educational process as the means to economic and social success. On the whole, these students did well academically and had a concrete goal—to succeed, to achieve a status which their parents could only dream of but which was now within their grasp. It was only necessary for them to pursue with vigor the path laid out before them.

It should be emphasized that the promised economic success awaiting post-war students was matched by the sheer achievement of being in college. They were perceived by their families (and consequently perceived themselves) as already having "made it." These students, therefore, had few if any problems in terms of knowing what they wanted and being confident they could achieve it. They were not concerned about being a number in a large university, because within their own families, at least, they were important and successful.

During the past 20 years, however, the situation of the typical college student has changed considerably. Despite the availability of scholarship aid, the price of education has increased drastically, and the family's contribution has gone up considerably. In contrast to the post-war 1940s, the overwhelming majority of students now are the sons and daughters of individuals who themselves went to college and who have enjoyed the fruits of middle-class affluence. It is worth emphasizing that the overwhelming majority of students involved in riots and unrest come from families who are economically successful and who usually have at least a college education. Campus disturbances have been more characteristic of the elite schools than of those institutions which draw their students from lower-middle-class backgrounds and which have had little or no student unrest. We believe, therefore, that the relative success of the parents is one of the important characteristics leading to student unrest.

Consider the situation of the student today. He has been raised in a materialistic and achievement-oriented society and he has been given all of the "advantages," which means that he has been provided with whatever he asked for without ever learning a clear relationship between his own behavior and any consequences which might flow from it. Characteristically, this is a generation raised by parents who did not want their children to experience the economic privations that they had endured and who were in a position to make this wish come true. As a result, many of today's students have satisfied most of their material wishes by making requests to their parents rather than by having to engage in useful work. Typically, the student will have had little or no gainful employment, and even if he worked a summer or two, it was made abundantly clear to him that his earnings would buy far less than that which his parents would willingly bestow upon him. Not only is this situation entirely different from that on a farm, where the child's assistance with chores was often essential to the well-being of the family, but it is even different from the situation of the lower-middle-class child who would need to work for whatever frills he desired over and above the essentials provided by his parents. In a real sense, the student by the time he reaches college has had little opportunity to learn to perceive himself as capable of providing what he needs by his own efforts. At best, he is aware of a very clear discrepancy between the amount of work and effort required to earn money and the apparent ease with which he can obtain it from his parents.

The relationship between any given action sequence and any given set of rewards tends to be complex. For example, the child may be given things he desires—not because he has worked for them, nor even because he has done something to please his parents—but because he has been particularly demanding and has succeeded in making his parents feel guilty about some real or imagined neglect. Too, he is often rewarded for *not* doing something rather than for a positive action, and he rarely gets the feeling that anything he might do is necessary for the well-being of the family. What we have been illustrating is one aspect of the situation in which the college student of today tends to find himself, namely, a situation that is different from the one that characterized his parents and one that tends to diminish his feelings of competence and self-reliance.

Other factors contrive to aggravate these problems. With the rapid development of new knowledge and increasing professionalization, which lead to greater and often unrealistic demands for specialized training, the time necessary to become competent to carry out many of the jobs which seem desirable to the student has increased greatly. It is generally recognized that a student upon finishing college is not ready to take a responsible position. If he goes into industry, he joins a management training program which will prolong his student role considerably. If he is interested in a profession, such as medicine, he is required to spend not only four additional years in medical school, but also another four or more years beyond that in internship and residency. Similar demands are made in preparing for law, the ministry, and the sciences. Inevitably the student already concerned with feelings of worthlessness is told that he will need to postpone by a matter of years any feeling of being either competent or adequately trained. It is perhaps relevant to observe that society's insistence on credentials and proof of competence is accompanied by an inevitable demonstration of incompetence in ways that are evident to the student. Rare is the teacher who is sufficiently master of all aspects of his field that shortcomings in his knowledge are not soon obvious to his students. Perhaps it is not surprising that the student, faced with this incongruity and failing to understand that the perfection he demands of his teachers is unattainable, should be concerned with "hypocrisy" and begin to ask questions about the relevance of his training.

It should also be noted that the student's status within his home and family is by no means as assured as it was in the case of his parents. The student whose parents have been to college does not gain the kind of respect that characterizes the first member of a family to undertake such training. Indeed, if he does well, his success tends to have been expected and is taken for granted. On the other hand, if he falters or is unfortunate enough not to attend a prestigious school, he may readily lose status. Not only must he cope with competitive pressure from kindergarten on, but the situation is contrived in such a way that failure leads to aversive consequences, whereas success, even if achieved with considerable effort by him, may scarcely be noted by his parents. Thus, while he is in college his family tends to think of him as having yet to show what he can do. Being in college or even completing college with some kind of distinction in no way assures him status either at home or in society at large. The ever-increasing proportion of the population which completes college insures this aspect of the situation. Another important but frequently overlooked fact is the demands made upon the student by the educational process. A level of performance is expected and received quite in excess of that which characterized the work of previous generations. There simply is more to learn and less time in which to do it. This pressure exists not only for the student but also for the faculty, and the increased pressure on faculty members decreases the amount of time and effort they are able to devote to students. In this context, of course, the inevitable consequences of increasing size in terms of diminishing close personal contacts between students and faculty hardly need comment; the deleterious effects are too well recognized.

The situation of today's student, then, is in many ways a difficult one. Materially he is well off. Few if any material demands are placed upon him now, or were while he was growing up. In an effort to provide everything for their children, the preceding generation avoided expecting substantive contribution to the home. As the student is given whatever he asks for without being required to work for his requests, inevitably a progressively greater load is placed upon him. If he is given everything so that he should be able to study, succeed, and be happy, the pressure on him to achieve competitively becomes progressively greater. Further, if he is not satisfied or happy, he is perceived as difficult or ungrateful. Students tend to become acutely aware of the paradoxical ways in which they are rewarded by their families. The highly successful film, *The Graduate*, provided an extremely insightful fictionalized account of the dilemma facing the middle-class individual who has successfully completed college without any great distinction and appears to be received by his family as the conquering hero. On the one hand, the family makes an overt show of enthusiasm and pride; on the other, they make it abundantly clear that they are preoccupied with their own problems and that the boy's achievement was not, in fact, particularly impressive to them. It is the inappropriateness of the rewards being offered that is perceived by the son or daughter as the parents' failure to understand, as lack of real interest, or as hypocrisy. Any or all of these interpretations may lead to a paralyzing kind of ennui.

It is fashionable to argue that middle-class children are neglected by their parents who are more concerned with material possessions and the trivialities of social success. It is unlikely, however, that previous generations, living in harder times that required considerably greater effort to survive, received more in the way of attention and love from parents who were working a 60-hr.-plus week. Rather, it seems probable that the difference lies in what was requested of the child. In situations where there is considerable hardship, the child is able to make a meaningful contribution from a very early age. He does not clean or assist in household chores simply as a favor which is appreciated, but because it is clearly essential for the well-being of the family. His contribution is actually *important* and everyone takes it for granted that he should make it as soon as he is able. As a result, he is not a supernumerary for whom everything is provided, and he correctly perceives himself as being someone who is necessary and important even if his parents are, in fact, too busy to observe and attend to the myriad successes and failures associated with his growth and development. It seems likely that a lack of opportunity or demand for some contribution to the family's welfare is what communicates to the individual that he is unnecessary and that nothing that he does matters.

By the time the individual becomes a university student, he has had many years of training in being unnecessary—unable to help others, and unable to do for himself. Not only is he not expected to perform a necessary function for the family, but when he tries to do so, he often will be told that it really does not matter. Unfortunately, modern city life requires almost no chores which if neglected would have dire consequences. There are no fires to be tended, no errands to be run, no chickens to be fed or cows to be milked—activities the importance of which become clearly evident if they are not properly executed at the appropriate time. When the child attempts to do things to help, given the complexity of appliances in modern living, he is very likely to complicate the situation and find his efforts strongly discouraged. It simply requires skills well beyond the average child to be capable of making a meaningful contribution to the family. Even housecleaning is often not expected from the child, and when such help is given ineptly, it is usually discouraged. The situation, therefore, contrives to give the student a large number of experiences where he is, in fact, told both explicitly and implicitly that his role is merely to entertain himself, preferably quietly, and to be "happy." Unfortunately, happiness is not a state of mind. Rather, it tends to be a consequence of achievements that are followed by appropriate social reinforcement. If a demand is made on a child which he can meet—preferably with some difficulty—then the reinforcer itself also becomes more meaningful. On the other hand, if the child is given whatever he requests without effort, these things, be they material objects, attention, or love, tend to become less effective reinforcers over time. To ask a child to be happy because he is given whatever he asks for creates the one kind of demand which the child cannot possibly meet.

One of the most significant consequences of the events that we have outlined is the nurturing of a feeling of helplessness which, by the time the individual becomes a student, has become extremely powerful. The educational process reinforces this feeling. Unfortunately, from the student's viewpoint, there is an infinite amount of material to be learned, and competence often seems unattainable. As we have already pointed out, he sees the time required for him to become competent in any endeavor where the rewards seem worthwhile as intolerably long. As a result, even in situations where the student is able to achieve something and where he might be able to make a meaningful contribution to his family or to society, he often feels impotent and paralyzed.

The problem outlined here has an interesting experimental analog in the research on learned helplessness in dogs (Seligman & Maier, 1967). The overwhelming majority of dogs in these experiments rapidly learn to avoid a painful stimulus in an avoidance conditioning situation. If they are in a box with two compartments, and a tone is sounded 10 sec. before the portion of the box where they are is electrified, they acquire the skill of jumping to the safe part of the box within the 10-sec. period. As a result, once they have learned this activity, they successfully avoid further shock. However, if the animals are first placed in a situation where the tone is invariably followed by a painful shock, and then are trained in the avoidance learning situation, they simply will not learn to avoid the shock. One interpretation of these observations is that the animals have learned they can *do nothing* about the shock, and once this has been learned, it becomes impossible for them to solve the problem of how to avoid the shock. One might say that they have learned to expect the shock as inevitable and, therefore, no longer try to avoid it even though the situation is changed so that the shock could be avoided. A similar kind of helplessness may be closely related to the dropping-out phenomenon in schools, which has become such a serious problem.

A good deal has been written about the existential problems of our day (see Maddi, 1970), that is, the kind of anxiety which presumably results from the meaninglessness in our everyday lives. Generally this is ascribed to the de-individuation rampant in our culture, the mechanization, the fact that we become a number, an object, and so forth. The search for meaning unquestionably is one of modern man's problems, and our comments are not intended to deny the substantive importance of these issues. On the other hand, it seems likely that one response to the situation of the individual who grows up in an environment which satisfies his every wish is to assert that there is little meaning in life, to complain that one cannot find any worthwhile satisfactions. Phrased in another way, such an individual is not being suitably reinforced by his environment.

The most straightforward manner of ensuring that an individual will gain gratification and satisfaction is to place him on some schedule of deprivation. If food is withheld from him, food becomes an effective reinforcer; if liquids are withheld, drink is reinforcing; if he is deprived of sleep, sleep is reinforcing; and so forth. Appetitive reinforcers require that the individual have an appetite for something. As long as the mere wish leads to immediate gratification, it becomes impossible to develop stimuli which serve as reinforcers. It is, of course, well known from animal studies that aversive or painful stimuli, such as electric shock, may also serve as powerful negative reinforcers, whereas escape from or avoidance of punishment acts as a reward. Modern child-rearing practices tend to avoid recourse to traumatic forms of punishment, or strong negative reinforcement. Modern society's elimination of severe physical deprivation, as well as extreme forms of corporal punishment, makes the kind of situation described above possible. Let it be clear that we are not advocating the reintroduction of physical want or corporal punishment. However, we do need to take a careful look at the present situation and to develop creative and appropriate means of dealing with the issues and results.

These problems, which are particularly striking in contemporary American society, are also clearly evident in the other prosperous industrial countries of the world, and student unrest can be seen as merely one symptom of many. In former times, there were, of course, always segments of society—the "upper classes"—the members of which had a surfeit of gratification. However, this group represented a relatively small segment of the population, the education of which was usually very demanding. While the children of the elite were, of course, without material cares, they were required to achieve considerable proficiency at a number of skills. Further, in the public schools of England, for example, there was little hesitancy in employing extremely powerful negative reinforcers; and for that matter, students were by no means overfed. At the same time, one of the factors which helped make the English public schools relatively successful is present in all forms of elitist education: namely, its limited availability, so that the group which partakes of this education appropriately feels itself to be privileged. On the other hand, it must be emphasized that, characteristically, the educational process made high demands. Rewards were given sparingly, intermittently, and only for considerable effort. Thus, high levels of both effort and achievement were demanded. Such an educational process simply was not designed for a majority which was concerned with merely surviving.

At the present time, and especially in the United States, we are faced with the paradox of providing education of an elite sort for a very large portion of the population. Furthermore, we face a situation where several large segments of the population no longer need be concerned about questions of survival. Most individuals can be assured of a reasonably high standard of living with relatively little effort, but few can still be characterized by a strongly developed elitist philosophy. Quite to the contrary, most middle-class individuals have worked hard to achieve their present security, and they do not want their children to struggle; after all, that is why they themselves have worked. This social situation, while unique in some ways to the United States, is found to a lesser degree in other industrial countries.

It would seem as though the absence of challenge, the lack of reality-induced stresses creates many of the problems of youth today. During a crisis one rarely observes depressive reactions, and even virtually incapacitated neurotics may function remarkably well. For example, during World War II there was a remarkably low incidence of psychiatric disturbance in London. Many individuals with almost incapacitating neuroses found themselves able to function successfully during the time of hostilities, only to suffer a relapse at the end of the war.

A particularly interesting example of some of the consequences of reality pressures is provided by the middle- and upper-middle-class immigrants who came to the United States during the 1930s to escape Hitler's Germany. This group included a considerable number of individuals who had been raised in favorable economic circumstances and whose children not infrequently manifested the kind of ennui and dissatisfaction that has been characterized as youth's problem of the 1960s. On their arrival in the United States, these individuals found themselves confronted with a new language, a new culture, and unanticipated economic difficulties. A remarkably high percentage of their children, however, managed to pursue higher education in the United States and to become successful in a wide variety of intellectual pursuits. Although the harsh realities of immigrating would seem to have complicated the careers of these individuals, such pressures, in fact, may have facilitated them by providing a necessary challenge. A certain degree of hardship made it possible for the children of these immigrants to be reinforced for succeeding in the new culture to a considerably greater extent than might have been the case otherwise. It is likely that the children of middle-class Cubans coming to this country may also become examples of the same peculiar paradox. Whether or not this indeed comes to pass should provide a fascinating outcome for social scientists to observe and interpret.

One way in which these several issues might be formulated is suggested by the behavior of individuals in experimental situations. We have observed that subjects who have participated in an experiment which involves some degree of stress, discomfort, or effort will tend to ascribe considerable importance and significance to the study (assuming, of course, that the investigators treated them reasonably as individuals). It seems as though the individual, having put forth effort or having tolerated pain, is particularly likely to perceive the experiment as having some importance. On the other hand, in an experiment where few demands are made upon the subject (even though he is well treated) it

is far more likely that he will consider the procedures to be trivial. Outside of
the laboratory this mechanism is equally easily recognized. The mountaineer
who pushes himself to the utmost is most likely to value his experience and seek
to renew it. Experiences that are recounted as significant, whether in athletics or
in intellectual pursuits, almost always tend to be those where great demands
were placed upon the individual—demands which he was able to satisfy only at
considerable cost and effort to himself. It is likely that the great hold the British
public schools exerted upon their former students was intimately related to the
totally unreasonable requirements made upon them during their training. One
might well wonder whether institutions such as hazing in a fraternity or the
plebe year at West Point might have served a similar function of making
membership in the group much more important to the individual. Some recent
research, in fact, points to this conclusion (see Aronson & Mills, 1959).

If an analysis as outlined above is at all valid, it suggests that many
individuals must master adversity at considerable effort and cost to themselves in
order to feel involved, committed, and successful. Behaviorally, we would say
that a certain amount of prior adversity is necessary to make success in certain
tasks a source of positive reinforcement. If society cannot provide acceptable
rites de passage which pose legitimate hurdles to overcome, then it may become
necessary for the individual to devise his own. It is tempting to interpret aspects
of the radical's technique of confrontation with authority, especially the police,
as an analog to the Indian youth who was required to demonstrate his prowess in
combat in order to become a brave.

Viewed in this manner, many faculty responses to student unrest appear
somewhat less than appropriate. Faculty members have tended to respond either
by girding themselves for confrontation with what they considered to be
wild-eyed fringe elements, or by rushing to join their students on the barricades.
Neither of these reactions provides the kind of leadership that is truly constructive. One posture ignores the legitimate needs of students and tends to deny the
reality of the students' perceptions of our social ills. The other position over-
looks the fact that much student protest might better be seen as a form of
"acting out," or a testing of the limits to which the adult society will permit
them to go. It seems incorrect to believe that students necessarily understand the
bases of their dissatisfactions, and, therefore, the response by some faculties has
generally raised more problems than it has solved. Too many faculty members
have assumed that they know what students want, have responded by attempting to give them what they want, and have then discovered to their surprise and
consternation that this was not what the students wanted after all. It now seems
clear that one thing students do not want is to be simply a number; perhaps
more than anything, they wish to be recognized as individuals. Nor do the
students want to receive a numbered degree for which they did not really work.
Unfortunately, the demands of students in this context have tended to be

confusing. Even in the medical schools they have asked for fewer or even no examinations while insisting on greater relevance. Some faculty members have responded by saying essentially, "If that's what the students want, let's give it to them." In the final analysis, however, the students themselves, given time for reflection, have become concerned with the consequences of relaxing academic standards. In due course, we believe it will become apparent that those faculties who have reacted impulsively by simply going along with the tide have failed in their responsibilities to their students as well as to their institutions.[2]

The faculties' behavior in this context is perhaps as important to understand as that of the students. Faculties who agree that no demands should be made upon the students or that academic performance should not be evaluated tacitly communicate that they themselves believe that what they are teaching is essentially trivial. When challenged by the students, their own doubts about the worthwhileness of their academic activities come to the fore. It is not surprising, then, that many students find their own academic responsibilities less attractive than demonstrating for causes that have little actual relevance to what universities are doing or could effectively do so far as political events are concerned. In other words, the faculty, by acquiescing to demands for lower standards, fewer or no examinations, immediate "relevance," and the abandonment of the search for new knowledge in favor of "better teaching," implicitly states that scholarly activity in their field is not very necessary. Yet it is precisely the opposite message that the student really wants to hear. More than anything else, he wants the faculty to reaffirm that what the students are doing is important. To do this, faculty members must have the courage of their convictions rather than seek to curry favor by adopting chimerical solutions that cannot help but aggravate the problem in the long run.

In this connection, the role of the junior faculty member is particularly important. Frequently, the junior faculty members themselves experience a period of conflict and difficulty. They have not yet achieved full academic recognition. Their own power within their departments is frequently limited and they often see themselves more as students than as faculty. Therefore it is not surprising that many members of the junior faculty identify with the students who, by their rebellion, act out those fantasies that the faculty themselves had hardly dared to think about. Their own feelings of helplessness are reconciled as they identify with a momentarily powerful student movement. A systematic study of the insecurities that characterize the junior faculty in "the better schools," the very schools which have been most plagued with student unrest, might shed considerable light on the mechanisms of unrest.

[2]This already has become apparent to enlightened student bodies. Two years ago, at Harvard Medical School, formal grades were abandoned in favor of descriptive remarks. This year the student body has petitioned the dean to return to letter grades.

As far as the students' actual wishes are concerned, remarkably little is known. While the vocal minorities have made a number of "nonnegotiable demands," what the majority of students actually think about some of the issues confronting them both as citizens and as members of the academic community has really not been explored. Apparently, few academicians have thought to take a poll of the students to try and find out what they actually are saying. A step in this direction was taken by the Harris Survey during the spring and fall of 1970 to determine whether the public at large correctly perceived the attitudes that students have toward several salient social issues. In all cases, the public misread the depth of student feelings on these matters. For instance, when the percentage of students expressing concern over a problem was compared with the estimate by noncollege respondents of this percentage, it became clear that the public seriously underestimated the number of students who felt, for example, that the Black Panthers could not get a fair trial, that the country is not serious about cleaning up air and water pollution, and that America is a repressive society. The public also underestimated the number of students who were against the use of violence and who were prepared to work for change from within the system rather than through revolution. As a result of similar misunderstandings, too many academicians have found themselves responding to nonnegotiable demands presented by 2% of the student body.

In conclusion, we rather belatedly take cognizance of Erikson's plea that one must undertake with diffidence to write yet one more paper on youth. Much of the literature on "contemporary 'unrest'. . . . reflects a profound unrest among adults" (Erikson, 1970, p. 154). They, in fact, exhibit "a traumatized state . . . that seeks catharsis in hurried attempts to reassert intellectual mastery over a shocking course of events [p. 154]." Both the concerned layman and the social scientist must contend with the proposition that not the fact of violence but the *legitimacy of violence*, as Erikson puts it, is the greatest single issue in youth's ideological struggle. Erikson (1970) sees many of the current protests as examples of regressive behavior that originates in the incapacity or the refusal of many youths to "conclude the stage of identity on the terms offered by the adult world [p. 172]"—a view which, while differently conceptualized, is not too dissimilar from the notion of learned helplessness.

We have tried to suggest that modern society must come to terms with a number of serious basic problems that require creative solutions. In order for an individual to feel satisfied with himself and develop a feeling of self-worth it is vital that he perceive himself as a necessary, contributing member of the community. In order to feel important, he must make a contribution that he feels is recognized as important.[3] The problem of the individual feeling neces-

---

[3] A not insignificant purpose of the recent strikes among municipal employees, e.g., garbage collectors, has been to show the community at large that they are needed.

sary becomes greatly aggravated in complex industrial societies. Ironically, as society becomes prosperous enough to provide the basic needs for all its members, problems of this kind intensify.

As we have pointed out, a very large segment of our population currently enjoys a high standard of living and a considerable degree of security in maintaining such a standard. Among this group in particular, the growing individual has rarely experienced the feeling of being needed. We suspect that the ubiquitous concern among this group for being wanted is likely to reflect a feeling of being unnecessary or superfluous. The length of time and the amount of training necessary to feel able to make a meaningful contribution within the family or within the society at large has progressively increased over the years, and only very recently have there been any attempts to revise requirements downward.[4]

Our society and that of other industrial nations, faces a unique problem in the history of man. A large segment of the population, likely to be the majority in the not-too-distant future, is in a material position which previously was enjoyed by only a very small elite. Elitist philosophies characteristically placed greater demands upon the growing individual and confronted him with many challenges, the mastery of which required considerable endurance and effort. Further, these challenges were socially legitimized as preparing the individual for his role of leadership. An elitist philosophy of this kind, however, is almost the precise opposite of the way in which the middle class approaches the problem of education: it should not be unduly difficult, it should not make undue demands, the wishes of the individual should be respected, and so forth. Children are protected against any arduous demands the system might make. Whereas an elitist philosophy is usually associated with considerable social control exerted by both parents and the schools, the middle-class parent generally eschews the exertion of authority. He is frequently more afraid of losing the favor of his child, than concerned that the child live up to the demands made upon him. This attitude is reflected in those school systems where, even in the lower grades, discipline has become an issue. As the student comes to the university, his difficulties with authority tend to be aggravated by faculties which frequently are unsure of the importance of their own work and, especially, by some members of the faculty who identify uncritically with the students' difficulties and fail to provide a suitable model.

In an analysis of this kind, it would be too easy to suggest a return to simple family virtues: chores for children, demands upon the growing individual, a tough, hard-nosed school system, and an equally adamant faculty in our universities as changes that would quickly resolve the problems. Not only is such a

---

[4] Finally, efforts are being made to shorten training for some of the professions; for example, medicine is in the process of eliminating the internship requirement.

solution unrealistic, it probably is undesirable. Rather, we are attempting to point to some of the basic issues which seem to underlie the worldwide phenomenon of student unrest. We would hope that modern man will ultimately develop creative new solutions. We would hope that the unreasonable demands formerly made by the English public schools, or the invidious and often vicious practices of hazing that were once so characteristic of our fraternities, need not be replaced by confrontation with the police or destructive violence. We would hope that alternative ways will be developed by which large segments of the population may benefit from an education no longer restricted to the elite, and that ways can be found by which man's need to be important, to master his environment, can be satisfied and channeled into socially productive ends. Perhaps the recent militant concern with issues of ecology, overpopulation, and similar problems reflects such a tendency.

Undoubtedly we are facing a period of major social change where the development of appropriate and meaningful new ways for the growing individual to become more immediately necessary to his fellow man is increasingly urgent. In this process of change the university too will gradually alter some of its functions—and perhaps even its form will gradually change. However, to the extent that faculties wish to exert positive meaningful influence, it will be essential not to opt for simple solutions, not to lose our integrity as scholars and scientists, but rather to grope with our students for constructive solutions which truly serve to satisfy their needs. In such a process dialogue between the students, the faculty, and the community will be essential. Genuine effort to understand what the student is saying and what he requires is crucial. However, the faculties cannot and must not expect the students to solve the university's problems. The responsibility for the form, nature, and quality of education must continue to rest with the faculty. To permit the student body to arrogate this responsibility to itself would be a gross disservice to the university, to the faculty, and, above all, to the present and future generations of students.

REFERENCES

Aronson, E., & Mills, J. The effect of severity of initiation on liking for a group. *Journal of Abnormal and Social Psychology*, 1959, **59**, 177-181.

Barr, S. Why students revolt. In *The establishment and all that.* Santa Barbara, Calif.: Center for the Study of Democratic Institutions, 1970. Pp. 67-70.

Bundy, McG. Were those the days? *Daedalus,* 1970, **99**, 531-567.

Erikson, E. H. Reflections on the dissent of contemporary youth. *Daedalus,* 1970, **99**, 154-176.

Flacks, R. The liberated generation: An exploration of the roots of student protest. *Journal of Social Issues,* 1967, **23**, No. 3, 52-75.

Halsey, A. H., & Marks, S. British student politics. *Daedalus,* 1969, **97**, 116-136.

Keniston, K. *The uncommitted: Alienated youth in American society.* New York: Harcourt, 1965.

Keniston, K. The sources of student dissent. *Journal of Social Issues,* 1967, **23**, No. 3, 108-137.

Lipset, S. M. Students and politics in comparative perspective. *Daedalus,* 1968, **97**, 1-20.

Lipset, S. M. American student activism in comparative perspective. *American Psychologist,* 1970, **25**, 675-693.

Maddi, S. R. The search for meaning. In W. J. Arnold & M. M. Page (Eds.), *1970 Nebraska symposium on motivation.* Lincoln: University of Nebraska Press, 1970. Pp. 137-186.

McGinnies, E. Some reactions of Japanese university students to persuasive communications. *Journal of Conflict Resolution,* 1965, **9**, No. 4, 482-490.

Morison, R. S. Some aspects of policy-making in the American university. *Daedalus,* 1970, **99**, 609-644.

Peterson, R. E. The student left in American higher education. *Daedalus,* 1968, **97**, 293-317.

Sampson, E. E. Student activism and the decade of protest. *Journal of Social Issues,* 1967, **23**, No. 3, 1-33.

Scott, R. E. Student political activism in Latin America. *Daedalus,* 1968, **97**, 70-98.

Seligman, M. E., & Maier, S. F. Failure to escape traumatic shock. *Journal of Experimental Psychology,* 1967, **74**, 1-9.

Shoben, E. J. Cultural criticism and the American college. *Daedalus,* 1970, **99**, 676-699.

Skolnick, J. H. *The politics of protest.* New York: Simon & Schuster, 1969.

Trent, J. W. & Craise, J. L. Commitment and conformity in the American college. *Journal of Social Issues,* 1967, **23**, No. 3, 34-51.

Harris, L. Poll finds public underestimates depth of student feeling. *Washington Post,* November 26, 1970, N3.

Wierzynski, G. H. New campus mood: From rage to reform. *Time,* November 30, 1970, 38-40.

Williams, C. V. Academic issues which should attract student protests in southern universities. In W. C. Snipes (Ed.), *The humanities and student revolt.* Ruston, La.: Southern Humanities Conference, 1970. Pp. 15-35.

5
The Tactics and Ethics
of Persuasion[1]

Philip G. Zimbardo
Stanford University

If one . . . has a layman's knowledge of practical psychology, and uses the salesman's approach, he can be successful in reaching into a man's brain and pulling out the facts he wants (Mulbar, 1951, p. 5ff).

The road to the top is steep and treacherous. To move up, you have to give 100 per cent of your energies and abilities at all times. . . . Whether you sell to industry, to wholesalers, to the retail trade, or to the individual consumer, you are dealing with people. Human beings are generally regarded as unpredictable and unfathomable but over the years the knowledge of human nature has been increased and clarified. Psychology has taught us much about getting along with and motivating people. The *Manual* will show you how to deal successfully with people and motivate them to make decisions in your favor (*Professional Salesman's Desk Manual*. Bureau of Business Practices, 1969, Introduction).

The police interrogator is recognized by society as an agent of change whose job it is to persuade witnesses and suspects to give evidence, admissions, and confessions of guilt. When he is successful, the individual may lose his freedom

---

[1] This paper represents an elaboration and integration of ideas developed in association with Robert Abelson and reflected in our book, *Canvassing for peace: A manual for volunteers*. Ann Arbor, Michigan: S.P.S.S.I., 1970. Other ideas come from my research on police interrogation techniques (an interest stimulated by Abraham Goldstein), which is outlined in "The psychology of police confessions," *Psychology Today*, June 1967, 17-27.

The action orientation to applying the knowledge from academic studies of communication and persuasion is more fully described in *Influencing attitudes and changing behavior*, Rev. ed. Reading, Massachusetts: Addison Wesley, 1970, co-authored with Ebbe B. Ebbesen.

or life, but society is presumed to be the beneficiary of this loss. The salesman's effective persuasion may or may not benefit either the "target" of his sales attempt or the society, but it certainly brings personal gain to the salesman and those he represents. What is similar about both is that they are "formal" persuasive communicators in so far as their goal to effect a specified change is explicitly formulated and their tactics often are laid down in training manuals used in their initiation. Examination of their tactics reveals a further basis of similarity—a willingness to employ virtually any means to achieve their goals. Indeed, for one, it has been necessary to establish Supreme Court rulings to limit the use of third-degree physical brutality and excessive psychological coercion; for the other, The Better Business Bureaus and Ralph Nader are needed to limit the excessive exploitation of the consumer.

Every social interaction, however, carries the burden of being a potential attitude change encounter. The ethical issues raised by deceptive business prac- tices or police coercion are often ignored in other equally compelling influence situations. Parents, educators, priests, and psychotherapists, for example, repre- sent some of the most powerful "behavioral engineers" in this society. It is rare that the appropriateness of evaluating what they do in ethical terms is even considered. This is largely because they are not perceived as formal agents of attitude and behavior change. They function with the benefits of socially sanctioned labels which conceal persuasive intent: parents "socialize," teachers "educate," priests "save souls," and therapists "cure the mentally ill."

There are two other characteristics of the influence situations in which they operate which minimize any issue of unethical, deceptive, or coercive persuasion. First, there is an illusion that the goal of the situation is defined in terms of the best interests of the target person: the child, student, sinner, sick patient. Second, an attribution error process typically occurs by which we judge that the individual could have resisted the pressures brought to bear upon him. One would want to believe that people change only when they want to or when they are subjected to overwhelming *physical* forces. The extent to which behavior is controlled by external social and psychological forces is denied in favor of the presumed strength of individual will power to resist. Given these three character- istics, then, the most persuasive communicators are not acknowledged as such, or are not recognized as exerting a potentially negative effect on the individuals with whom they interact.

Upon closer analysis, however, these underpinnings of this naive view of such attitude-change agents lose some of their foundation. For example, all of them can be viewed as "salesmen" for the established *status quo* with the best interest of society placed before the best interest of the individual. "Socializa- tion" to be a Hitler *Jungn*, "socialization" to repress impulses, to be a good child, to do what one is told, to be seen and not heard, to be patriotic, to be polite, not to question elders, and so forth are goals of the adults in the society, which may be at odds with the child's personal growth. "Education" can mean to bias, to present prejudiced opinion as scientific or accepted fact, to perpetuate preferred ways of thinking. For example, the Russians teach the doctrine of Lysenko, some United States schools reject Darwinism, teachers can be models of racial prejudice, and the like. To save sinners may involve making people feel guilt, shame, anxiety—deny the pleasure of physical contact; accept the poverty and *status quo* of this world for a pie in the sky when you die. To cure the mentally ill sometimes involves communicating what the person must do in order that society not label him a "deviant" and cast him out into a madhouse. Psychotherapy can be seen as conformity training in which there is a unilateral influence attempt to make the patient's "abnormal" behavior "normal" (like everyone else's) again.

Such a predisposition to make the attribution error of overestimating internal relative to external causality is seen repeatedly in those phenomena which most intrigue and fascinate us. Hypnosis, voodoo deaths, brainwashing, placebo effects, Asch's conformity, and Milgram's obedience findings all share this property. Dramatic changes in behavior occur in others, which we believe we personally could resist. The strength of the situational forces are not appreciated, while our own ability not to be tender minded, or weak willed, or suggestible, or controlled by words is magnified.

Research from many disparate areas clearly reveals how easy it is to bring behavior under situational control. Hovland (1959) has noted that it is almost impossible *not* to get positive attitude change in a laboratory study of attitude change. Orne (1962) despairs at being able to find a task so repulsive and demeaning that "experimental subjects" will *not* perform it readily upon request. Milgram (1963) shows that the majority of his subjects engage in extremely aggressive behavior in a situation which psychiatrists had believed would only have a weak effect in inducing blind obedience. We comply, conform, become committed, are persuaded daily in the endless procession of influence situations that we enter, yet each of us continues to maintain an illusion of personal invulnerability. It is only when the situational forces become so obviously unfair—so physically suppressive or psychologically repressive—that we question the ethics of the change situation.

In this sense, then, one may talk about the politics of persuasion since an influence attempt backed by society is persuasion sanctioned by established policy. If a *communicator* advocates change which is not acceptable to the power structure controlling the resources of the society, then pressure is applied to change the communicator. Attempts are made to bring him back in line or, failing this, to reject him through relabeling as a "revolutionary," "radical," or "traitor."

Society in the United States is now in a state of confusion because agents of change whose persuasive influence once was sanctioned by society are no longer granted dispensation to use the approved labels "educator," "pediatrician," and so forth, or to be immune from persuasion attempts themselves. It then becomes obvious to former "targets" that there was previously an implicit contract of complicity and that there still is with other agents. When people become aware of this duplicity and cognizant of the hidden situational forces, they lose trust in parents, educators, politicians, and all those who now reveal themselves as undercover agents of change. They become cynical toward a system which professes to function for the people when, in fact, it functions for the communicator and his powerful backers, the "Society." Finally, when the illusion of individual assertiveness, resistance, and willpower disintegrates under the realization of the overwhelming forces operating to keep even their "personal" communicators in line, then feelings of hopelessness come to the surface.

If a society, through its political power base, wanted to make war and not peace, and most of its traditional communicators have supported this view (or did not openly oppose it), how could the society ever be changed? The two alternatives are revolution, which destroys the established base of power, or persuasion, which redirects available knowledge and tactics and utilizes former "targets" as new agents of communication.

The remainder of this paper presents one attempt to apply the research findings of social psychology and the salesman's intuition to just this problem. Can "students" and young people effectively persuade adults, who collectively have the power to change the system, to use their voting power in an effort to promote peace?

Tactics and strategies designed to achieve this goal will be formulated explicitly, and then, for purposes of comparison, the tactics of the police interrogator will be outlined. The ethical issues involved in attempting "to turn a society around" by working through its system will not be discussed, but the question of using "Machiavellian" techniques on an individual in order to do so will be raised.

PERSUADING FOR NEW POLITICS

Preparing for the Initial Contact

A. *Be informed.* Get as much accurate, up-to-date, reliable evidence as you can. Commit important facts, arguments, statistics, and quotations to memory so they are "natural" when you need them. You should see yourself as more expert on the particular issue of concern than the people you will try to persuade. Your perceived competence is a very important source trait. However, *do not use information as a put-down.* Do not overkill. Hold your storehouse in reserve and select only the facts you need.

B. *Learn as much as you can about those you will engage.* Be familiar with their neighborhood, local issues, basic values, language style (use of diction, cliches, homilies), source of local pride and discontent, the nature of usual influence media, attitudes on the issue in question, and the like. You can obtain this information from local businessmen (barbers, cab drivers, grocery store employees, bartenders, and others), salesmen, letters to the newspaper, and distinguishing characteristics of the neighborhood or the individual home. You can also encourage people to state their opinions on preliminary telephone surveys. When you are in this learning phase, do not try to exert influence.

C. *Actively role-play with a friend the anticipated situation.* Imagine and then work through as realistically as possible the persuasion situation in which you will operate. If available, tape-record or videotape such dress rehersals and then critically analyze your performance. Switch roles and try to be the target person in the situation where he is experiencing the pressure to comply to a request for some commitment.

D. *Do a critical self-appraisal.* Analyze your own personal strengths and weaknesses, your appearance, and discuss any source of fear, anxiety, anticipated embarrassment, and so forth with one or more persons with whom you feel comfortable before you actually start out.

E. *Be confident.* Expect that you will be effective more often than not. You must expect some setbacks, but you must be dedicated to winning, to making the "sale." If you do not handle the situation carefully, you may produce the undesirable effect of increasing the person's resistance to any further influence attempts by others, or you may generate a backlash effect yourself. If you blow it once or twice, or if you get doors slammed in your face before you even start talking (this will surely happen in some neighborhoods), keep trying. If you lose your confidence, however, or you get negative results in a variety or neighborhoods with a variety of techniques, then perhaps you are not suited for face-to-face confrontations and your talents could be put to better use elsewhere.

F. *Be sensitive to the varied reasons underlying the attitude(s) in question.* Attitudes are formed and maintained because of needs for information, for social acceptance by other people, or for ego protection from unacceptable impulses and ideas. Deeply held attitudes probably have all three of these motivational bases. Information *per se* is probably the least effective way of *changing* attitudes and behavior. Its effectiveness is maximum at the attitude-formation stage when the person has not yet taken a stand and put his ego on the dotted line. Your general approach must acknowledge that the individual is more than a rational, information processor—sometimes he is irrational, inconsistent, responsive to social rewards, or primarily concerned about how he appears to himself and to others.

G. *Even as a stranger you can exert considerable influence.* You can be an effective agent for change by serving as a model for some behavior by publicly engaging in it, selectively reinforcing some opinions rather than others, and providing a new source of social contact, recognition, and reward for many people.

Gaining Access to and Establishing the Contact

A. Before you can persuade, you must get the person to acknowledge your presence, to attend to you and to follow your presentation. People are wary of an assault on their privacy and "life space" by an unknown person on their doorstep. You might want to consider an initial phone call or letter to contacts to be made at home.

B. If you are making a home contact, be aware of the particular situation you have encountered. Be sure that the person is willing to give you the required time. You might be interrupting dinner, a phone call, a family quarrel, a visit with guests, or some bad news. You do not want the dominant motivation of the homeowner to be to get rid of you as soon as possible.

C. Although strangers can influence everyday behavior, persuasion is enhanced when the target perceives some basic similarity with the source. This "strategy of identification" (practiced by all good entertainers and politicians) involves finding something in common between you. Physical similarity is the most obvious: age, sex, race, ethnic features, dress (distribution of hair). In addition, similarity is inferred from voice dialect, regionalisms, and appropriate slang, jargon, or group-membership-identifying phrases (for example, "such a lot of *chutzpah* he's got, that Vice President," or "People like us who work for a living have callouses on their hands; a politician like X who talks about working for the people, probably has them only on his mouth.") Canvassing should be arranged to optimize this perceived similarity by selecting neighborhoods and locations which are approximately matched to the available canvassers. The canvasser should try to uncover as many points of similarity as possible because similarity breeds familiarity, which breeds liking and enhances credibility and greater acceptance of the message.

D. Students are not seen as credible sources on most issues that concern them directly, and to be effective, it is important that they increase their source credibility. This may be accomplished in a number of ways:

1. Impress the audience with your expertise, concern, and dedication, being forceful but not overbearing.
2. Make some points which are against your own best interest: indicate the sacrifices you have made and would be willing to make.
3. Have a respected person introduce you, make the contact for you.
4. Begin by agreeing with what the audience wants to hear, or with whatever they say first.
5. Minimize your manipulative intent until you ask for the commitment.

E. Avoid group situations where the majority are known or expected to be against you, since they will provide support for each other and their cohesion might make salient the group norm that you appear to be attacking (which they never cherished so much before your attack).

Maintaining, Intensifying, Directing the Interpersonal Relationship

Once you have managed to get the person to receive you, then you must hold this attention, while trying to get your message (and yourself) accepted.

A. You have the power to reinforce many behaviors of the target person, a power you should use judiciously but with conscious awareness of what and how you are reinforcing.
1. Listen attentively to what the other person has to say about anything of personal interest. This not only "opens up" the person for a dialogue, and helps in establishing what are the primary values, beliefs, and organization of his (or her) thinking, but establishes you as someone open to what others have to say. (The opportunity to tell a college student where to get off is very rewarding for many people.)
2. Maintain eye contact with the person and as close physical proximity as seems acceptable to the person.
3. Individuate the person, by using names (with Mr. or Mrs. or titles where there is an age or status discrepancy). Make the person feel you are reacting to his uniqueness and individuality—*which you should be*—and are not reacting in a programmed way to your stereotyped conception of a housewife, blue collar worker, etc. Similarly, help the other person to individuate you, to break through the categorization and pigeon-holing process which makes you just an anomymous canvasser. At some point, describe something personal or unique about your feelings, background, interests, and so forth (which you expect will be acceptable). However, once accomplished, then do not allow yourself to be the exception to the stereotype—say "most other students are like me in how we feel about X."
4. Reinforce specific behaviors explicitly and immediately, by nodding,

saying "good," "that's an interesting point," and the like. Reinforce more general classes of behavior by smiling, and by making it obvious you enjoy the interaction and by being impressed with the person's openness, sensitivity, intelligence, or articulateness. As a student with a lot of "book learning" you can still learn a lot from people who have gone to the "school of hard knocks," who have "real-life learning" and "street savvy" to offer you. Let them know that this is how you feel when talking to someone who has not had the benefit of your degree of education.

5. The person must perceive that you personally care about and are enthusiastic about the item(s) under discussion; moreover he/she must perceive that *you* as a person really care about the complaint act—at a personal level and not merely as part of your role.

6. Your reinforcement rate should increase over the course of the interaction, so that ideally, at the end of the time, the person is sorry to see you leave.

B. Be aware of sources of resentment against you for what you represent by your physical appearance, group membership (as a student), and the like; work first to differentiate those biased and often unfounded feelings and reactions from those reactions you want to elicit by your influence attempt.

Working class people in particular will resent you for having an easy life. They have worked with their hands, strained their backs, calloused their knees, scrubbing, lifting, sweating, struggling, ekeing out a measly subsistence, while you (as they see it) sit on your butt and have every need catered to. You can blunt this resentment in at least two ways: (1) by showing respect, even awe, for how hard they work, acknowledging that you found it really tough that summer you worked as a hod-carrier, and so forth; (2) by offhandedly noting what a sweat you had studying for that last calculus exam, that while other students may have a lot of money, *you* don't and you don't know whether you can afford to make it through college, and the like—whatever you can honestly say to undercut the perception that you are privileged and spoiled.

In contrast, middle class office workers are likely to resent you for a different set of reasons: that (according to the stereotype) you do not show respect for your elders, that you are an uncouth, dirty, disruptive, pot-smoking libertine, and so forth. A neat appearance and considerate, respectful manner will do much to combat this stereotype.

C. Plan the organization of your approach well enough so that it seems natural and unplanned, and be flexible enough to modify it as necessary.

1. Do not surround your best arguments with tangential side arguments or a lot of details. Arguments that come in the middle of a presentation

are remembered least well. Put your strongest arguments first if you want to motivate or interest uninvolved people.

2. Draw your conclusions explicitly. Implicit conclusion drawing should be left for only very intelligent audiences.

3. Repeat the main points in your argument, and the major points of agreement between you and the target person.

D. Tailor your approach to the target person.

1. Do not put him on the defensive, or even encourage or force a public defence of (and thus commitment to) any position against you. Opposing beliefs are seen as providing the opportunity for open discussion, and as a starting point to find areas of common agreement. If the person is for you, then get a public commitment early, and try to make that commitment more stable and more extreme than it was originally.

2. If possible, have the person restate your ideas and conclusions for himself, in his own words (encourage active participation).

3. If the person appears to be very authoritarian in manner and thinking, then he will probably be more impressed by status sources, decisiveness, and one-sided generalizations than by informational appeals, expert testimony, unbiased presentation of both sides of the issue, and so forth. Make any approach responsive to the dominant personality and social characteristics of the person to whom you are talking.

4. Work in pairs. Although a more personal relationship can be established in a two-person interaction, there is much to be gained from teamwork. Working in pairs provides each student with social support, lowers apprehension about initiating each new contact, and allows one of you to be "off the firing line" appraising the situation, to come in when help is needed, to refocus the direction, or respond to some specific trait detected in the target person. There are several ways in which teams can be composed to produce interesting effects. There is a general principle covering them all, namely, *the two members of the team should differ in some obvious characteristic, such as temperament, age, or sex.* There are two reasons behind this principle: first, it maximizes the chances that either one or the other member will be similar to the target person and therefore can gain a persuasive advantage at the appropriate moment; second, it promotes the subtle idea that even when people differ in outward characteristics, they can still agree on the important issue of peace—therefore, the target person, who may differ from both persuaders, can be encouraged to agree also. The obverse of this "team difference" principle is also important: *it is very inefficient for similar canvassers to accompany each other.*

Getting the Commitment and Terminating the Contract

Do not insist that the person accept and believe what you have said before he makes a behavioral commitment. Get the behavioral commitment anyway, and attitude change will follow. The ideal conclusion of the contact will also leave the person feeling that the time spent was worthwhile and his self-esteem will be greater than it was before you arrived.

A. Do not overstay your welcome or be forced to stay longer than is worthwhile according to your time schedule. Timing is essential both in knowing when to ask for the commitment and in knowing when to quit with an intractable person. For a person who needs more time to think, encourage him if you get a promise to allow you to come back.

B. Provide several levels of possible behavioral alternatives for the person: pushing the most extreme is likely to get a greater level of compliance even if the extreme is rejected.

C. Be clear as to what actions are requested or what has been agreed upon or concluded.

D. Use a "bandwagon" effect, if called for, to indicate prestigious others who have joined in the action.

E. When you believe the target person is about to make the commitment (or after a verbal agreement is made), stress the fact that the decision is his own; it involves free choice, no pressure. This maximizes the dissonance experienced by the decision made and forces the individual to make his behavior internally consistent by generating his own intrinsic justification for his behavior. Each person is his own best persuader. After the final commitment, honestly and openly thank the person and reinforce his behavior.

F. Broaden the contact in two ways. First, get the name of one or more neighbors who would agree with that person's position—you will talk to them too and use the person's name if that is O.K. with him. Second, honestly react to something about his person which is irrelevant to the main social/political issue at hand—the house, decor, hair, clothes, and avocation mentioned, or a favor which you can do related to something mentioned.

G. Extend your influence if you can get the target person also to be an agent of influence. Try to enlist his aid in getting at least one other person to agree to do what he has just done. He should be motivated to proselytize at this time, especially if he is an outgoing person good at persuading others. If he convinces others, that will reduce his own doubts about whether he has done the right thing.

MACHIAVELLIAN STRATEGIES

Just how far should you go to make the "sale," to get the commitment? The answer to such a question depends ultimately on a complex interplay of ethical, ideological, and pragmatic issues. Each individual must establish his own set of weighting coefficients to determine how much pressure he is willing to exert. Assuming that your approach will achieve your purpose, is it "right," "proper," "decent," "humane," "moral" for you to deceive someone, to hit him below his unconscious, to arouse strong negative feelings of guilt, anxiety, shame, or even positive feelings of false pride? Behaving unethically for whatever reason pollutes the psychological environment by replacing trust, understanding, and mutual respect with deceit, lies, and cynicism.

Police interrogation manuals state: "When you break a man by torture, he will always hate you. If you break him by your intelligence he will always fear and respect you" (Kidd, 1940, p. 49). This generalization may hold only when he does not realize that you, in fact, have broken him by intention. When deception techniques are employed by a sophisticated, trained practitioner, the "victim"—be he a criminal suspect, collegiate experimental subject, or "mark" in a pool hall hustle—does not realize he has been conned. But *you* always know what your intention was and that you "broke a man" thus. What effect does such knowledge have upon you? Do you respect yourself more because of it? Do you begin to depersonalize other human beings as they become notches on your gun handle, "hits/misses," "easy cases/tough customers"? Thus, you must reflect upon the psychological effects of behaving unethically, both upon the target person and upon yourself. If you are so ideologically committed to your cause or goal that any ends justify the means, then ethical issues will get a zero weighting coefficient. But that alone should give you pause.

    (a)   Will it be possible to restore ethical precepts after your ends have been achieved?

    (b)   If you have been converted to such an extreme view, can others be similarly moved without recourse to deception?

    (c)   Have you not been duped into the extreme position you now hold?

    (d)   Are you being honest with yourself in recognizing that you are about to be dishonest with others, and are not covering up the fact with rationalizations about "the other side did it first" (if that's true then the poor victim gets it from both ends).

Finally, if you cast ethics to the wind, yet proceed firmly convinced that Goodness, Justice, and Truth are what you stand for, then ask one more practical question: "Is it likely to work?" How much effort, training, staging, and time will it take to carry off the caper? Are you the type of person who can be effective at this game? What happens if the person discovers the gimmick? Will each "miss" turn into a "boomerang" or a backlash that will actively work against your cause? Will you then get only the immediate, small behavioral compliance, but blow the hoped-for bigger subsequent commitment and attitude change? Have you "ruined" the person for further persuasion attempts (or experiments) by your colleagues?

Having posed and answered such questions to your own satisfaction, and if you still want to go for broke, then the time has come to go Machiavellian. Once such a decision has been made, your only concern is to find the weak points of the target person, and learn what conditions to manipulate and how best to exploit the unsuspecting victim.

Before describing several concrete examples of how Machiavellian tactics can be utilized in even such an incongruous situation as a "peace campaign," let us see how they are already effectively being used.

The Police Interrogator Misrepresents a Little Bit

Confessions are often obtained by either minimizing the seriousness of the offense and allowing the suspect a "face-saving" out, or by the opposite through misrepresenting and exaggerating the seriousness of the crime.

The first approach can be accomplished through "extenuation"—in which the investigator reports that he does not take too seriously a view of the subject's indiscretion, since he has seen thousands of others in the same situation. Or he may "shift the blame" to circumstances, the environment, or a subject's weaknesses, any of which might lead anyone to do what the suspect did. A more morally acceptable motive may be suggested for the crime, such as self-defense, an accident, a mistake, heat of passion, and so forth. In order to "open up" a suspect, it is recommended that good "bait" is to blame anyone who might be associated with the crime other than the suspect, for example, an accomplice, a fence, a company, loan sharks, or even the victim.

Some provocative examples of the way in which experts use this approach in order to misrepresent the nature of the crime to the suspect in order to get him to talk about it are:

1. A 50-year old man accused of having taken "indecent liberties" with a 10-year-old girl was told:

   "This girl is well developed for her age. She probably learned a lot about sex from the boys in the neighborhood and from the movies and

TV; and knowing what she did about it, she may have deliberately tried to excite you to see what you would do" (Inbau & Reid, 1962, p. 45).

2. Or, in forcible rape cases, "where circumstances permit, the suggestion might be offered that the rape victim acted like she might be a prostitute . . . that the police knew she had been engaged in acts of prostitution on other occasions" (Inbau & Reid, 1962, p. 46).

3. "During the interrogation of a married rape suspect, blame may be cast upon the subject's wife for not providing him with the necessary sexual gratification. 'When a fellow like you doesn't get it at home, he seeks it elsewhere' " (Inbau & Reid, 1962, p. 51).

Once the suspect is in a state of emotional confusion, then "he is unable to think logically and clearly, since his sense of values has been disturbed and his imagination is distorting his perspective. It is possible for the investigator to obtain admissions or even a confession from the suspect by further misrepresenting the picture" (O'Hara, 1956, p. 105).

This misrepresentation can take the form of a "knowledge bluff"—revealing a few known items and pretending to know more, or lying to the suspect that his fingerprints, blood, etc. were found at the scene of the crime (even show him falsified samples and records). In some cases of murder, it might be stated that the victim is not dead or, as happened in Minneapolis, a youthful offender, John Biron, might be told that he will be tried as a juvenile when it was known that he is legally an adult (see *Time Magazine,* December 3, 1965 p. 52; April 29, 1966, p. 65).

The exaggeration of fears can be successful with some types of suspects, as in statutory rape cases, where the suspect is told that his "victim" has testified to being forcibly raped. When thefts and embezzlement are involved, it is suggested that one increase the reported value of the loss and thus the consequences. "To make it look more authentic" it is suggested that a letter typed on company stationery be prepared reporting the false, larger loss to the police and the insurance company, and it should be "folded and refolded several times" to increase its believability.

Such misrepresentation by the police has two more extreme forms:

1. *The fixed line-up,* in which the interrogation is interrupted while alleged witnesses (in alliance with the police) finger the suspect as the offender, after which the interrogation is resumed, with the interrogator adopting an air of confidence.

2. *A reverse line-up* again has the suspect falsely accused by paid witnesses, but for a real or ficticious crime more serious than that under investigation. Confession to a burglary may seem like a simple way out when accused by seemingly reputable citizens in a police station of murder, rape, or kidnapping.

Since modern interrogation involves establishing "rapport" or a meaningful interpersonal relationship between the suspect and the interrogator, it must involve a distortion of the social-psychological situation. Even before the questioning begins, the interrogator is urged to role-play the position of the subject in order to be able to respond to him—"man to man, not as policeman to prisoner" (Inbau & Reid, 1962, p. 19).

Under this category would fall all the appeals which depend upon the interrogator being friendly, kind, sympathetic, understanding, "a Dutch uncle," or an older brother. He is the one who provides social approval and recognition, who accords the suspect status, and is aware of and able to manipulate the suspect because of his social values, feelings of pride, and class or group membership.

The police manuals recognize that "It is a basic human trait to seek and enjoy the approval of other persons." Therefore, it is wise to flatter some subjects, for example, by complimenting an accused driver of a getaway car for his maneuvering and "cornering," or by comparing a juvenile with his movie idol, or a member of a racial group with a respectable, outstanding member of that group. This approach apparently works best with "the uneducated and underprivileged," since they "are more vulnerable to flattery than the educated person or the person in favorable financial circumstances."

A slightly different approach is needed for the white-collar first offender, which includes clerks, managers, cashiers, office workers, professionals, and teachers—in short, most of the audience of this book. Since these people traditionally subscribe to orthodox ethical principles and conventional moral standards, the calm, dignified approach of the physician is respected and effective. One police manual author states rather boldly: "The character of a person in this category is weak and must be exploited fully" (O'Hara, 1956).

To create rapport, the interrogator could pat the suspect on the shoulder, grip his hand, or offer to do a favor for him—get water, talk to his wife, employer, etc. O'Hara says (1956): "Gestures of this type produce a very desirable effect. They import an attitude of understanding and sympathy better than words."

For suspects who have pride in their family, if an attempt to get their parents to cooperate fails, their attention is called to a (faked) circular being prepared for broadcast and distribution throughout the country. It not only describes the fugitive, but lists all of his known relatives' names and addresses as possible leads for approaching him. Cooperation quite often is obtained in this way.

The reader may recall that in the famous case of George Whitmore, Jr. (who confessed to the slaying of two society girls in New York in 1963), he gave a 61-page typed confession after 20 hr. of interrogation. He virtually sentenced himself to death or life imprisonment with this confession—which later was proved false and coerced when the true murderer was subsequently exposed.

Although the Whitmore case gained much notoriety, it is by no means an isolated exception. Alvin Mitchell confessed to a murder after being interrogated by the police, only to have it repudiated when another man, Winston Mosley, took the stand at Mitchell's trial to admit that he was the killer. A Bronx, New York, factory worker, who spent a year in jail after having confessed to the murder of a woman, subsequently was proven innocent and released.

In Whitmore's case the techniques reportedly used involved the arresting detective instilling fear in him, while the interrogating detective was protective, supportive, and sympathetic. Whitmore responded to this technique, which the police call the *Mutt and Jeff* approach, by actually believing that "Jeff" was sincerely concerned about his welfare. Mutt is typically a big, cruel, relentless investigator, while Jeff is a kind-hearted family man, perhaps with a brother in a similar scrape once. Jeff asks Mutt to leave the prisoner alone and get out of the room. He then confides that he, too, detests Mutt's tactics (which unfortunately will get worse), and the suspect's only hope is to cooperate quickly with his friend Jeff by telling the truth and confessing. Whitmore is reported to have said that Detective Aidala (Jeff) was nicer to him than his own father ever was!

An extension of this device, used primarily with prostitutes who may be concealing information about clients, agents, or underworld connections, is called "face-saving." If the girl refuses to cooperate, the officer begins to degrade her by calling her vile names. Just then another officer enters, throws the first officer out of the room, apologizes, tells the girl that the first officer can lose his job for the way he behaved toward her, and if she cooperates with him by confessing, then he will see what he can do in this matter. Once she does, of course, he does nothing in return.

If two or more persons are suspected of committing a crime, one of the following tactics is recommended:

1. Put both men in the same cell, then remove the weaker (or follower) of the pair for an hour, during which time *nothing happens*. When he is returned to the cell and he tells the other suspect that "nothing has happened," this will create suspicion. Then question the other man, telling him that his accomplice squealed.
2. If the suspects are father and son and they refuse to talk, separate them, question the father, and, regardless of what he says, get him to send a note to his son saying, "I have told the truth, you should do the same."
3. A very effective technique, called *bluff on a split pair*, involves removal of the weaker member to the interrogation room while the other sits outside able to hear only muffled voices. After a while the secretary is called on the intercom and told to bring in her stenography pad. When she reenters the waiting room, she begins typing from her "notes,"

interrupting herself only to check with the waiting suspect the spelling of his name or to get some other background information from him. When he is finally questioned, the interrogating officer waves before him the alleged (typed) confession of his friend, which purportedly puts all the blame on the waiting suspect. Often resentment toward this "squealie" will result in a confession in order to even the score.

While practicing one or more of these tactics on the suspect, the interrogator is cautioned to be on the alert constantly to recognize "moments of indecision, during which [the suspect's] struggle to avoid the consequences of his criminal act will be partially overcome by, or temporarily deadlocked with, his impulse to confess" (Inbau & Reid, 1962, p. 76).

This is the time to "move in" on him. If he is a youngster, the interrogator can play on shame by asking him if or how often he masturbates. This is so embarrassing for most youngsters that they will be eager to change the topic of conversation, and can easily be led into talking about the crime.

On the other hand, with sex offenders of the so-called "intellectual type," it may be helpful to note that the Kinsey reports reveal human beings to be not so different from animals in matters of sex. Because female sex victims are usually reluctant to talk about the activities which transpired (and some may even be feeling some guilt at not being more disturbed than they are after having been raped), the interrogator may have them write out details rather than speak them, or he may ease the situation for them by asking them to view him as their gynecologist whom they are consulting about "a sex organ problem."

Fears of novel contrivances allow the police to capitalize on the public's belief in the validity of lie detector tests, truth serums, and the like. The suspect is told he will have to undergo such tests and they will prove conclusively his guilt. If he refuses, then he is told that this too is taken as a sign of his guilt. It is suggested that a "knowledge bluff" be used in which false fingerprint comparisons are presented to the suspect, or falsified ballistics reports, blood stains, lie detector records, and so forth. While this evidence obviously cannot be used in court, a confession based on it is admissible.

MAKING MACHIAVELLI WORK FOR PEACE

The following hypothetical examples do not have the time-tested validity of those reported in the police interrogator's literature; rather, they merely illustrate how such tactics can be adapted to suit virtually any cause. The content of our cause will be related to "canvassing for peace," but one could imagine an adversary who could use them to canvass for war.

A. *Mutt and Jeff.* The so-called "Mutt and Jeff" technique of police interrogation involves a sneaky one-two punch in grilling suspects. A rough analog of this tactic in political persuasion can be devised. One persuader is militant in style and extreme in his position; the second persuader is moderate and reasonable as if to save the listener from the excess of the first, but in fact exacts a considerable concession by virtue of his soothing performance.

A very skilled and aggressive antiwar debater, who is dying to be turned loose but who may sometimes turn people off, can be paired with a sympathetic gentlemanly type who can gently chide him in the presence of the listener with remarks such as, "My friend may be overdoing it a little because he feels so strongly about the war, but what I would say on this point is that the war is much too expensive. I think that this is a position with which most hard-headed Americans can agree." Thus, the "moderate" brings the listener over to his side by using the "militant" as a foil.

This technique at best must be used very delicately and sparingly. It is double-edged. Too much "Mutt" militance on the doorstep will drive the listener up the wall, and both may get thrown out before Jeff can intervene. Furthermore, it takes a couple of good ham actors to carry it off, and too much "con" in the canvassing operation would be unfortunate, especially if neighbors compare notes.

B. *The stigmatized persuader.* Recent research has found that a person with a visible stigma (such as blind or crippled) elicits a mixed reaction. There is sympathy and a tendency to want to help in some way, but also considerable tension from guilt, revulsion, and resentment (the disabled person has intruded himself upon the complacent life space of the individual). These basic motives to help and to ignore can both be elicited by having a person with a real or faked stigma appear on the doorstep (for example, a pretty girl with a scar, a boy on crutches, a team of whom one member is apparently blind). After the general introduction, the person with the stigma clearly states the level of commitment desired and then suggests that if the person does not want to act on it now, they could perhaps spend some time together talking it over. Embarrassed sympathy will make it difficult to terminate the interaction brusquely, but if an easy way out is provided by the canvasser, it will be the preferred way of resolving the conflict. They may sign now to avoid facing the stigmatized of the world any more than is necessary.

C. *The "overheard" communication.* It is a well-known result of studies of persuasive communication that a message accidentally overheard can be more effective than when the speaker is aware of the listener's presence. In the "accidental" case, the listener has no reason to be suspicious that the speaker is trying to manipulate him.

The following setup tries to utilize this advantage of overhearing. Since it is an artifice, it is not recommended for widespread use.

In a possible one-person version, a coed enters a busy laundromat with a basket of laundry, puts the clothes in the machine, and asks another customer for change of a quarter to make a phone call to her mother. While pretending to call Mom she describes the chores she is doing and checks on the groceries she is to buy at the supermarket. "A daughter like that, I should only have," is the kind of thought running through the heads of the women there. "Good Daughter" then proceeds to talk to her mother briefly about the war and agree with her mother that it is awfully important to end this terrible war very soon and that she is happy that the mother has written to her congressman, and hopes she will also vote for Candidate X. She talks loudly enough to let the target audience hear, but goes about her business when she is finished, unless someone in the audience initiates a conversation.

Variations on this idea can be adapted for use in bus stations, drug stores, barber shops, and other such places, although this technique suffers from the general difficulty that the same person cannot wash the same bundle repeatedly, call the same Mom over and over, or get more than a few hair cuts a day without seeming very peculiar indeed.

The two-person version is more practical. This can be enacted when riding back and forth on crowded subways or buses, never traveling the same line at the same hour of a weekday. A Student and an older person (his uncle or Dad, presumably) make the ideal team. The two get into a spirited argument about today's mood of campus protest. Even though they argue, it is obvious that they have a great deal of affection for each other, and the Student (or Son) slips in references to good behaviors ("When I was fixing our sink last night with that rusty drainpipe, I was thinking down the drain, down the drain, boy, all the money we're spending in Vietnam is just going right down the drain, totally wasted"). Their voices are raised just enough so that people can hear, but not enough to be obnoxious. The Dad complains that students aren't working hard like he did in his day (avoid references to riots, drugs, and the like—the most intense antistudent issues). The Son agrees that this may be true, but the reason is that they are disillusioned because America is fighting an expensive, faraway war when there are all these problems that need working on at home. The Dad tentatively offers a few lukewarm arguments in favor of present war policy, but soon changes his mind when the student confidently (but not arrogantly) cites facts and arguments for quick withdrawal. The Dad agrees to write against the war to his congressman, but counterattacks with gusto on the issue of student laziness. The Son now concedes this point (it would not leave a good taste with the listeners if the cocky Son triumphed completely over the wishy-washy Dad). The Son resolves to get back to his campus and get all his buddies more involved in their own education and in constructive action. He complements his Dad on his understanding and on all he has done all these years for his Son. They now chat amiably about other things.

POSTSCRIPT

The fundamental thesis of this paper is reflected in Bandura's (1969) perceptive concern for the potential misuse of the therapist's influence in his one-way power relation with those labeled "patients."

As behavioral science makes further progress toward the development of efficacious principles of change, man's capacity to create the type of social environment he wants will be substantially increased. The decision process by which cultural priorities are established must, therefore, be made more explicit to ensure that "social engineering" is utilized to produce living conditions that enrich life and behavioral freedom rather than aversive human effects. [p. 112] .

REFERENCES

Bandura, A. *Principles of behavior modification.* New York: Holt, 1969.

Hovland, C. I. Reconciling conflicting results derived from experimental and survey studies of attitude change. *American Psychologist*, 1954, 14, 8-17.

Inbau, F. E., & Reid, J. E. *Criminal interrogation and confessions.* Baltimore: Williams & Wilkins, 1962.

Kidd, W. R. Police interrogation. *The Police Journal.* New York, 1940.

Milgram, S. Behavioral study of obedience. *Journal of Abnormal and Social Psychology*, 1963, 67, 371-378.

Mulbar, H. *Interrogation.* Springfield, Illinois: Thomas, 1951.

O'Hara, C. E. *Fundamentals of criminal investigation.* Springfield, Illinois: Thomas, 1956.

Orne, M. On the social psychology of the psychological experiment: With special reference to demand characteristics and their implications. *American Psychologist*, 1962, 17, 776-785.

Time Magazine, December 3, 1965, p. 52.

Time Magazine, April 29, 1966, p. 65.

6

Conflict Strategies Related to Organizational Theories and Management Systems[1]

Rensis Likert and David G. Bowers
The University of Michigan

Human nature, it is said, never changes. This leads some persons to conclude that wars and other forms of violent conflict are inevitable since they believe the urge to fight is part of human nature.

If we define human nature as that which man brings into the world with him when he is born, that is, his inherited capabilities and motives, human nature has changed little, if at all, in tens of thousands of years. However, there has been a tremendous change in the past thousands of years in what man has learned and has passed on from one generation to another. Moreover, these changes continue as experience and insights enrich learning.

Mankind's ability to organize human effort, activity, and cooperation has undergone a tremendous development in recorded history. Ernest Dale describes one significant step:

> Delegation is a major problem which goes back to Biblical days. The lack of it was the major cause of Moses' failure to reach the Promised Land in his Exodus from Egypt. Having wandered for 40 years in the desert, he found he had covered only half the distance between Egypt and Palestine. He consulted his father-in-law, Jethro, and when the latter saw that Moses 'stood by the people from morning unto evening,' he said:
>
> > 'The thing that thou doest is too heavy for thee . . . thou and thy people will surely wear away.'

[1] This paper is a condensed version of Chapter 2 of *Managing Conflict* by Rensis Likert and Jane Gibson Likert, to be published by McGraw-Hill Book Company, Inc. in 1972. It was presented and discussed at the symposium on Attitudes, Conflict, and Social Change, by David G. Bowers.

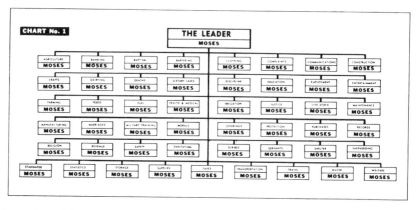

Figure 1 Original organizational scheme under Moses. From: *Organization . . . an illustrated outline;* ©1960 by Ernest Dale. Reprinted by permission of the author.

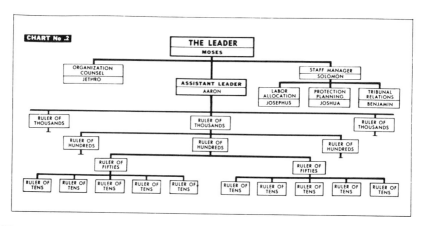

Figure 2 Jethro's scheme of reorganization. From: *Organization . . . an illustrated outline;* ©1960 by Ernest Dale. Reprinted by permission of the author.

Moses, as leader, had all the departments reporting to him. Figure 1 shows the structure.

Organization counsel, in the person of Jethro, prescribed the remedy. Figure 2, straight from the Bible, shows the new organization he devised. . . . Moses no longer needed to settle all the details himself; he was provided with staff assistance. This is the earliest example of a general staff.

What were the results? The organization plan was adopted at Flath, about halfway from the Red Sea to the Promised Land. It took almost 40 years to accomplish the first half of the journey before the organization plan was introduced; only a few months for the last half.[2]

PROGRESS IN RECENT CENTURIES

For a long period of human history the use of naked power by individuals or small social units was common. Whenever a disagreement or conflict occurred and one of the parties had sufficient power to settle it in the way he wished, and had no qualms about using this power ruthlessly, he forced the solution he desired on the other party. The defeated party may have been resentful, bitter, and motivated to strike back whenever the opportunity occurred, but for the moment the conflict was suppressed or "settled." To resolve a conflict in this manner, the victor had to have sufficient power to win, his values had to be such that he had no scruples in using this power, and he had to feel that he could live safely with such consequences as the continued or increased hostility and bitterness which his behavior created in the defeated party.

Mankind appears to have found power used in this kind of ruthless and unchallengeable way unbearable. This power had a highly corrosive effect on those who possessed it, and their behavior became intolerable. To prevent this, mankind, over many centuries, has sought, fought for, and largely won the establishment of checks and balances as a safeguard against the abusive use of power in political, industrial, and governmental systems. Related major social inventions such as majority rule and parliamentary procedures also were created in mankind's struggle for freedom and justice. The history of the development of political systems and their administration and that of industrial enterprises reflect this gradual, painful change from unchecked power to organizations and systems which rely on such social inventions as checks and balances, majority rule, and parliamentary procedures.

The invention of checks and balances, majority rule, and parliamentary procedures represented great human progress. Gaining the acceptance of each was a major step forward in mankind's social evolution. There is need, however, for further social evolution since checks and balances, majority rule, parliamentary procedures employing *Roberts' Rules of Order,* and the advocacy concepts of the law are all based on the win-lose approach to resolving conflicts. This approach does not result in all parties being pleased by the outcome and prepared to live by it. Because one gains at the others' expense, hostility continues and may become even more intense after the apparent resolution of the dispute. Since the win-lose approach is seriously inadequate for managing

---

[2] From: *Organization . . . an illustrated outline.* Published by the author, Ernest Dale, 30 Berkeley Avenue, Yonkers, N.Y., 1960.

conflict, any system—political, industrial, or other—based on it is equally inadequate and needs to be revised or replaced by more effective ways. The evidence is widespread in today's society of the need for further social evolution and the creation of new social inventions which can cope much more constructively with the existing serious and numerous conflicts.

PROGRESS USUALLY STARTS IN ONE AREA OF HUMAN ACTIVITY

Mankind's progress over the centuries has not occurred at a uniform rate nor in a uniform manner. Improvement in such different areas as (a) political, legal, and governmental activities, (b) business and commercial activities, and (c) military activities typically has not occurred simultaneously, equally, or in a parallel fashion. Sometimes the progress has occurred first in one area of activity. At another time and in a different society, it has occurred in one of the other areas.

Examples of each come readily to mind. Rome represented a great step forward in man's capacity to organize his military activity as well as to rule through governors whose operations were coordinated but decentralized. The French and American Revolutions and the political thinking of that period was an era of important progress in political life. The principles of Adam Smith and the Industrial Revolution and, much later, the American corporation were major developments in mankind's commercial and business activities.

In every society, however, there seems to be a general trend toward establishing and maintaining a basic consistency in values, principles, and procedures among all of its different areas of activities—political, legal, governmental, educational, business, and military. When any one area of activity, for whatever reason, develops a significantly better mode of operation, this improvement and the underlying concepts and philosophy upon which it is based is generalized sooner or later and applied to all of the other activities of that society. This may require a considerable span of years, but, within a society, such a trend among areas of activity toward an internal consistency appears to occur, eventually.

THE NATURE OF A SOCIETY IS REFLECTED IN
ITS MANAGEMENT OF CONFLICT

This general trend toward a consistent pattern means, of course, that the strategies and principles used by a society and all of its organizations for dealing with disagreements and conflict reflect the basic values and philosophy of that society. A primitive society uses primitive procedures for coping with differences and conflict; a feudal society employs feudal concepts and principles. The approach of a modern, industrialized nation to the management of disagreements and conflict reflects its basic philosophy, values, and social system as do all of the other principles and procedures employed by organizations within that society.

This same consistency also is found within large organizations. All of the component activities within an organization, such as its leadership, decision-making, communication, motivation, and control, tend to be consistent, one with the other, as well as to reflect the values and organizational concepts of the society of which it is a part. A large number of organizational studies of leadership, management, and organizational performance demonstrate that organizations in all of their operating characteristics, including their customary procedures for resolving disagreements and conflicts, display orderly and internally consistent patterns.[3]

Since the management of conflict is a major function of every organization, all aspects of the manner in which conflict is handled tend to be consistent with the organization's basic management philosophy, principles, and interaction processes. This applies to conflicts within the organization and to conflicts between it and other organizations. Progress by an organization in developing and using more effective organizational theory and systems will lead, consequently, to improvement in its handling of conflict, since organizations tend to maintain internally consistent procedures.

QUANTITATIVE RESEARCH ACCELERATES DEVELOPMENT OF IMPROVED SOCIAL SYSTEMS

Social science research is accelerating vastly the social evolution of appreciably more effective but more complex organizational systems. This research, using quantitative methods, was started about three decades ago shortly after the basic methodology required for it became available (Likert & Willits, 1940). It substituted rigorous quantitative measurement for crude judgment and trial and error. Since 1945 the volume of this research on leadership, management, organizational performance, and organizational theory has increased greatly.

The bulk of the research has been done by universities, and most of it has been conducted in business organizations because of the precise measurements of performance which can be obtained in many business enterprises. Other studies, however, have been undertaken in governmental agencies, hospitals, and nonbusiness organizations.

Probably the most extensive and sustained research on organizational systems and theory since 1945 has been done by Institute for Social Research at

[3] These data have been reported by Likert (1967, Chapter 7, Appendix I).

the University of Michigan. The central objective of this research has been to discover more effective ways for a human organization to define and accomplish its goals efficiently, and has been basic to the discovery of more effective ways to organize and operate a human enterprise or institution.

The Institute for Social Research's studies show that in widely different industries and for widely different kinds of work, on the average, the same basic principles for managing human activity are used by the managers who achieve the highest production, lowest cost, and most financially successful operations. These principles differ significantly from those used by those managers who achieve below-average productivity, costs, and earnings.

Although the principles used by the highest-producing managers are essentially the same from industry to industry or for different kinds of work, the specific methods for applying them usually differ markedly from situation to situation. These principles are applied in what might be called a culturally relative manner. Able managers use methods for applying the basic principles that are appropriate for that particular industry, job, and personnel, and are consistent with the traditions of the individual firm.

A GENERAL THEORY BASED ON PRINCIPLES
OF THE BEST MANAGERS

The basic principles used by the highest-producing managers have been integrated into a general organizational theory. A brief description of this theory follows:

The human organization of the firm is made up of interlocking work groups with a high degree of group loyalty among the members and favorable attitudes and trust among peers, superiors, and subordinates. Sensitivity to others and relatively high levels of skill in personal interaction, group problem-solving, and other group functions also are present. These skills permit effective participation in decisions on common problems. Participation is used, for example, to establish organizational objectives which are a satisfactory integration of the needs and desires of all members of the organization and the persons functionally related to it. Members of the organization are highly motivated to achieve the organization's goals. High levels of reciprocal influence occur, and high levels of total coordinated influence are achieved in the organization. Communication is efficient and effective. There is a flow from one part of the organization to another of all the relevant information important for each decision and action. The leadership in the organization has developed a highly effective social system for interaction, problem-solving, mutual influence, and organizational achievement. This leadership is also technically competent and holds high performance goals.

This organizational theory, which is based upon the principles used by the highest-producing managers and makes full use of cumulative cooperative motivational forces, has been labeled "System 4" for ready reference.

In comparison with more traditional organizational theories and systems of organizing human interactions and activities, System 4 is a more highly developed and complex system and represents further social evolution. It requires those using it to learn more complex leadership and interaction skills. As might be expected, however, it displays all the characteristics of a more effective form of organizing human interaction and efforts. A rapidly growing body of research findings shows that it is appreciably more effective in enabling an organization to decide upon its objectives and to accomplish them efficiently (for example, Seashore & Bowers, 1970; Bowers, 1963; Bowers & Seashore, 1966; Guest, 1962; Likert, 1967; 1969; Marrow, Bowers, & Seashore, 1967; Roberts, Miles & Blankenship, 1968). When an organization shifts to System 4 from a traditional organizational theory, performance improves, costs are reduced, and improvement occurs in the satisfaction and health of the members of the organization (Coch & French, 1948; Marrow et al., 1967).

Recent results reveal that the greater effectiveness of System 4 in comparison with more traditional organizational theories is much more clearly demonstrated when *trends over time* in productivity, costs, earnings, and other end-result variables are examined rather than measuring all variables simultaneously (Likert & Bowers, 1969).

A small but growing body of research findings supports the view that in every kind of organization, a shift to System 4 significantly improves the capacity of the organization to achieve its goals successfully. The System 4 theory, moreover, provides more effective processes than traditional organizational theories for successfully handling all the different kinds of conflicts that arise in organizations.

HUMAN ORGANIZATIONS CAN BE DESCRIBED QUANTITATIVELY

The extensive research over the past quarter of a century, which has provided the findings from which the System 4 theory was derived, also has yielded the methodology for measuring any organizational system. Any management or organizational system, consequently, can be measured and described in terms of well-defined variables. Moreover, the scores of an organization on these variables can be related to measurements of its performance, its success in achieving its goals, and its capacity to resolve conflicts constructively.

The methodology for measuring the management system of any organization employs an orthogonal framework for two of its major dimensions. This framework can be applied to any organization in an industrialized or

TABLE 1 MOTIVATIONAL FORCES OF DIFFERENT MANAGEMENT SYSTEMS[a]

	System 1	System 2	System 3	System 4
1. Underlying motives tapped	Physical security, economic security, and some use of the desire for status	Economic and occasionally ego motives, e.g., the desire for status	Economic, ego, and other major motives, e.g., desire for new experience	Full use of economic ego (e.g., desire for a sense of personal worth or importance) and other major motives, as, e.g., motivational forces arising from group processes
2. Manner in which motives are used	Fear, threats, punishment, and occasional rewards	Rewards and some actual or potential punishment	Rewards, occasional punishment, and some involvement	Economic rewards based on compensation system developed through participation and involvement in setting goals, improving methods, appraising progress toward goals, etc.
3. Kinds of attitudes developed toward organization and its goals	Attitudes usually are hostile and counter to organization's goals	Attitudes are sometimes hostile and counter to organization's goals and are sometimes favorable to the organization's goals, and support the behavior necessary to achieve them	Attitudes may be hostile but more often are favorable and support behavior implementing organization's goals	Attitudes generally are strongly favorable and provide powerful stimulation to behavior implementing organization's goals

TABLE 1   MOTIVATIONAL FORCES OF DIFFERENT MANAGEMENT SYSTEMS[a]

	System 1	System 2	System 3	System 4
4. Extent to which motivational forces conflict with or reinforce one another	Marked conflict of forces substantially reducing those motivational forces leading to behavior in support of the organization's goals	Conflict often exists; occasionally forces will reinforce each other, at least partially	Some conflict, but often motivational forces will reinforce each other	Motivational forces generally reinforce each other in a substantial and cumulative manner

[a] Adapted from *New Patterns of Management* and *The Human Organization: Its Management and Value* by Rensis Likert. Copyright © 1961 and 1967 by McGraw-Hill, Inc. By permission of McGraw-Hill Book Company, Inc. No further reproduction or distribution authorized without permission of McGraw-Hill.

110

TABLE 2 PROFILE OF ORGANIZATIONAL CHARACTERISTICS[a]

Organizational variable	System 1	System 2	System 3	System 4
1. To what extent do superiors have confidence and trust in *subordinates?*	Have very little confidence and trust in subordinates	Have some confidence and trust, such as master has in servant	Quite a bit of confidence and trust	A great deal of confidence and trust
2. To what extent do superiors behave so that subordinates feel free to discuss important things about their jobs with their immediate superior?	Subordinates do not feel at all free to discuss things about the job with their superior	Subordinates do not feel very free to discuss things about the job with their superior; do it guardedly	Subordinates feel rather free to discuss things about the job with their superior but may be somewhat cautious	Subordinates feel very free to discuss things about the job with their superior and do so candidly
3. How much responsibility is felt by each member of the organization for achieving organization's goals?	High levels of management feel responsibility; lower levels feel less; rank and file feel little and often welcome opportunity to defeat organization's goals	Managerial personnel usually feel responsibility; rank and file feel relatively little responsibility for achieving organization's goals	Substantial proportion of personnel, especially at higher levels, feel responsibility and generally behave in ways to achieve organization's goals	Personnel at all levels feel responsibility for organization's goals and behave in ways to implement them
4. To what extent do superiors willingly share information with subordinates?	Provide minimum of information	Give subordinates only information superiors feel they need	Give information needed and answer most questions	Seek to give subordinates all relevant information and all information they want

TABLE 2   PROFILE OF ORGANIZATIONAL CHARACTERISTICS[a]

Organizational variable	System 1	System 2	System 3	System 4
5. Are there forces leading to accurate or distorted upward information?	Powerful forces to distort information and deceive superiors	Many forces to distort; also forces for honest communication	Occasional forces to distort along with many forces to communicate accurately	Virtually no forces to distort and powerful forces to communicate accurately
6. How much cooperative teamwork is present to achieve organization's goals?	Practically none	Slight amount	A moderate amount	Very substantial amount throughout the organization
7. To what extent are subordinates involved in decisions related to their work?	Not at all	Practically never involved in decisions; occasionally consulted	Usually are consulted but ordinarily not involved in the decision-making	Are almost always involved in decisions related to their work
8. To what extent is there an informal organization present and supporting or opposing goals of formal organization?	Informal organization present and opposing goals of formal organization	Informal organization usually present and partially resisting goals	Informal organization may be present and may either support or partially resists goals of formal organization	Informal and formal organization are one and the same; hence support efforts to achieve organization's goals

[a] Adapted from *New Patterns of Management* and *The Human Organization: Its Management and Value* by Rensis Likert. Copyright © 1961 and 1967 by McGraw-Hill, Inc. By permission of McGraw-Hill Book Company, Inc. No further reproduction or distribution authorized without permission of McGraw-Hill.

moderately industrialized nation. It has been used successfully for this purpose in such areas of the world as the United States, Western Europe, Eastern Europe, Asia, and Latin America.

Employing the customary x and y axes, organizations are arrayed on the y axis according to the degree to which they employ the elementary concepts of functionalization. Organizations at the lower end of this axis are relatively amorphous masses. There is little differentiation in function, an excessive span of control, considerable confusion about each person's role, and, in extreme cases, chaos and anarchy. These organizations, as shown in Figure 3, are viewed as using System 0 (zero).

The x, or horizontal axis, is used to reflect the *basic motivational forces which the organization seeks to employ, the manner in which they are used, and the extent to which they are cumulative and reinforcing.* In essence, this axis reflects the degree to which the basic human motive sources are employed by the organization in a socially evolved rather than in a primitive manner. In a modern, highly industrialized nation, the more socially evolved management systems, that is, those more toward the System 4 end of the continuum in Table 1, achieve appreciably higher motivational forces focused on accomplishing the organization's goals than do the less evolved, more primitive systems, or those toward System 1.

The items in Table 1 indicate the nature of the motive sources which different management systems use and the resulting motivational forces and consequences. At the "System 1," or left, end of the continuum, the motivational forces rely on punitive treatment of members of the organization. At the right end, labeled "System 4," the motivational forces are based on supportive treatment. Punitive treatment yields hostile attitudes and restriction of production. Supportive treatment yields favorable attitudes and cooperative, responsible behavior which seeks to accomplish the organization's goals.

The Jewish nation prior to the time that Moses, using Jethro's advice, reorganized it, would be classified, of course, as a System 0 organization. It would fall at the lower end of the y axis (see Figure 3).

After the reorganization, it would fall much higher on the y axis, but since Moses and his nation relied heavily upon fear and punishment as major motive sources, his organization would have fallen well over to the left end of the x axis, that is, toward Sytem 1. The punitive character of the Mosaic Law reflects this orientation.

The operating characteristics of the different management systems are revealed in greater detail by the items in Table 2. As observed, the range along the x axis in Table 2 varies from the left end of System 1 to the right end of System 4. Each organizational variable in the table displays this same range. Under each system heading, there is a brief statement describing that system for that particular variable.

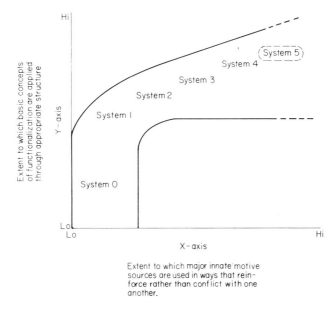

Figure 3   Schematic location of Systems 0-4 in relation to
motivational forces used.

An examination of Table 2 reveals that any organization which has sufficient functionalization and corresponding structure to fall within the System 1-to-System 4 band can be categorized readily on that continuum. In a modern nation, the overwhelming majority of organizations in business, government, education, and elsewhere will be found, of course, to have sufficient functionalization and structure to fall somewhere along the System 1-to-System 4 continuum.

In Figure 3, System 5 is shown in a dotted ellipse. This is intended to suggest that social science research will help create an even more effective, complex, and socially evolved management and social system in the next few decades. Some experiments already are providing a glimmering of what this system may be like.

RELATION OF INTERACTION-INFLUENCE NETWORKS TO CONFLICT MANAGEMENT

The profile of an organization obtained by using Tables 1 and 2 is a quantitative description of that organization's interaction-influence network and the manner in which it functions. The interaction-influence network of an organization is

TABLE 3   CHARACTERISTIC PATTERNS OF CONFLICT MANAGEMENT[a]

	System 1	System 2	System 3	System 4
1. How open, candid, and unguarded is the communication and interaction between the conflicting parties?	Extremely guarded	Quite guarded	Some guarded; some candid	Open, unguarded, and candid
2. To what extent do the conflicting parties seek to deceive or to inform the other correctly?	Parties try hard to deceive	Parties often try to deceive	Sometimes try to deceive; sometimes try to inform correctly	Strive to inform correctly
3. To what extent are efforts made to build or restrict channels of communication, interaction, and influence between conflicting parties?	Extensive efforts to restrict except through top leaders	Some efforts to restrict; little interest in building	Sporadic efforts to build, especially at top level.s of organization(s)	Extensive efforts to to build at all levels of organization(s)
4. What methods of resolving conflicts are used?	Suppression	Some suppression; win-lose confrontation and compromise	Win-lose confrontation, negotiation, and bargaining	Creative problem solving using consensus

TABLE 3 CHARACTERISTIC PATTERNS OF CONFLICT MANAGEMENT[a]

	System 1	System 2	System 3	System 4
5. To what extent is each conflicting party striving to gain power *over* others or seek mutually satisfactory solutions *with* others	Strives ruthlessly for power over others	Strives primarily for for power over others	Seeks some mutually satisfactory solutions but still strives for power over others	Seeks mutually satisfactory solutions through joint efforts with others
6. How well are the solutions accepted and implemented?	Strong covert resistance except by victor	Some overt acceptance; appreciable covert resistance	Over acceptance; some covert resistance	Overt and covert acceptance; full implementation sought

concerned with its structure and with the character of all such processes within the organization as those dealing with leadership, communication, motivation, control, decision-making, coordination, goal-setting, evaluation, and conflict management.

One of the essential functions of the interaction-influence network of an organization is coping with conflict wherever it may occur, either within the organization or between it and others. The manner in which an organization copes with conflict is consistent with the operating characteristics of its interaction-influence network and the management system upon which its interaction-influence network is based. Table 3 presents many of the variables involved in a conflict situation and describes for each variable the characteristic mode of dealing with it in organizations using different interaction-influence networks ranging from those based on System 1 to those based on System 4.

Table 3 was set up in the same manner as the original version of Tables 1 and 2, which were published previously in a longer form (Likert, 1961, Table 14-1, pp. 223-233). These tables were created by examining, in a large number of studies, the pattern of relationships among the kinds of items included in the tables and also the relationship of these items to such performance variables as productivity, costs, and earnings. Based on the general pattern observed, the specific wording for each item was prepared for each of the different management systems. Table 3 is, essentially, a detailed elaboration of the conflict portion of Tables 1, 2, and other longer tables (see, for example, Likert, 1967, Appendix II, which presents in considerable detail an array of items dealing with conflict).

CONFLICT MANAGED BEST IN MOST HIGHLY
DEVELOPED SOCIAL SYSTEM

There is an orderly progression in the development of social or organizational systems from System 0 to System 4. To date, System 4 is the most socially mature and developed form of human interaction and provides the most highly developed and effective means of managing conflict, while System 0 is, of course, the most primitive. Without doubt, this development over time will continue, and as suggested previously, an even more sophisticated, complex, and effective system will emerge gradually in the form of a "System 5" and provide even better resources for handling conflict constructively.

Each of these systems and its corresponding interaction-influence network, moreover, has its own characteristic way of handling conflict. This was made evident by the comparison of Tables 1, 2, and 3 (suggested above).

These different patterns of managing conflict illustrate the major propositions of this paper:

1. Every conflict, other than those internal to a particular individual, involves an interaction among persons, groups, organizations, or larger entities and occurs through an interaction-influence network.

2. The extent to which a conflict is likely to be resolved constructively depends directly upon the effectiveness of the interaction-influence network used during the conflict.

3. The effectiveness of an interaction-influence network depends upon its social maturity as measured by the extent to which it approaches System 4.

4. The nearer an interaction-influence network is to System 4, the greater is the probability that the conflict will be resolved constructively.

5. To function well, a completely new interaction-influence network has to shake down into a well-knit, smoothly running entity. Cooperative working relationships need to be established.

6. Effective, synergistic interaction-influence networks based on System 4 can be created and can be used in every conflict situation by those who wish to have the conflict resolved more constructively and successfully.

    (a) The use of System 4 interaction-influence networks requires an understanding of System 4 principles and skills in applying them effectively.

    (b) A period of time is required to build an effective social system and have its full potential ready to use in a difficult, emotion-laden conflict. For this reason, it is desirable to anticipate major crises and create a social system based on the System 4 model before the conflict erupts.

OBSOLETE SOCIAL SYSTEMS USED IN ATTEMPTS TO RESOLVE CONFLICT

Some feeling of the potential for improvement in the management of conflict through the use of more effective interaction-influence networks based on System 4 can be obtained by answering Table 3 to show how a particular conflict is being handled *now* and answered a second time to show how you would *like* it to be. Do this by selecting any major conflict you wish and answering Table 3 with an *n* on each line to show how you feel the conflict is being dealt with now. After completing Table 3 in this manner, answer it again with a *w* on each line to show how you would like it to be managed. Draw a line connecting all of the *n*s and another line connecting all of the *w*s. You are very likely to find your *n* profile much to the left of your *w* profile. If this is the case, the implication for changes to improve the management of the conflict is clear.

This use of Table 3 in a conflict situation reveals inadequacies which may be present both in the structure of the interaction-influence network and in its operation. When such inadequacies become evident in an existing interaction-influence network, substantial improvement can be made in the management of the conflict by strengthening the interaction-influence network at the points of revealed weakness.

EFFECTIVE INTERACTION-INFLUENCE NETWORKS ABSENT IN COMMUNIST CHINA-UNITED STATES RELATIONSHIPS

The interaction-influence network used by the United States and Communist China to cope with their differences is so primitive and inadequate that it is surprising the conflict has not worsened. News such as the following extracts from an Associated Press dispatch from Warsaw, Poland, dated January 8, 1970, describe the present situation:

> WARSAW, Poland (AP)—U.S. Ambassador Walter J. Stoessel, Jr. and Lei Yang charge d'affaires at the Communist Chinese Embassy, conversed over tea for two hours at the American Embassy here today, but the session was not classified officially as a formal meeting.
>
> There was immediate speculation that the conversation may have centered around a date for the resumption of full-scale Chinese-American ambassadorial talks, which have been held in Warsaw since 1958 but were canceled by the Peking government in the last two years.
>
> The last session-the 134th-was held exactly two years ago.
>
> The United States and Red China do not recognize each other diplomatically.
>
> Officials in Washington indicated a few days ago that the United States was ready to resume the talks. Asked by a newsman, the U.S. spokesman said today's meeting was not the 135th.
>
> But it was the third contact between Stoessel and Yang since last Dec. 3 when the American sought out the Chinese diplomat at a Yugoslav reception and apparently suggested a resumption of talks.
>
> The two met again Dec. 11 at the Chinese Embassy. The subject matter of these contacts was never disclosed.

If one uses Table 3 to score the existing relationships between the United States and Communist China, many of the items yield a System 1 score. Several other items which deal with the adequacy of the interaction-influence network between the United States and Communist China make one realize that a System 0 score is most appropriate because of the virtual absence both of this interaction structure and of efforts to build it.

BLACK-WHITE RELATIONSHIPS LACK EFFECTIVE
INTERACTION-INFLUENCE NETWORKS

A picture almost as dismal as the United States-Communist China interaction-influence network emerges if black-white relationships in major metropolitan areas are scored. In the cities where major riots have occurred, such as Los Angeles (Watts), Cleveland (Hough), Newark, and Detroit, there was a huge interaction-influence void between the white and black communities and between the more affluent and the poverty-stricken sectors of these urban areas. Even today one is impressed, unfortunately, more by the gaps in the interaction-influence network of our big cities than by its strength. With regard to black-white relationships, this applies to both the gap *between* the black and white communities and the many gaps in the interaction-influence network *within* each of these heterogeneous sectors of urban life. Systems 0, 1, and occasionally System 2 appear to be much more characteristic of the pattern of black-white relationships than System 4. This conclusion is equally true of the pattern of relationships between the affluent and the poverty-stricken in our urban areas.

LARGE UNIVERSITIES LACK EFFECTIVE
INTERACTION-INFLUENCE NETWORKS

A similar picture emerges if we analyze, with the aid of Table 3, the interaction-influence networks of our large universities, especially those where disruptive or destructive student riots or sit-ins have occurred, often with some faculty support. The scores on Table 3 reveal that the formal interaction network between each of the three major sectors of the university—students, faculty, and administration—is seriously deficient. None of our large universities appears to have an interaction-influence network embracing all parts of the university through which efficient communication and problem-solving can occur. Moreover, once decisions are reached, the interaction-influence networks of these universities *do not create the levels of motivation and felt responsibility among all, or virtually all, students, faculty, and administrators to assure that the decisions will be effectively implemented.* The present interaction-influence networks of our large universities are as inadequate for creating widespread felt responsibility as they are in their communication capabilities. These are serious communication and responsibility gaps.

   The kinds of conflicts which we have just examined using Table 3 give painful evidence that the present management of some of our most serious conflicts relies upon obsolete models of social systems and interaction-influence networks. The present interaction-influence networks are extremely inadequate and reflect very primitive forms of social systems. There is, obviously, an opportunity for improving the management of these conflicts substantially. If more effective interaction-influence networks were used based on more socially evolved social systems such as System 4, the improvement would be great.

Substituting a System 4 interaction-influence network for a System 1 or System 2 type, however, is not done easily, especially in complex conflict situations. Fortunately, findings from current research on the dynamics of changing attitudes and behavior are directly applicable. This is especially true of studies in business firms on how to aid an organization to shift to System 4 most efficiently. These studies are yielding principles and procedures which can accelerate substantially a shift to System 4 in the management of any conflict and thereby resolve the conflict faster and better than is otherwise possible.

REFERENCES

Bowers, D. G. (Ed.) *Applying modern management principles to sales organizations.* Ann Arbor, Michigan: Foundation for Research on Human Behavior, 1963.

Bowers, D. G. Organizational control in an insurance company. *Sociometry,* 1964, **27**(2), 230-244.

Bowers, D. G. & Seashore, S. E. Predicting organizational effectiveness with a four-factor theory of leadership. *Administrative Science Quarterly,* 1966 **11**(2), 238-263.

Coch, L., & French, J. R. P., Jr. Overcoming resistance to change. *Human Relations,* 1948, 1(4), 512-532.

Dale, E. *Organization . . . an illustrated outline.* New York, 1960. (see footnote, p. 103).

Georgopoulos, B. S. ,& Mann, F. C. *The community general hospital.* New York: Macmillan, 1962.

Guest, R. H. *Organizational change.* Homewood, Illinois: Irwin, 1962

Jerovsek, J., Mozina, S., Tannenbaum, A. S., & Likert, R. Testing a management style. *European Business,* 1970, **27**, 60-68.

Kahn, R. L. Human relations on the shop floor. In E. M. Hugh-Jones (Ed.), *Human relations and modern management.* Amsterdam: North-Holland Pub., 1958. Pp. 43-74.

Kahn, R. L., Wolfe, D. M., Quinn, R. P., Snoek, J. D., & Rosenthal, R. A. *Organizational stress: Studies in role conflict and ambiguity.* New York: Wiley, 1964.

Katz, D., &Kahn, R. L. Some recent findings in human relations research. In E. Swanson, T. Newcomb, & E. Hartley (Eds.), *Readings in social psychology.* New York: Holt, 1952. Pp. 650-665.

Katz, D., & Kahn, R. L. *The social psychology of organizations.* New York: Wiley, 1966.

Kerr, C., Dunlop, J. T., Harbison, F., & Myers, C. A. *Industrialism and industrial man.* Cambridge, Massachusetts: Harvard University Press, 1960.

Likert, R. *New patterns of management.* New York: McGraw-Hill, 1961.

Likert, R. *The human organization: Its management and value.* New York: McGraw-Hill, 1967.

Likert, R. The relationship between management behavior and social structure—improving human performance: Better theory, more accurate accounting. *Proceedings of the fifteenth International Management Congress,* 1969, 136-146.

Likert, R., & Bowers, D. G. Organizational theory and human resource accounting. *American Psycholigist,* 1969, 24(6), 585-592.

Likert, R., & Willits, J. M. *Morale and agency management.* Hartford, Connecticut: Life Insurance Agency Management Assoc., 1940. 4 vols.

Marrow, A. J., Bowers, D. G., & Seashore, S. E. *Management by participation: Creating a climate for personal and organizational development.* New York: Harper, 1967.

Myers, C. A., & Harbison, F. *Management in the industrial world.* New York: McGraw-Hill, 1959.

Roberts, K. H., Miles, R. E., & Blankenship, L. V. Organizational leadership, satisfaction, and productivity: A comparative analysis. *Academy of Management Journal,* 1968, 11, 401-414.

Seashore, S. E., & Bowers, D. G. Durability of organizational change. *American Psychologist,* 1970, 25(3), 227-233.

Tannenbaum, A. S. *Control in organizations.* New York: McGraw-Hill, 1968.

Part Three
Racial Attitudes and Social Change

In the area of racial and ethnic attitude change, we include three chapters: "The Impact of Social Change on Attitudes" by Harry Triandis; "The Mass Media and Social Change" by Walter Weiss; and "Contextual Models of School Desegregation" by Thomas Pettigrew and R. T. Riley. These three contributions span the continuum from the 'micro" level (the individual or small group) to the "macro" level (mass communication and behavior in major social strata: racial groups, educational groups, rural versus urban groups, and so forth). Regardless of the particular level(s) upon which it focuses, however, each of these contributions is concerned with racial attitudes and opinions—with the ways they are originally formed, the subsequent influences that change them, and their relationship to other social variables of interest.

In the first contribution, Triandis attempts to conceptualize the variables involved in forming or changing racial attitudes. In his analysis, Triandis combines individual psychological variables, or concepts (like habit), with social psychological ones like customs, norms, attitudes, and social change. Following Smelser's (1963) paradigm, he elaborates such entities into a framework composed of four levels: values, norms, roles, and facilities. This hierarchial model allows him to predict effects on intergroup conflict—or cooperation—of disagreements at any given level in this structure.

A particularly interesting part of Triandis' paper involves his appraisal of the relative contributions of the sociological variable, "norms," and the psychological variable, "personality." Contrary to the finding of researchers who work in the tradition of *The Authoritarian Personality* (Adorno *et al.*, 1950), Triandis finds that norms are "twice as important" as personality in accounting for social distance phenomena.

Norms, of course, are learned during social interactions, particularly those involving primary or face-to-face groups. This leads us to a second major aspect of Triandis' paper: it rests on an infrastructure consisting of the principles of

123

learning. Throughout his paper, we find Triandis invoking the concepts of reinforcement, schedules of reinforcement, trial and error, habits, rewards, and the like.

In this respect, Triandis' approach agrees with that of our other contributors who typically award a central position to these variables in their writing (even though this emphasis may not stand out particularly in their papers in this volume). In the other contributions to Part Three we see a particular relationship (with regard to use of learning concepts) to Guthrie's paper. Guthrie, too, stresses the importance of reinforcement schedules in explaining behavior changes in the context of social change. Like Triandis, Guthrie deals largely with attitudes and behavior commonly represented in large groups, or classes, of people. The reader will also notice a compatible emphasis on learning approaches in the chapters by Abelson and by Orne and McGinnies.

While he uses reinforcement as a central variable in considering ways to change prejudiced attitudes and behavior, Triandis combines it with a sociological emphasis on institutional arrangements. In other words, he finds a potential remedy for prejudice in new institutional conditions such that racial exploitation will not be reinforced.

We also should note Triandis' position on the relationships between attitudes and behavior. He recognizes that either one can change behavior by first changing attitudes, or one can modify behavior first, thereby producing consequent changes in attitudes. Of these two directions of causality, Triandis finds the latter (from behavior to attitudes) a more powerful influence, in general. This position, of course, ties in closely with his recommended strategy for changing attitudes: change behavior and institutions first. It also agrees with the positions taken by Abelson, herein, and Guthrie, as well as the implicit assumptions in a number of our other chapters.

The contribution by Walter Weiss focuses explicitly on broad social influences, particularly as they are manifested in, or changed by, the mass media. While he recognizes the importance of personal channels of communication, Weiss concerns himself primarily here with "macro" phenomena: mass communication, public opinion, and social change as they bear on changing racial attitudes.

The starting point for any analysis of the impact of mass media on social change in general, or racially linked attitudes, in particular, must be the generally accepted conclusion that the mass media are typically effective only within rather narrow limits. Klapper, a representative spokesman for this viewpoint, has summarized the sociological and psychological evidence bearing on the impact of the mass media in his book, *The Effects of Mass Communication* (Klapper, 1960). He concludes there that mass media are typically effective only within narrow limits: "Mass communication *ordinarily* does not serve as a necessary and sufficient cause of audience effects, but rather functions through a nexus of mediating factors and influences [p. 8]."

A more recent, more psychologically oriented treatment of mass media phenomena recently has been published by Weiss (1969). On the basis of his review of the literature, Weiss agrees with Klapper in concluding that, under the usual conditions (that is, an open society), mass media do not typically produce the drastic changes in attitude that have been labeled "conversions." He finds, nevertheless, that the mass media do produce significant attitudinal effects, particularly in closed societies and developing nations. The impact of these media may involve reinforcement of existing views (thereby helping the individual to resist other influences pressing toward change), provision of supportive reasons for the person's attitudinal position, or transformation of uncertainty (or lack of awareness) into a definite attitudinal position (Weiss, 1969, pp. 101-102). In this volume, Weiss considers the ways that mass media content relates to social change in general and to racial attitude change in particular. He is concerned here with the ways in which the black social "revolution" in the United States has manifested itself in the mass media, focusing on *Ebony,* a magazine appealing primarily to blacks.

We note some parallels between Weiss' analysis of mass media content and the classical studies of Thomas and Znaniecki (1918). They, of course, analyzed letters, diaries, and the like, as opposed to mass media content. However, in both cases, the analysis reveals the impact of social conditions and social change on the attitudes and behavior of minority groups in the United States. In both cases the major analytic tool is content analysis. In each case, we end up with observations and conclusions relevant to acculturation or assimilation phenomena.

Pettigrew and Riley, like Walter Weiss, deal with racial attitudes (or opinion) and behavior at the aggregage or mass level rather than the individual or small group level. Their approach involves the integration of census data and responses to surveys of public opinion and attitudes. Following the model provided by Pool, Abelson, and Popkin (1964), they developed a means of studying changes in the climate of opinion over time without having to conduct an opinion survey each time such an assessment or prediction was desired. Perhaps one of the most important characteristics of their approach in our present context is the "interdisciplinary" nature of their conceptual and empirical approaches in which they merge psychological, ecological, and economic variables into fruitful combinations.

Obviously a multivariate approach of this sort provides more extensive—and usually more reliable—information than a small-scale study designed to determine whether a single independent or experimental variable affects a single dependent variable or criterion. A design like Pettigrew's also permits a partitioning of variance such that the relative contribution of the independent variables to the determination of the dependent variable stands out. In this case, it permits one to determine whether attitude data contribute anything to the prediction of the characteristics of the desegregation process independently of demographic and status variables. Certainly, attitude data in real life become worthwhile only if they make such an independent contribution and, in this volume, we are concerned with the relevance of attitudes to real-life social problems.

One other aspect of the present paper by Pettigrew and Riley deserves mention here—its reliance on a form of simulation of attitudes (or the climate of opinion). Since conducting repeated opinion surveys in many locations over a period of time is prohibitively expensive, we badly need a means of simulating the climate of opinion, or of extrapolating from past data, at a given point in time. This, of course, is essentially what Pettigrew and Riley have done—they have used past opinion survey data to arrive at a useful index of present attitudes and opinions.

Such an approach, of course may involve the risk of incurring other costs as a result of nonlinear or otherwise unexpected changes in the climate of "public" opinion—a problem which has plagued public opinion polling organizations on several notable occasions. Nevertheless, the emphasis on this simulation approach does deserve mention as one of the potentially most important developments in the area of attitudes and opinions. For additional information on the use of simulation techniques in the social and behavioral sciences, the reader would do well to consult Pool, Abelson, and Popkin (1964), or Abelson (1969).

REFERENCES

Abelson, R. P. Simulation of social behavior. In G. Lindzey and E. Aronson (Eds.), *The handbook of social psychology,* Reading, Massachusetts: Addison-Wesley, 1969.

Adorno, T. W. Frenkel-Brunswik, E., Levinson, D. J., & Sanford, R. N., *The authoritarian personality.* New York: Harper, 1950.

Klapper, J. T. *Effects of mass communication.* Glencoe, Illinois: Free Press, 1960.

Pool, I., Abelson, R. & Popkin, S. L. *Candidates, issues, and strategies.* Cambridge, Massachustts: M.I.T. Press, 1964.

Smelser, N. J. *Theory of collective behavior.* New York: Free Press, 1963.

Thomas, W. I. & Znaniecki, F. *The polish peasant in Europe and America.* Boston: Badger, 1918.

Weiss, W. Effects of the mass media of communication. In G. Lindzey and E. Aronson (Eds.), *The handbook of social psychology,* Reading, Massachusetts: Addison-Wesley, 1969.

7

The Impact of Social
Change on Attitudes

Harry C. Triandis
University of Illinois, Champaign

It is implicit in the thinking of many social scientists and laymen that attitudes are among the "causes" of social behavior. Yet the evidence that has been accumulating during the past 15 years of social psychological research suggests that the reverse direction of causality is more powerful. (For a review, see Triandis, 1971). People do something first, then bring their attitudes in line with their behavior. Actually, it is best to think of attitudes and behavior as interacting in a reciprocal process, but the more powerful influence involves that from behavior to attitude, the less powerful, that from attitudes to behavior.

A review of the literature suggests that many social psychologists may have oversimplified in their conceptualization of the relationship among attitudes and behaviors. There are many additional variables to those found in the literature intimately involved in this relationship. Some of these variables emerge directly from characteristics of the cultures in which people happen to live. Before returning to such theoretical relationships, it may be useful to place this discussion in a general framework involving social change, since social change is one of the focal points of this volume.

Campbell (1960) remarked that cultures evolve in much the same way as organisms. In the course of living humans have to solve many day-to-day problems; when these problems include novel elements, they employ a trial-and-error approach to the solution of these problems. Some solutions happen to get reinforced. The reinforced solutions persist, and become accepted as cultural elements, to be transmitted to the next generation. Of course, many cultural elements which were effective at one point in time may be quite ineffective at another point in time; yet humans may engage in all sorts of defensive reactions to protect these cultural elements. As a result, an old cultural element may or may not be reinforced through environmental feedback, but in such cases is usually reinforced by other members of the culture who hold the same views of reality.

Now, let us follow this cycle as it influences those variables of interest. The solution of a problem involves doing something. By chance some behaviors are reinforced. They then will become *habits,* at the individual level, and *customs* at the sociocultural level. Related to such customs are ideas justifying such behaviors, and norms stating that it is appropriate for members of the culture to engage in these behaviors. As one generation of humans dies and another occupies the arena of action, what is transmitted consists primarily of norms, and secondarily of the justifications parents may employ when they explain norms to their children.

These norms influence behavior directly and indirectly, the indirect influence being through attitudes and values. Essentially, "norms" specify which behaviors are appropriate. "Attitudes" contain (*a*) ideas (cognitions) justifying the norms, (*b*) affect consistent with such justifications, and (*c*) behavioral intentions to act according to the norms, and refer to relatively specific objects in the environment. However, attitudes are distilled into values that refer to abstract conceptions of the environment. Values change at slower speed than attitudes, thus providing some continuity in the typical behaviors of individuals. When the environment changes, some norms no longer may be functional. However, individuals who manage to surround themselves by other members of the culture who hold similar views may manage to maintain their attitudes, in spite of the fact that these attitudes are no longer functional.

Now a broad panorama of influences may be unfolded among various classes of variables. At the most distal level, physical events, environmental resources, and historical events mold the kinds of economic, social, and political activities which are likely to become cultural elements, via ordinary mechanisms of reinforcement. An individual engages in economic (occupational) behaviors maximally rewarding to him, in social behaviors that get rewarded by his ingroup, in political behaviors that he perceives as leading to future rewards. He explains what he is doing to himself by developing cognitive structures that are internally balanced and effectively predict his future rewards. He exposes himself to attitude objects associated with rewards and avoids objects associated with punishments. To understand his specific actions, it is necessary to examine (*a*) his expectations of reinforcement that follow from each specific action and the value of this reinforcement to him, minus the costs of events that likely follow a particular behavior (Lewin, *et al.,* 1944; Tolman, 1951; Vroom, 1964; Steiner, 1970), (*b*) his abilities to perform the behavior, (*c*) his habits concerning this action, and (*d*) his behavioral intentions concerning the attitude objects involved in the particular social situation. His behavioral intentions reflect both norms and affect toward the behavior (Fishbein, 1967).

One could trace back those influences, which lead to his expectations, abilities, habits and behavioral intentions. For example, it could be stated that his expectations may reflect previous schedules of reinforcement, his abilities may result from environmental and genetic variables, his habits be patterned after previously experienced instrumental learning and the like. However, for the purposes of this contribution it does not seem necessary to elaborate the full range of the nomothetic network involving those variables. With this very roughly sketched network of variables and relationships we now can understand what happens when there are significant changes in a person's environment.

What does social change imply? "Social change" is defined here as a new set of social relationships and social behaviors that is most likely to lead to rewards. The causes of such change may be found in the physical environment, for instance, when a resource is exhausted and new economic activities are needed for survival, or in the social environment, as happens when a new institution emerges, or a particular social group acquires greater power, as happens after conquest, war, or revolution. Related to such social changes are political changes which usually involve the redistribution of power—changes in the locus of reinforcements.

Conflict is the inevitable outcome of such changes. Inconsistent behavioral tendencies result in conflict. Such tendencies may emerge at the economic, social, or political level, and are translated most easily into terms of *who* controls reinforcements, for *whom, when,* and *where.*

One of the most interesting problems is interpersonal conflict, particularly that occurring when two persons hold dissimilar attitudes. There is a good deal of support for the proposition that interpersonal attraction is a function of interpersonal similarity, particularly with respect to attitudes (Byrne, 1969). Nevertheless, there are very few experimental demonstrations of what intuitively appears to be very obvious—namely, that disagreement with another person about some trivial issue should have less of an effect on interpersonal attraction than disagreement on some fundamental and important issue. In fact, studies by Byrne and Nelson (1964, 1965) have not confirmed this intuition.

One possible explanation of this negative finding is as follows: A person uses disagreement on a trivial issue as a cue of disagreement on a fundamental value; hence, the effect of disagreement on something unimportant is as great as the effect of disagreement on something important. It should be made very clear here that the following discussion concerns first impressions and the effect of disagreement on interpersonal attitudes during the formative stage of such attitudes. Disagreement in stable interpersonal relations may follow other laws.

One theoretical framework which has been helpful in dealing with this problem is the one provided by Smelser (1963). A free translation of Smelser's arguments into my language would be that disagreement at the level of *values* is more damaging to interpersonal attraction than disagreement at the level of *norms,* which in turn is more damaging than disagreement at the level of *roles,* which in turn is more damaging than disagreement at the level of *facilities.* An example may help.

Suppose two workers meet in a machine shop, and one claims that "honesty is for suckers" and the other believes that "honesty is always the best policy" on normal grounds. This disagreement, which is at the level of values, is likely to lead to considerable tension between them, if they are fully aware that they have conflicting views. Now suppose that two workers meet in the same shop, and one thinks that cleaning one's workplace after work is necessary, while the other believes that it is unnecessary. This difference will also create tension, but the theory specifies that the latter disagreement, which is at the level of norms, will not divide the two workers as much as the former, which is at the level of values. Consider now two more workers, one of whom believes that the other should do a particular undesirable job. This disagreement, which is at the level of roles, will again be serious, but not quite as serious as disagreement at the previous levels. Finally, two workers may disagree at the level of facilities, such as is the case if they disagree on whether a job ought to be done using one set of tools or another set of tools. The last kind of disagreement is probably the least difficult to resolve.

It should be clear that each of these levels of disagreement are at different levels of abstraction. Disagreement about the use of tools does not normally have implications about broad issues, such as what kind of person the other is; disagreement at the level of values has broad implications. A dishonest person may act in a reprehensible way not only in the shop but also in his family, his church, his children's school, his neighborhood, and so forth. Thus, disagreement at the level of values is most serious, while disagreements at the levels of norms and roles is intermediate in seriousness.

Now, if the Smelser argument is correct, the hypothesis that disagreement at one level of abstraction is always used as a cue for disagreement at a higher level of abstraction becomes plausible. In short, if two people disagree at the level of facilities, it seems likely that they will interpret their disagreement as a cue that they disagree at the level of roles, perhaps even at the levels of norms or values. It is a matter of empirical investigation to see how far the disagreement spreads, but I suspect that there is such a *projection of the disagreement to a higher level of abstraction*, and this is the explanation of the negative results obtained by Byrne and Nelson. In short, disagreement on something trivial has as much affect as disagreement on something important because the trivial is projected to become important.

Another hypothesis concerns the *spread* of the effects of disagreement. It is assumed that disagreement at the level of values will have more widespread effects than disagreement at a more specific level, in the sense that the persons in conflict will see a wider range of their behaviors as being in conflict with the behaviors of the other person. For example, disagreement about cleanliness might imply disagreement about the importance of health measures, while disagreement on how to wash dishes will not necessarily spread to such a different domain of disagreement.

If these arguments are sound, they have very specific implications about ways to reduce conflict. One is that people should learn to diagnose the level of abstraction of the conflict, and also learn to guard against its projection to a higher level of abstraction. Techniques could be developed to train people to deescalate the meaning of a disagreement, and to realize that they have a tendency to exaggerate the significance of a disagreement. Such training will tend to make conflict less of a zero-sum game and more fitted to a problem-solving analysis, in which the two sides of the conflict see it as *our* problem.

The discussion has been very abstract thus far, and it seems appropriate to utilize a particular focus for illustration. The interracial tensions that characterize American society seem suitable.

Let us look at the source of so-called white racism. One point is very clear in the literature on interpersonal attitudes among racial groups—norms are much better predictors of the variance of such attitudes than any other predictor that might be employed (Triandis & Triandis, 1960, 1962, 1965). Triandis and Triandis (1962) tried explicitly to divide the variance between cultural influences, such as norms, and personality influences, such as insecurity, anxiety, authoritarianism, and the like. According to the data, about twice as much variance was controlled by "norms" than by all personality variables put together. Thus, it seems that norms are twice as important as personality variables, although both norms and personality variables predict significant amounts of the variance of social distance scores. The kinds of people who had higher social distance scores tended to conform to social institutions (that is, norms) more strongly than other subjects, agreed with prevailing viewpoints, and accepted the values of their ingroup somewhat more readily and uncritically than the other subjects. Therefore, the personality variables themselves reflected the extent to which the individuals conformed to norms

In samples from the United States, the most powerful determinant of social distance scores was the *race* of the *other*. In other cultures other characteristics, such as religion, social class, and so forth, were the important determinants of social distance (Triandis, Davis, & Takezawa, 1965). A little historical reflection will show why race is so important in the American context. There has been exploitation across racial lines for the past 200 years. As Dollard (1937, 1957) has documented, this exploitation took economic, sexual, and social forms. Even today, the discrepancy in the earning power of lower-class blacks versus whites testifies that there is exploitation in the economic domain. There also is an obvious advantage in social prestige, leading to what might be called "social exploitation." Such exploitation clearly leads to increased reinforcements. In short, for at least 200 years, it was reinforcing to be a racist. Of course, not all obtained such reinforcements. Some obtained greater reinforcements because institutional arrangements, such as slavery in the South, allowed greater reinforcements in both the economic and sexual domains. Others obtained sufficient rewards from expanding industrialization in the North and were less dependent on reinforcements across racial lines. At any rate, specific customs involving the institutionalization of exploitation developed.

The attitudes of those living with such institutions simply reflected, explained, and justified these institutional arrangements to them. Their values also involved distilations of these attitudes and emphasized *Freedom* (to exploit) and deemphasized other aspects of the "American Creed" (Myrdal, 1962).

It is obvious that, for a racist, there is some dissonance between that part of the "American Creed" that specifies that "all men are created equal . . . " and his exploitative behaviors. Abelson (1959) might have used this example in describing his several mechanisms for the resolution of belief dilemmas. The resolution can take many forms. The racist can claim that (a) "All men are *not* created equal—this is obviously a Communist line, a part of the conspiracy to overturn the American government, etc., etc." or, he can argue: (b) "Blacks are not exploited—why, they like to get less pay" or, he can state: (c) "There is no connection between the two beliefs; the American Creed refers to ideal relationships, but in actual life you have to pay wages according to how much you get from your workers, and blacks are bad workers . . . " or, (d) he might claim that "the American Creed refers to white men" or even worse, he might claim that "niggers are not men," and/or (e) finally he can justify his exploitative behaviors by bolstering them with a variety of cognitions, ranging from the quality and quantity of work produced by blacks to such matters as their dependability, costs of training, and so forth. Those familiar with Abelson's terminology will recognize that arguments (a), (b), and (c) are forms of *denial;* argument (d) is a form of *differentiation;* and argument (e) involves *bolstering.*

This analysis traces some of the sources of the cognitions of a racist, but also implies what can be done to reduce this racism—create institutional arrangements in which exploitative behaviors are no longer reinforced. In fact, theories of cognitive consistency (Abelson *et al.,* 1968) would predict that if an individual is forced to show preferential behavior toward blacks, his attitudes will develop in such a way to justify this behavior. It is unnecessary to explain here that the forcing must be done rather subtly, because when a person thinks that his behavior is against his will, the behavior is no longer dissonant with his attitudes. Furthermore, it is well known that the person must see little justification for his behavior (Festinger, 1957; Brehm & Cohen, 1962; Kiesler, Collins, & Miller, 1969).

To force a person to give preferential treatment to blacks under such circumstances seems very difficult, but may not be impossible. One of the important characteristics of racists is that they conform to whatever norms they see as important in their environment. If the impression can be created that others have adopted new norms of favoritism toward blacks, such an impression may go a long way toward reducing racism. Another hopeful bit of evidence comes from the interracial studies of Irwin Katz (for example, Katz et al., 1958, 1960), in which it was shown that the prejudiced white subjects, in the New York University samples, behaved more positively toward blacks in the mixed groups than did the unprejudiced subjects. It seemed as if the prejudiced subjects did not want to reveal their prejudice in an environment in which racism was disapproved, and bent over backwards to be nice. At any rate, in such situations significant shifts in attitudes might be expected, since behavior is inconsistent with the attitudes.

In sum, if the conditions of reinforcement of the white racist are changed by making it economically less rewarding for him to engage in exploitative behaviors, racism will be reduced. The theoretical arguments presented earlier then would suggest the following chain of events. First, the shift in reinforcements will shift the racist's behavior, and will lead to a new set of habits; second, his attitudes will change to become consistent with his behavior; third, his values will start realigning themselves to become consistent with his attitudes.

Some of these changes already are taking place. Legislation requiring that employers pay the same wages for equal work, regardless of race or sex, is a step in this direction. It does not handle, however, the "Negro jobs," which is a more subtle method of economic exploitation. This condition probably can be solved only by making such jobs so economically rewarding that many whites would like to do them. Salary schedules could be readjusted with this point in mind. For instance, good arguments can be presented for paying garbage collectors and grave diggers much more than they get now. The effect of such a wage change would be forced mechanization of this type of work, and the elimination of many jobs in this category. At the same time, however, the remaining jobs would become highly desirable, and more importantly the conception that these are "Negro jobs" thus would be eliminated. Of course, changes of this sort must be coupled with an intensification of efforts in manpower training. A very definite strategy exists here—a strategy that needs *only* money. The fundamental point is that economic changes lead to significant psychological changes in a given society, and the theoretical model outlined above suggests the nature of these changes.

Related to the problems discussed previously is the role of the blacks themselves in the initiation of the kinds of social change needed to reduce white racism. Here my analysis, derived from Smelser's (1963) theorizing, is relevant. When the blacks challenge the white community at a given level, the whites are likely to see the challenge at a higher level of abstraction, and the conflict thus is escalated. Let us look at this point more specifically. Most conflict between whites and blacks, at least in the Nothern ghettoes involves facilities and roles—who is going to do what work, using what facilities. However, the projections of this conflict by whites at a higher level of abstraction make the conflict look like a disagreement at the level of values. For example, the black says "I want a good job" and the white interprets it as "you want to reduce the standards and qualifications for this job" or "you do not consider efficiency important." If *high standards* or *efficiency* are middle-class values, then the disagreement has been projected to the level of values.

There is no evidence that blacks disapprove of efficiency *in principle,* or would like to lower standards. It is true that some behavior by blacks may suggest that they do not value efficiency as highly as some middle-class whites. However, in order to value efficiency, one must be rewarded for such behavior. There are few, if any, rewards for efficiency in the ghetto—note the high rate of unemployment and the long welfare roles. It is easy to understand that efficiency does not emerge as a black characteristic simply because the particular environment of the black ghetto does not reward it. In short, if contingencies of reinforcement are set up that maximize rewards for efficiency, in a particular institutional setting, both blacks and whites probably will respond to this reinforcement schedule.

After this slight digression, let us return to the issue of projection of the disagreement at higher levels of abstraction. It is assumed that this is a general, human characteristic. The black who challenges the Establishment at the level of facilities will be perceived by whites as challenging it at the level of values.

Evidence, meager though it is, suggests that blacks and whites have similar values (Lott & Lott, 1963). Both want freedom, equality, a good life, respect, happiness, peace, brotherhood, and so on. The blacks are burning the establishments that do not give them respect, that exploit them, that deny their freedom, that prevent them from reaching a good life. Yet their actions are interpreted as challenges to fundamental values. This is not to deny that there are some blacks whose values are inconsistent with those of the majority of Americans, but they are a very small minority, probably about 8% of the population of the ghetto, and a much smaller percentage of the total black population. Let us also remember that there are about as many whites whose values are in fundamental contrast to the values of the majority. My view is that these groups are relatively small. The problem lies elsewhere, namely, at the level of translation of these common values into appropriate roles and into equitable distributions of resources.

The tragedy of American society is that there is so little communication of the communality of fundamental values, so little understanding among the silent majority of the problems of the ghetto, so much readiness to escalate the conflict, and so much feeding of one escalation on previous escalations. If this volume helps to clarify some of these phenomena, it will have been most useful.

REFERENCES

Abelson, R. P. Modes of resolution of belief dilemmas. *Journal of Conflict Resolution*, 1959, 3, 343-352.

Abelson, R. P., Aronson, E., McGuire, W. J., Newcomb, T. M., Rosenberg, M. J. & Tannenbaum, P. H. *Theories of cognitive consistency: A source-book.* Chicago: Rand McNally, 1968.

Brehm, J. W., & Cohen, A. R. *Explorations in cognitive dissonance.* New York: Wiley, 1962.

Byrne, D. Attitudes and attraction. In L. Berkowitz (Ed.), *Advances in experimental social psychology.* New York: Academic Press, 1969. Pp. 35-89.

Byrne, D., & Nelson D. Attraction as a function of attitude similarity-dissimilarity: The effect of topic importance. *Psychonomic Science*, 1964, 1, 93-94.

Byrne, D., & Nelson, D. The effect of topic importance and attitude similarity-dissimilarity on attraction in a multistranger design. *Psychonomic Science*, 1965, 3, 449-450.

Campbell, D. T. Blind variation and selective retention in creative thought as in other knowledge processes. *Psychological Review*, 1960, 67, 380-400.

Dollard, J. *Caste and class in a southern town.* New York: Anchor, 1957. (Originally published in 1937.)

Festinger, L. *A theory of congitive dissonance.* New York: Harper, 1957.

Fishbein, M. Attitude and the prediction of behavior. In M. Fishbein (Ed.), *Readings in attitude theory and measurment.* New York: Wiley, 1967. Pp. 477-492.

Katz, I., & Benjamin, L. Effects of white authoritarianism in biracial work groups. *Journal of Abnormal and Social Psychology*, 1960, 61, 448-456.

Katz, I., Goldstone, J., & Benjamin, L. Behavior and productivity in biracial work groups. *Human Relations*, 1958, 11, 123-141.

Kiesler, C. A., Collins, B. E., & Miller, N. *Attitude change.* New York: Wiley, 1969.

Lewin, K., Dembo, T., Festinger, L., & Sears, P. Level of aspiration. In J. M. Hunt (Ed.), *Personality and the behavior disorders.* New York: Ronald Press, 1944. Pp. 333-378.

Lott, A. J., & Lott, B. E. *Negro and white youth: A psychological study in a border-state community.* New York: Holt, 1963.

Myrdal, G. *An American dilemma.* New York: Harper, 1962.

Smelser, N. J. *Theory of Collective Behavior.* New York: Free Press, 1963.

Steiner, I. Perceived freedom. In L. Berkowitz *Advances in Experimental Social Psychology.* New York: Academic Press, 1970. Pp. 187-248.

Tolman, E. C. A psychological model. In T. Parsons & E. A. Shils (Eds.), *Toward a general theory of social action.* Cambridge, Massachusetts: Harvard University Press, 1951. Pp. 279-359.

Triandis, H. C. *Attitude and attitude change.* New York: Wiley, 1971.

Triandis, H. C., & Triandis, L. M. Race, social class, religion and nationality as determinants of social distance. *Journal of Abnormal and Social Psychology,* 1960, **61**, 110-118.

Triandis, H. C., & Triandis, L. M. A cross-cultural study of social distance. *Psychological Monographs,* 1962, **76**, No. 540.

Triandis, H. C., & Triandis, L. M. Some studies of social distance. In I. D. Steiner and M. Fishbein (Eds.), *Current studies in social psychology.* New York: Holt, 1965. Pp. 207-217.

Triandis, H. C., Davis E. E., & Takezawa, S. I. Some determinants of social distance among American, German and Japanese students. *Journal of Personality and Social Psychology,* 1965, **2**, 540-551.

Vroom, V. H. *Work and Motivation.* New York: Wiley, 1964.

8

Mass Media and
Social Change [1]

Walter Weiss
Hunter College,
The City University of New York

Any general examination of the relationship between mass media and social change must begin by acknowledging a few salient cautions. First, the concepts, being *portmanteau* terms, are too diffuse to be lodged in other than gross and imprecise statements of relationship. Both terms require specification so that the aspects operative as influences or responsive as consequences can be more precisely delineated. In negative paraphrase, media are not media are not media. They differ in structure and contents, in traditions, organization, and utility as shaped by societal and competitive needs, in the psychological requirements of interaction, and, by virtue of the preceding, in the profiles of the attracted audiences. Also, among examples of a particular medium, there are sufficiently marked differences in these attributes that general assertions about a medium should be viewed as imprecisely defined in reference. Again in paraphrase, the press is not the press is not the press. In regard to social change, the conceptual problem is similar, in view of the open-ended diversity and heterogeneity of potential and actual changes. Unfortunately, there is no systematic dimensional analysis of kinds of effects on types or groupings of receivers to which units of media stimuli can be related. Complicating all is the temporal dimension for the operation and assessment of effects. The empirical and analytical problems added by time are deepened by the absence of base-line data derived from continuous systematic assessments of relevant social changes. Hence, it is only by a conceptual leap and more than a touch of faith and hope that categories emerge for empirical and theoretical relationships. Nevertheless, general and loosely drawn statements of relationship have been made and found useful in some degree, and constitute the thin understanding currently available of this societally significant topic (see Weiss, 1969, 1971).

[1] Preparation of this paper was aided by Contract NONR 4309(00).

Second, while discussions of the relationship tend to refer to the mass media, at whatever level of analysis, the effective concept implicitly is exposure to the media. The usual elliptic reference implies exposure, but the absence of explicit recognition can lead to confusion between availability and what people are actually aware of, between analyses of content and the psychological import of the media experience, and between physical units of media and the media's social impact (Weiss, 1969, 1971).

Third, the media are themselves societal institutions (see DeFleur, 1966). Hence, questions about media and social change are intrinsically questions about the relations between a dynamic and potent societal institution and other societal institutions, aspects or activities. For instance, the media operate within social contexts of personal relations, feeding and interacting with personal channels of communication, and contribute with other influences and institutions to the facilitation or obstruction of change. Also, as an institution, changes in the media themselves constitute societal changes and are responsive to general societal changes.

This acknowledgement leads to a fourth and critical caution. The general relationship between mass media and social change can be viewed from the perspective of the contribution of media to social change or in terms of the effects of social change on the media. The dynamics and fluidity of the relationship undoubtedly require a shift from one perspective to another whenever the relationship is examined over time. However, the mutual interaction between the two always must be kept in focus. Furthermore, to complete and complicate the transactive relationship, the influence of other factors on both should also be entertained. For example, technological developments such as advances in communication satellites and computer technology can have strikingly pervasive, if not revolutionary, effects on both (Schramm, 1968).

GENERAL FUNCTIONS OF THE MEDIA

Societal functions of the mass media have been conceived as threefold: the media act as public 'watchman,' by providing surveillance of the near and far environment; they aid social decision making by providing information, opinions, and appraisals of events and persons; and they teach by providing information and skill-related knowledge to the general public or by formal use in educational settings (Schramm, 1964). Essentially, all three functions constitute outcomes of the general informational-educational utility of the media. Although not mentioned in this narrowly instrumental catalog, the coordinate function of providing entertainment, diversion, and relaxation and a leisure-time resource for personal development has received emphasis in recent writings (Dumazadier, 1967; Stephenson, 1967). However, from a functional perspective that reflects a behavioral or receiver-determined focus, no media experience is solely informative or solely entertaining. What is predominantly diverting and relaxing inevitably carries some information or cultural potential, offering new facts, ideas, and images. And what is basically informative and educational may also be diverting, having entertainment values or providing personal gratification, self-enhancement, or the raw pleasure of vicarious social contact.

In modern industrialized countries, the full diversity of the media's actual and potential contributions are somewhat obscured and narrowed. This is a consequence of the current societal complexity in which the media operate, their *seriatim* development over time within an evolving matrix of other institutions, and the very pervasiveness of mass communications in modern society. Some responsibilities and potential have been absorbed, or preempted by, or are shared with other institutions (for example, education). Hence, it is in the developing areas of the world that the wide spectrum of the media's contributions and functions can be most vividly appreciated.

NATION BUILDING

The key role of mass media in nation building and national development can perhaps best be instanced by considering the general development model proposed by a number of analysts. Despite some divergences among them, a collation and abbreviation of their views would lead to the following model (the arrows should be read as "fosters"): economic adequacy, manifested by the Gross National Product (GNP) or indexes of urbanization and industrial development → educational resources and the spread and upgrading of education, with a consequent reduction in illiteracy and with the production of a variety of educational effects (for example, on cognition, intellection, attitudes, values, personality) → the expansion of means of mass communication and their greater use by the populace → a variety of modernization outcomes. The elements of this part model are bound in mutually interactive relationships, such that changes in one reflect back as well as ahead of other elements in this linear array. Also the model is not merely descriptive but implies action decisions; for example, it suggests that the effective use and development of the mass media, a necessity for successful modernization, requires the prior establishment of an adequate economic and educational base. (A significant report by Guthrie (1970) underscores the constraining influence on innovational behavior in the developing country of existing social norms and reinforcement contingencies, despite the acceptance of modern-oriented attitudes.)

To effect nation building, the contents of the direct and indirect informational functions of the media are crucial (Schramm, 1964; Lerner & Schramm, 1967). It is by virtue of information and news about development projects and related governmental actions, decisions, and policies that development activities can be fostered through popular understanding and support. General informa tion about the wider environment which need mean no more than news about other communities or areas of the country, as well as about other nations, contributes to a wide-angled perspective and makes far-off and abstract events locally and personally relevant. References to national activities of all kinds fosters a sense of national identity or at least of identity with a wider social entity than the village or tribe. And a fuller awareness of nationhood can induce support for national policies that may require local or personal deprivations or commitments of resources. In addition, national media provide governmental or societal-wide interpretations and evaluations of significant events and persons (Lane, 1969). This accepted picture of the surrounding world is not only important for broad support of governmental policies but also aids in producing cohesion among socially and geographically disparate groups, and gives to the believing individual a necessary sense of social support for his views and hence an organized perception of a complex world. Additionally, the media's role in the development of national identity and the diffusion of national policies and interpretations has the crucial function of providing the ground for governance of large and physically dispersed populations. Through the media, coordination of efforts and actions over the country or over wide areas becomes possible, even though mere behavior and not assent is the key requirement, and even when coercion is available. The importance of the support of public opinion hardly need be belabored; while media do not guarantee it, even in a closed society, without the means of rapid, repeatable mass communication such understanding and active public support becomes much more difficult of attainment.

RISING ASPIRATIONS AND DEFERRED GRATIFICATION

As the modernization process becomes established, direct personal contacts with the wider environment as well as vicarious, mediated contacts through mass communications lead to rising aspirations (Lerner, 1958). Here the key is presumed to be a psychological state of empathy which permits a person not merely to observe new possibilities but to adopt an "as if" perspective in relation to himself as a participant in a new way of living. However, rising aspirations can become a volcano of rising frustrations, if unrealistic expectancies are developed or instant changes demanded. Hence, another function of the media is to channel rising aspirations into activities that will facilitate development and to impress a realistic stamp upon them (Dube, 1967; Lerner, 1967; Rao, 1966). The principal channeling is in terms of the fostering of the value of deferred gratification and its supporting behaviors; that is, people must understand and accept the importance of taking actions now that will not bring immediate gratifications but whose full fruition will occur some time in the future. Of course, other societal institutions are involved and probably more centrally in the development of such a value. In fact, education itself is the grand example of the acceptance of deferred gratification, as well as its fosterer. But, aside from exhortation, the media can also contribute by providing information and appraisals for realistic actions and expectations, for deferred gratification requires risk-taking and to engage in sound risk-taking requires valid information about possibilities and likelihoods.

PERSONAL CHANNELS

Since developing countries have long-standing traditions of oral transmission of news and views, the mass media, even without planning, become linked to personal channels of communication (Weiss, 1969, 1971). That the linkage is unplanned is unfortunate, for the multiplying effect of media transmission of information can be made more efficient and potent if skillfully connected to existent modes and contexts of person-to-person transmission. Given that personal transmission is crucial in developing countries and will continue to be so for some time, a mapping of conversational linkages and personal contacts would be of particular value for when personal contacts and hence the flow of information by word of mouth is vertical, diffusion of news is rapid and reasonably complete over a wide segment of the populace. In contrast, when it is horizontal and within socially segmented strata of society, diffusion is limited; as a result, the more modern-oriented people who are in contact with the media and with extralocal sources of information do not contribute their full potential to national development.

Personal contact in the diffusion process is important not only for the rapid flow of information but also for behavior and attitude changes that require social support or group action. One technique for overcoming traditional ways has been the development of organized group exposure to radio and television, followed by group discussion and decision-making (Weiss, 1969). Although most such forums have focused on community projects or the acceptance and adoption of agricultural innovations, some have been designed to induce changes in other kinds of behavior and attitudes (for example, hygiene and child care) or have such effects as a derived outcome of changes in traditional ways of living and thinking (Weiss, 1971).

The significance of person-to-person transmissions also invites caution with regard to assessing the spread or reach of mass media in terms of the number of newspapers circulated or sets available per some fraction of the population. The linking of media to personal channels multiplies considerably their potential significance. For instance, a single newspaper copy often is read by a number of people and may be read out loud to many others who are illiterate. Similarly, even without organized listening and watching, group exposure to broadcast media occurs. For instance, programs broadcast through the one radio set in a coffee house or a village meeting place may reach a fair number of listeners. It is because of this one-many linkage between media units and exposure contacts, as well as the general significance of personal channels in the diffusion of news, that the social impact of the mass media in developing countries will be underestimated by indexes composed of physical units per some amount of population (Weiss, 1971).

MODERNIZED AREAS

Turning to industrialized and modernized countries, we find that all media functions and contributions noted in regard to developing countries can be discerned here too. However, some no longer are dominant or that evident on casual glance, as a result of the prior development of supporting traditions and values and the sharing of responsibilities with other vital institutions. Nevertheless, it takes but a breakdown in the availability of the regularly used media to reveal people's deep dependence on them (Berelson, 1949; Kimball, 1959). Their general informational and entertainment functions are vividly etched on the modern scene. They even have utility as a means of symbolic social contact or as a means of relating ourselves to others. Also, they are used in supplementing fashion and, except under special circumstances, are the principal sources of and resources for both topical and background information and knowledge (Bogart, 1968-1969; Wade & Schramm, 1969).

The significance of the media for national interpretations and coordination of national actions and attitudes and, thereby, for governance is well understood. But the media also provide a means of transmitting information and views from the public to government and from one segment of the public to relevant others. In these days, this is accomplished not merely by the reporting of ordinary happenings but by the reporting of pseudoevents or public demonstrations designed to achieve media access for the views of special interests or inadequately publicized groups. In a sense, the media provide two-way channels of communication to connect different societal units, although the frequency and efficiency of transmission is not likely to be the same in both directions (see Chaffee, 1967).

Personal channels do not loom as large in industrialized as in developing countries. They operate primarily on personal or highly involving or dramatic matters and, even then, are often complementary to the mass media (Weiss, 1969, 1971). Here too, little is known concerning routine or regular conversational linkages or the ordinary substance of conversations. In industrialized countries, two other means of personal communication, though not literally face to face, are regularly used: the telephone and the mails. However, their roles have not been given adequate recognition or systematic attention. It takes interference with their use to vivify the considerable part they play in modern communication systems.

The usual media content, including advertising, continues to influence wants and aspirations. Empathy and deferred gratification, while fostered by the media, are initiated and sustained principally by other societal institutions and traditions. However, deferred gratification requires some assurance of the stability or predictability of the future, as well as a sense of being able to cope through personal or group efforts. Hence, the media can and do contribute significantly to the requisite future orientation, by providing valid knowledge and objective appraisals of situations, resources and likelihoods so that risk taking can be put on a more realistic basis.

MIRROR VERSUS MOLDER

In view of the functions of the media and their interconnections with other societal institutions, it is evident that, in the most general way, the media are both mirrors and molders of society. However, in any given instance of social change or lack of change or tension for change, the role of the media cannot be simply assayed or extracted from the manifold of operative influences. To say that the Orson Welle's broadcast, "The War of the Worlds," caused a panic in New Jersey is true in that, if the production had not been broadcast, no panic would have occurred. But differential receptivity and susceptibility to the broadcast, the occurrence or absence of checking behavior, and the kinds of behavior elicited following belief in the broadcast must all be given their due in the total outcome (Cantril, 1940). National publicity given to the civil rights movement in its early days undoubtedly facilitated further civil rights actions, affected the response of civil officials and police, and encouraged civil rights changes. However, if the times were not propitious, would changes have occurred? Consider what probably wouuld have been the result if the same actions occurred 20 or 30 years earlier, even if television had been available. Similar complexities of analysis apply to the relationship between public taste and the entertainment function of the media (Weiss, 1969).

Even the very nature of the events selected from the welter of all possible ones for reporting and analysis is conditioned by a variety of factors. Some of those involved are the nature and professionalism of news personnel, the presence of a diverse assortment of "gate keepers" or influentials, the organizational and financial structure of the industry, and the meaning of newsworthiness and normative dimensions of appropriateness for news (Weiss, 1971). Since the economic base of the media is essentially predicated on audience use, media contents cannot diverge too far from audience views, expectations, needs, and interests. However, should the latter change as a result of the influence of other factors (for example, rising education), so will the formats and contents of the media (DeFleur, 1966; Potter, 1966). In sum, economic or political dependence on mass audiences means that the standards, values, and requirements of the general public are controlling in regard to media content and form, and constitute the context to which the media adapt and within which they function.

In addition, the media as a societal institution will reflect the general values and standards of the society. At best, they may lead society slightly or sporadically with a few brave or deviant ventures. When social change does occur, however, the media, as is true of any public institution or activity, will also be affected. It is in this sense that the media both reflect and lag social change. Nevertheless, by giving voice and publicity to the first stirrings of change, they can influence its trend and speed.

THE MEDIA AND THE BLACK SOCIAL REVOLUTION

In the United States, the reflection of the black social revolution in the media should exemplify these posits. Although quantitative content analyses have not been done, there is no doubt that during the past 15 years the major media have devoted considerable space and time to news reports and analyses of civil rights activities. This continuous publicity principally for salient events has kept black strivings in the focus of public attention and kept them from being swept under the societal rug, and has inspired black groups and given to black voices sometime access to public thinking and the public conscience. However, it has also had an adverse effect on the weekly black press, which had previously depended on its function as the almost sole source of black news for its principal appeal to a large group of black readers (Lyle, 1967; Roshco, 1967). Circulation has dropped markedly; and the only black-oriented news service, the long-lived Associated Negro Press, terminated when the major wire services began to provide regular news on black activities to the black press (Beard & Zoerner, 1969). However, the black weeklies are still the only source of news of the ordinary run of events of interest to a black audience and the principal locus of a continuing Negro perspective on the news. Interestingly, the limited achievement of greater economic, educational, and residential mobility of Negroes has also caused the black press to lose an important core of readers. The psychological and physical movement away from the ghetto has led to a less geographically bound interest in black news and hence to a reduced use of the ghetto press (Lyle, 1967; Roshco, 1967).

The complex of economic, social, and legal changes that have occurred in the status of blacks in American society have already had their effects on media depictions of Negroes. These are visible in two forms. First, the number of black professionals in the news media have increased, although they still constitute an insignificant percentage of the total. Second, Negroes have become more visible in movies and television and are portrayed in many different roles. Also, depictions of Negroes in national advertising directed at the general public have shown a twelvefold increase over 18 years (6-71%) in their representation as skilled or white-collar workers, in place of their former dominant representation as unskilled or service personnel (Cox, 1969-1970). One commentator has suggested that these visible changes in the employment and depiction of Negroes in the media serve not only to encourage black aspirations, pride, and dignity but more significantly to contribute to a greater acceptance by whites of the idea that blacks belong in the mainstream of American life (Colle, 1968).

The effects of the black social revolution should not only be reflected in the media addressed to the general public but also in the media directed at black audiences. Since black media are also economically dependent on their audiences, they cannot be too discrepant from them in expressed views or themes or values. Consequently, analyses of the contents of black media should intimate Negro perspectives and salient concerns and thereby the effects of their changed and changing status. However, there has always been a dearth of attention to the contents and functions of media vehicles designed for specific ethnic, racial, or religious groups. Instead, research has focused almost exclusively on the media for the general public. Hence, it is not unexpected, although unfortunate, that despite the black social revolution there has been relatively little research on the Negro press or other media addressed to black audiences.

In order to examine the changes over time in media contents for a black audience, Michael Chapko[2] and I undertook an exploratory content analysis of the advertising in *Ebony* magazine. Our choice of advertising as the content was predicated on the assumption that major advertisers use market research and copy testing as an intelligence operation for determining how best to appeal to an audience. Hence, changes in audience views and values should affect their responses to advertisements and therefore should be taken into account by the advertiser. This argument could even be pushed to the point of suggesting that advertising research might turn up attitudinal changes that are not yet publicly visible. But even without such an assumption, it is reasonable to expect that over time advertising directed to a black audience would exhibit changes in accord with the development of black dignity and pride and the unfreezing of the social status of blacks.

[2] Mr. Chapko, a City University doctoral student, gathered and organized the data. His contributions merit consideration as a coauthor of the reported content analysis.

Ebony and Life

Lacking close competition, *Ebony* is the premier national Negro magazine of its kind. Its readers number more than 900,000, are almost exclusively black and, compared to the general Negro population, are better educated, have higher incomes, and hold proportionately more white-collar jobs (Hirsch, 1968). Although appealing to a middle-class segment of the Negro community, *Ebony* also draws from the lower-class sector, with 31% of its readers earning less than $5000 per year and 41% not completing high school. Its editors admit to a responsive sensitivity to the views, desires, and aspirations of the majority of its readers (Hirsch, 1968).

In general appearance, size, and format, *Ebony* resembles *Life* magazine. While the readership profiles of the two diverge in the same manner as do the general black-white profiles in the country, both readership groups are higher socioeconomically than their respective general population groups. Because of the similarities between the magazines, the general types of advertisements found in *Life* were used as a base line against which to reflect some of the data gathered from *Ebony*.

Issues sampled. Issues from 1964, 1966, and 1968 were analyzed. Since *Ebony* is published monthly, all 12 numbers from each of these years were included. For *Life*, a weekly, the first issue of each month was used. Hence, the total sample comprised 36 issues of each magazine over the period from 1964 to 1968.

Categorization of advertisements. Each advertisement that was at least one quarter of a page in size was included in the analysis. The *Ebony* ads were categorized in terms of type of product, race(s) and sex(es) of the model(s), and the relative lightness-darkness of the black model(s). Since only a few *Life* ads contained a black model, only type of product could be used as a basis of categorization.

The ratings of lightness-darkness of the black model(s) were made in the following way. From *Ebony's* advertisements, a sample of 16 models representing a wide diversity of skin tones of black models were rank ordered from lightest ("1") to darkest ("16") by ten judges. Based principally on mean rankings and degree of consensus in ratings, four of these photographs then were selected as the reference standards for scoring the advertisements in Ebony. Their mean rankings were 1.0, 5.8, 12.0, and 14.2; for convenience, they will be referred to as A, B, C, and D, respectively. If the skin tone of a model in an advertisement was judged to fall between A and B, the model received a rating of "1"; if between B and C, a rating of "2"; if between C and D, a rating of "3"; and if darker than D, a rating of "4." When more than one black model appeared in an ad, the average skin tone of the models was used as the rating for the ad as a whole.

TABLE 1   DESCRIPTIONS OF PRODUCT CATEGORIES

Category	Description	Examples
Personal appearance		
Afro	Any product that is used for personal appearance and the Afro look.	Afro hair spray
Wigs	Any advertisement for wigs or falls	
Straightener	A product used to straighten the hair	
Skin lightener	A product used to lighten skin color	
Personal—female	Any product used for personal care by a female, including makeup, skin care, hair care	Lipstick, powder, hairspray
Personal—male	Any product used for personal care by a male, including skin care, hair care, shaving	Hair lotion, razor blades
Personal—both	Any product used for personal care by both male and female	Deodorant, soap
Clothes	All clothing and accessories	Pants, underwear, hats, dresses, jewelry
Alcohol		
Wine	Any wine	
Beer	Any beer, ale, or malt liquor	
Liquor	Any alcoholic beverage having an alcoholic content over 20%	Whiskey, gin, vodka, brandy
Automotive		
Autos	Any new automobile	
Truck, skooter	Any new truck or skooter	
Auto products	Any product used for the running or upkeep of a car	Gasoline, tires, oil
Home		
Kitchen	Products to be used in the kitchen for cooking, and cleaning products for the home	Pots, silverware, detergent, pet products, cleaners
Household	Products used by the family for play, work, or school	Toys, lawn equipment, furniture, pens, carpets, T.V.
Large appliances	Any large appliance	Refrigerator, washer, stove, air conditioner

147

TABLE 1 (continued)

Category	Description	Examples
Food	All food products except those included in other categories	
Smoking		
Cigarettes	Any cigarette	
Other tobaccos	Any tobacco product excluding cigarettes	Cigars, pipe tobacco
Soft drink	Any carbonated nonalcoholic beverage	Cola
Travel	Any mode of travel or destination	Airline, bus, rent-a-car, Bermuda, England
Drugs	Products found in a drugstore and not included in other categories	Aspirin, cough drops, female sanitary products
Books, magazines, records	Any book magazine, or record	Book of the Month Club, Columbia Record Club
Job solicitation	An advertisement, usually placed by a large corporation, containing the name and address of individual to contact for job application	
Insurance	Advertising for some type of insurance	

Categorization of type of product was initially as discriminating as possible. Then functional groups were employed to aggregate very infrequently occurring subcategories. Finally, these were coalesced further to yield larger but meaningfully interrelated clusters. Table 1 contains the final groupings of product types employed in the analyses of the advertisements.

Ebony versus *Life*

Although on the average *Ebony* contains 1.7 times as many pages as *Life*, approximately 9% fewer of its pages contain ads of a quarter page size or larger. Table 2 presents the percentages of ads placed in the major content categories for each magazine. Particularly striking is the dominance in *Ebony* of ads

TABLE 2 PERCENTAGES OF ADVERTISEMENTS IN DIFFERENT PRODUCT CATEGORIES

	Ebony				Life			
	1964	1966	1968	All	1964	1966	1968	All
Personal appearance	32.9	34.6	35.8	34.3	15.3	12.2	12.2	13.4
Alcohol	22.0	18.2	15.6	18.6	7.9	11.4	8.1	8.8
Automotive	4.5	5.0	5.4	5.0	14.5	14.8	15.5	14.8
Home products	16.3	13.4	13.8	14.6	30.3	28.4	34.9	30.8
Smoking	4.4	3.4	3.8	3.8	7.0	5.8	5.6	6.2
Soft drink	1.9	2.5	2.0	2.1	2.9	3.1	1.2	2.6
Travel	2.0	2.8	3.6	2.8	1.2	4.2	1.9	2.6
Drugs	9.0	9.3	6.0	8.1	7.1	5.7	4.0	5.7
Books, magazines, records	2.4	2.6	4.8	3.3	2.4	1.7	3.7	2.5
Job solicitation	1.6	3.3	3.4	2.7	0.0	0.1	0.5	0.2
Insurance	1.0	2.3	2.2	1.8	3.0	3.7	3.0	3.3
Miscellaneous	2.1	2.9	3.6	2.8	8.5	8.8	9.5	9.0

pertaining to personal appearance, slightly more than one out of three falling into this category and with percentages averaging 2.5 times that of *Life*'s. Even when products specifically designed for the black market are removed, the differences, though diminished, are still considerable. Also, the trend for this category is upward in *Ebony* over these years, in contrast to the downward turn in *Life*.

But these results, which are based on the conglomerate category of personal appearance, obscure some contrasting trends. While skin lighteners declined steadily from 3.6 to 1.5%, hair straighteners showed a consistent upward trend from 1.4 to 3.8%. Ads displaying wigs also increased continuously from 2.0 to 5.2%, and only a few of the wigs displayed were of the Afro kind, even in 1968, the first year for the appearance of Afro products; in that year, the latter products constituted less than 2% of all ads. Hence, in terms of ads principally for women, the appeal of the natural black look was evidenced at best in the avoidance of skin lighteners; but an opposing trend appeared with regard to hair straighteners and wigs.

Ads for alcoholic drinks was the second largest category for *Ebony*, and it was the only other one in which *Ebony* had a considerably higher percentage of ads than did *Life*. Of particular interest is the steady downward trend of such ads in *Ebony* but not in *Life*, perhaps suggesting related shifts in attitude on the part of *Ebony*'s readers. *Ebony*'s persistent weakness relative to *Life* in ads for automotive and household products was also found by Berkman (1963). Two trends in *Ebony* worth noting, since they are reflective of changes in black mobility, are the consistent increases in ads for travel and for job opportunities.

TABLE 3   PERCENTAGES OF ADS SHOWING ONLY BLACK MODELS
(Based Only on Ads in Which a Model Appeared)

	1964	1966	1968	1964-1968
Personal appearance	92.8	93.5	90.3	92.3
Alcohol	69.8	82.4	78.4	78.4
Automotive	20.0	20.0	15.0	18.8
Home products	94.5	82.6	72.1	84.1
Smoking	97.7	86.1	89.2	91.4
Soft drink	100.0	85.0	55.0	78.2
Travel	90.0	56.0	51.4	62.5
Drugs	95.9	91.1	98.2	94.7
Job solicitation	80.0[a]	100.0[a]	71.4	79.2
Insurance	83.3[a]	36.7	83.3	67.4
Books, magazines, records	81.2	100.0	94.7	92.3
Miscellaneous	24.1	50.0	53.8	53.6
Average	85.2	83.9	81.8	84.2

[a] $N < 10$.

Use of black models.   Since the percentage of ads using models varied both by
product category and by year, data on the race of models are based on
percentages of ads that contained one or more models of either race or sex.
Table 3 reveals that more than four out of five ads in any year contained only
black models, but also that there was a slight but steady overall decline in the
use of such ads. A similar decline occurred for white-only ads; whereas, ads
displaying mixed racial models showed a continuous overall increase from 3.5 to
9.4%.

As can be seen, there is a considerable range over product categories in the
use of black-only models from an overall low of 18.8% for automotive products
to a high of 94.7% for drugs. Although the data are not fully consistent, it seems
as though the product categories whose ads feature the use of the product by
one person or in limited social settings involving primarily pairs are the ones with
the high percentages of black-only models. This factor of social setting, with its
implication of wider black mobility and acceptability, is most clearly evidenced
in travel and soft drink ads, where there is a sharp and steady decline in
black-only models coupled with a compensating increase in the use of mixed
racial models.

Home products which exhibited a steady decline in black-only models also
evidenced a rise in the use of both white-only and mixed racial models. Although
approximately three out of four of all automotive ads contain only white
models, the percentage of such all-white ads has declined from 77.1 to 65.0%;

TABLE 4   PERCENTAGES OF ADS CONTAINING "RELATIVELY
LIGHTER" BLACK MODELS (Ratings 1 and 2)

Racial composition	Sex of model	Year			
		1964	1966	1968	1964-1968
Black only	Only female	86.0	87.7	73.9	82.7
	Only male	59.0	53.9	49.7	54.2
	Both sexes	71.8	72.3	60.5	68.3
	Average	75.0	74.0	63.6	71.0
Mixed	Only female	83.3	72.2	41.7	58.3
	Only male	37.5	37.5	16.1	25.5
	Both sexes	42.8	75.0^a	45.0	52.2
	Average	50.0	60.9	32.0	44.3

^{a}Small N.

but, rather than an increase in the use of black-only models, there has been a sharp upswing in ads with mixed racial models. In general, the trend seems to be toward the introduction of white models where the categories in 1964 were dominated by black-only models (even personal appearance shows a slight but steady rise in the use of mixed racial models; drugs is the main exception to this conjecture) and the introduction of black models into the one category dominated by white-only models. The overall result, as previously noted, is a slight but steady movement toward the use of mixed racial models in ads.

Relative lightness-darkness of black models.   Although models were rated on a four-category scale, the data will be presented in terms of the percentages of models assigned to either of the lighter two categories (ratings 1 and 2). Table 4 contains these percentages broken down by year, racial composition of ad, and sex of the model(s). The general trend is toward a decrease in the use of relatively lighter models. The major decline occurred from 1966 to 1968, the likely period of growing emphasis on the "black is beautiful" sentiment. However, in ads containing only black models, the models were lighter than in ads of mixed racial composition. Also, the models in ads containing only females tended to be lighter than the models in mixed-sex ads, which in turn were lighter than the models in ads containing only males. This pattern, which is essentially due to a female-male difference, probably fits existent sex-related differences in the population, although it may also reflect evaluative standards of feminity and masculinity.

Commentary

The preceding trends and patterns generally appear in most of the product categories. As might be expected, the percentages vary over the product categories, from a high of 84.7% for personal appearance (which includes 25.0% for Afros) to a low of 49.0% for home products. The latter category contains a sharp difference between 68.0% for ads for large appliances or household items and 38.2% for ads for food and kitchen products. This predominant use of darker models in ads for products associated with mundane homemaking routines contrasts with the trend for all other product categories (excepting Afros) and is suggestive of an image-related association involving the lightness-darkness dimension.

Although a diversity of speculative inferences are easily generated by different segments of the total data, such posits have been eschewed at this time. To give them greater validity or to draw the most plausible probes from the data requires, at the least, an input of knowledge of the empirical and policy bases of the advertisers' decisions, the value perspectives and attitudinal reactions to the ads of *Ebony*'s readers, and the editorial policies of the magazine's editors (see Hirsch, 1968 for the latter). Nevertheless, it is evident that by 1968 *Ebony*'s ads still exhibited relatively little impact of a militant version of the publicly salient themes of black dignity. The modest increase in the use of racially mixed models and the trend toward darker models, along with some modifications in the advertising weight given to selected product categories seem the principal responses to changes in black socioeconomic status, social mobility, and pride. Although it should be kept in mind that *Ebony*'s readers constitute a special, self-selected segment of the general black population, it is probable that the customary reaction of advertising to evolving social changes is one of delay and tentativeness.

The general value of any approach to an examination of the relations between the media and social change depends fundamentally on its being used continuously, systematically, and routinely. One-shot, limited, or sporadic efforts cannot provide the knowledge base for the broad and varied conceptual perspectives needed, if mass communications research is to flourish.

REFERENCES

Beard, R. L., & Zoerner, C. E., III. Associated Negro press: Its founding, ascendancy and demise. *Journalism Quarterly*, 1969, 46, 47-52.

Berelson, B. What 'missing the newspaper' means. In P. F. Lazarsfeld and F. N. Stanton (Eds.), *Communications research* 1948-49. New York: Harper, 1949. Pp. 111-129.

Berkman, D. Advertising in "Ebony" and "Life": Negro aspirations vs. reality. *Journalism Quarterly*, 1963, **40**, 53-64.

Bogart,L. Changing news interests and the news media. *Public Opinion Quarterly,* 1968-1969 (Winter), **32**, 560-574.

Cantril, H. *The invasion from Mars.* Princeton, New Jersey Princeton University Press, 1940.

Chaffee, S. H. The public view of the media as carriers of information between school and community. *Journalism Quarterly,* 1967, **44**, 730-734.

Colle, R. D. Negro image in the mass media: A case study in social change. *Journalism Quarterly*, 1968, **45**, 55-60.

Cox, K. K. Changes in stereotyping of Negroes and whites in magazine advertisements. *Public opinion Quarterly*, 1969-1970 (Winter), **33**, 603-606.

DeFleur, M. L. *Theories of mass communication.* New York: Mackay, 1966.

Dube, S. C. A note on communication in economic development. In D. Lerner and W. Schramm (Eds.), *Communication and change in the developing countries.* Honolulu: East-West Center Press, 1967. Pp. 93-97.

Dumazadier, J. *Toward a society of leisure.* New York: Free Press, 1967.

Guthrie, G. M. *The psychology of modernization in the rural Phillipines.* Quezon City, Phillipines: Ateneo de Manila University Press, 1970.

Hirsch, P. M. An analysis of Ebony: The magazine and its readers. *Journalism Quarterly,* 1968, **45**, 261-271, 292.

Kimball, P. People without papers. *Public Opinion Quarterly,* 1959, **23**, 389-398.

Lane, J. P. Isolation and public opinion in rural northeast Brazil. *Public Opinion Quarterly*, 1969, **33**, 55-68.

Lerner, D. *The passing of traditional society.* Glencoe, Illinois: Free Press of Glencoe, 1958.

Lerner, D. Communication and the prospects of innovative development. In D. Lerner and W. Schramm (Eds.), *Communication and change in the developing countries.* Honolulu: East-West Center Press, 1967. Pp. 305-317.

Lerner, D., & Schramm, W. (Eds.) *Communication and change in the developing countries.* Honolulu: East-West Center Press, 1967.

Lyle, J. *The news in megalopolis.* San Francisco: Chandler Publ. Co., 1967.

Potter, D. The historical perspective. In S. T. Donner (Ed.), *The meaning of commercial television.* Austin: University of Texas Press, 1966. Pp. 51-68.

Rao, V. V. L. *Communication and development.* Minneapolis: University of Minnesota Press, 1966.

Roshko, B. What the black press said last summer. *Columbia Journalism Review,* 1967, 6, 6-9.

Schramm, W. *Mass media and national development.* Stanford, California: Stanford University Press, 1964.

Schramm, W. *Communication satellites for education, science, and culture.* New York: UNESCO Publ., 1968.

Stephenson, W. *The play theory of communication.* Chicago: University of Chicago Press, 1967.

Wade, S., and Schramm, W. The mass media as sources of public affairs, science, and health knowledge. *Public Opinion Quarterly,* 1969, 33, 197-209.

Weiss, W. Effects of the mass media of communication. In G. Lindzey and E. Aronson (Eds.), *Handbook of social psychology.* Vol. V. Reading, Massachusetts: Addison-Wesley, 1969. Pp. 77-195.

Weiss, W. Mass communication. In P. Mussen and M. Rosenzweig (Eds.), *Annual review of psychology.* Palo Alto, California: Annual Reviews, 1971. Pp. 309-336.

9
Contextual Models of School Desegregation[1]

Thomas F. Pettigrew and Robert T. Riley
Harvard University

Racial change over the past generation has not developed uniformly over the South. Some areas readily complied, for example, with the 1954 Supreme Court ruling against *de jure* racial segregation in the public schools. Other areas resisted until direct pressure was brought to bear upon them. Many others have resisted strenuously throughout the intervening years. What underlies this pattern of acceptance and resistance? Is it predictable? This contribution will attempt to account for this pattern of change, first, in ecological terms alone, second, in attitude terms alone, and, finally, in contextual terms employing both ecological and attitude data.

PREVIOUS RELEVANT ECOLOGICAL RESEARCH

The factors which ecological research has consistently isolated as critical in Southern race relations can be subsumed heuristically under four interrelated classifications: (*a*) urbanism, (*b*) the Negro, (*c*) economc prosperity, and (*d*) traditionalism. For a review of past research in this area, see Pettigrew, Riley, and Ross (in press).

THE TEXAS ECOLOGICAL MODEL

For a comprehensive attack upon this problem, we focused upon one key southern state and enlarged upon previous studies in two ways: a systematic

[1] The research reported in this chapter was performed under Contract OEC-1-6-061774-1887 with the United States Office of Education's Bureau of Research. Points of view or opinions stated do not necessarily represent official Office of Education positions or policy. A more detailed treatment of this and related racial research will appear in Pettigrew, Riley, & Ross, 1972.

TABLE 1   ORTHOGONAL FACTORS FROM 150-CENSUS
VARIABLE FACTOR ANALYSIS OF TEXAS
COUNTIES, 1960[a]

Factor	Approximate label	Latent root	Rotated sums of squares
I	Population size	37.2	34.4
II	Urban-rural	11.8	5.1
III	Commercial farming	4.9	4.3
IV	Mexican American	4.4	2.4
V	Prosperous, young white residents	3.7	10.9
VI	Farming-manufacturing	2.6	5.4
VII	Negro American	2.1	3.7
VIII	Housing quality	1.9	3.2

[a]Principal components factor analysis was conducted followed
by factor rotation subject to the varimax criteria.

expansion of the independent variables; and subregional as well as state-wide
analyses. We chose Texas because it has a large number of units for analysis (that
is, 187 counties with 1% or more Negro population in 1960), sharp subregional
variation within it, and the only established state-wide survey agency in the
South.

Expansion of Independent Variables

Much of the previous research in this area is characterized by an un-
systematic approach to the selection of the independent variables. Usually
only a few census indicators are tested; yet the 1960 census directly provides
approximately 150 variables at the county level, and more could be constructed
from the original 150. Most of these 150 measures, of course, tap the same basic
dimensions. Were we to regress the entire set upon the school desegregation
measure, a large number of the predictors would be strongly multicollinear.
Hence, there is an initial need to reduce this sizable array down to a small
number of orthogonal (independent) dimensions. Rather than attempt this
crucial reduction on strictly *a priori* grounds, we employed a principal components factor analysis of the entire array and obtained through varimax rotation
the eight orthogonal factors listed in Table 1.

Five of the factors are already familiar from the work of past studies:
population size, urban-rural, manufacturing-farming, the Negro, and housing
quality. One factor, Mexican Americans, is among Southern states special to

TABLE 2   FACTOR SCORE ASSOCIATIONS WITH THE
EXTENT OF SCHOOL DESEGREGATION IN
TEXAS, 1965

		Extent of school desegregation	
Factor	Approximate label	Standardized beta weights	Unique contributions
I	Population size	+.17	2.9
II	Urban-rural	+.36	13.2
III	Commercial farming	+.43	18.3
IV	Mexican American	+.18	3.8
V	Prosperous, young white residents	−.06	.4
VI	Farming-manufacturing	−.04	.2
VII	Negro American	+.13	1.7
VIII	Housing quality	−.07	.3

R^2 (percentage of variance explained) = 40.8%[a]

R (multiple correlation) = .64

[a]Since the eight factors are orthogonal, multicollinearity is no issue here and R^2 is a simple sum of the contributions of each factor in accounting for desegregation variance by counties.

Texas. Two others are partly discoveries of this factor analytic approach—commercial farming and areas with prosperous, young white residents. The former turns out to be a highly significant predictor.

The Dependent Variable

We chose an index of the extent of the school desegregation process as our dependent variable: *the percentage of public schools in biracial districts within a county which boasted biracial student bodies in 1965.*

Complications were introduced by the fact that Texas has many more public school districts (2024) than counties (254). Fortunately district lines do not cross county lines, and we faced only the task of aggregating the data from the biracial school districts within each of the 187 counties whose populations in 1960 were 1% or more Negro. In aggregating over school districts within counties, we weighted the contribution of each district by its number of students. Thus, large districts have proportionate weight in the percentage of a county, and the final index is consequently not a precise percentage of the biracial schools in a county. Furthermore, we eliminated all districts within which no Negroes reside.

Factor Scores and Desegregation

Table 2 provides the correlations between the eight ecological factors and our measure of school desegregation. About two-fifths of the variance of desegregation is accounted for by these eight ecological factors. The extent of school desegregation is greatest in Texas counties with a large number of commercial farms and a large portion of its population living in *rural* areas. This surprising result may be partly a function of our particular measure of desegregation. Since rural counties have fewer schools to desegregate, it should be easier for them to attain a higher percentage of biracial schools. On the other hand, these findings also reflect the fact that so-called *de facto* segregation is less of a problem for rural than urban areas, and thus once again the process can proceed more swiftly.

Specific Variables and Desegregation

The technique of regressing orthogonal factor scores, as shown in Table 2, is analytically "clean" in that it avoids problems of multicollinearity and incompleteness. However, it hinders precise theoretical interpretation, because a wide range of variables may load heavily on more than one factor. Moreover, subregional variation cannot be accounted for with this technique. Factor structures shift from Black Belt-like East Texas to sparsely populated West Texas, for example, and this undermines the basis of intersubregional comparisons.

To avoid these problems of interpretation inherent in the technique of regressing factor scores, another series of regressions was performed using census variables directly. Unlike previous efforts, however, variables were selected carefully to meet three criteria: (*a*) each variable had a high loading on a critical factor; (*b*) each critical factor was represented by at least one key variable; and (*c*) each variable had a statistically significant zero-order correlation.[2] Since two factors, IV (the Mexican-American factor) and VIII (the housing quality factor), had neither significant relationships with desegregation nor any highly loaded variables which significantly related to desegregation, they are not represented in the list of variables.

Table 3 reveals the six key variables chosen to meet these criteria together with their zero-order correlations and standardized beta weights. The six variables chosen are: population change, median Negro education, total commercial farms, median house value, retail sales, and percentage of Negroes. The three variables tapping economic prosperity and urbanism all render highly significant zero-order correlations with the school desegregation indicator once they are transformed, as noted in Table 3. However, two emerge as the dominant

---

[2]Two exceptions, median Negro education in 1960 and percentage of Negroes in 1960, are made to this third criterion because of their theoretical importance.

TABLE 3   SIX-VARIABLE PREDICTIONS OF THE EXTENT OF TEXAS
SCHOOL DESEGREGATION BY COUNTIES[a]

Variable[b]	Zero-order correlations	p	Standardized beta weights	p[c]
1. Population change 1950-1960	+.164	<.05	+.017	n.s.
2. Median Negro education, 1960	−.102	n.s.	−.061	n.s.
3. Total commercial farms, 1960	+.439	<.001	+.315	<.001
4. Median house value, 1960	+.290	<.001	+.100	n.s.
5. Retail sales, 1958	+.509	<.001	+.367	<.001
6. Percent Negro, 1960	+.058	n.s.	+.010	n.s.

R^2 (percentage of variance explained)   =   34.5%
R (multiple correlation)   =   .59 p <.001

[a]Includes all 187 Texas counties which had Negroes comprising 1% or more of their 1960 populations.
[b]The three economic variables (3, 4, and 5) were all transformed by a log transformation both to obtain less skewed distributions and for conceptual clarity. Arc sine transformations were attempted for the remaining variables (nos. 1, 2, and 6), but they did not improve the distributions significantly and were not used. Consequently, variables 1, 2, and 6 are used in their raw census form.
[c]These probabilities are derived from two-tailed t tests.

predictors when all six variables are regressed simultaneously on desegregation: *total commercial farms and retail sales.* Together, these two variables account for a giant portion of the 35% school desegregation variance explained by this set of ecological factors. Note that this percentage of explained variance is only 6% below that of the ecological factor scores of Table 2.

At least three possible explanations for these results exist. Two are partly artifactual and involve the nature of the indicator. Commercial farms, as a rural prosperity predictor, may reflect that our desegregation measure makes it possible for smaller counties with fewer schools to obtain more easily higher percentages with the desegregation of comparatively fewer schools. Likewise, one can speculate on the role of the vast number of military installations in Texas. A district with many school children of military personnel is "federally impacted" and receives special school aid from the federal government; but this aid can be cut off under Title VI of the 1964 Civil Rights Act if segregation is maintained. Hence, military bases may cause an area to be both high on retail sales and a leader in school desegregation.

More fundamental, however, the two correlates of Table 3 appear to tap a social structure especially conducive to relatively rapid implementation of desegregation once begun. Checking the census correlates of total commercial farms and retail sales, we find counties characterized as high on these variables are concentrated in Central Texas and are moderately urban with intermediate percentages of Negroes. Such counties appear to lie near major cities and serve them agriculturally. Their secret of extensive desegregation may be that they combine the less traditional norms of prosperous urban communities without the city's problem of so-called *"de facto"* segregation brought about by sharp residential separation of the races.

Subregional Differences

The results already suggest sharp subregional differences in the Texas pattern of public school desegregation. We have just observed the relatively rapid spread of the process in the prosperous counties of Central Texas with large numbers of commercial farms, and shall explore these leads further with "dummy" variables for each subregion. This merely means that they were formed by assigning one point to each county within a given subregion and zero to all other counties. Formed in this manner, Central Texas boasted the greatest spread of school desegregation (+.240, $p < .05$), East Texas less (+.047, n.s.), and West Texas the least (−.191, $p < 10$).

Can the same six variables predict the school desegregation process not only over the whole state of Texas but also within sharply different subregions of the state as well? Table 4 presents the relevant data for East and Central Texas.[3] Both of the predictions are successful, with the six key census variables accounting for about two-fifths of the desegregation variance in each subregion. The total number of commercial farms remains an important correlate in both subregions, especially in Central Texas. Prosperity is critical in East Texas, represented by retail sales, and growth is critical in Central Texas, represented by populations change.

What do these contrasting patterns signify? First, it means that subregions within Texas constitute a vital factor in shaping the desegregation process, a factor obscured in statewide analyses. The two areas are ecologically diverse, and this diversity conditions the ecological structure of desegregation in a pointed demonstration of a "contextual effect."

Second, the findings of Table 4 provide us with detailed pictures of the range of desegregation patterns. Combined with the economic descriptions of these areas by Bogue and Beale (1961), we can see how racial change in the public schools spread in a more refined manner than is possible at the state level. Consider, for instance, East Texas. Educational desegregation developed furthest in the prosperous counties of the subregion characterized by large oil refineries

---

[3] West Texas is omitted for two reasons. First, it contains exceedingly few Negroes. Second, because of this, the census seldom provides the median of Negro education for West Texas counties. However, we did perform an analysis of West Texas without median Negro education, and obtained a multiple correlation of +.63, with the heaviest beta weights on commercial farms and median house value.

TABLE 4   BETA WEIGHTS FOR SIX-VARIABLE PREDICTION OF TEXAS
SCHOOL DESEGREGATION WITHIN SUBREGIONS[a]

Variable[b]	East Texas	p	Central Texas	p[c]
1. Population change 1950-1960	+.077	n.s.	+.414	$<$.02
2. Median Negro education, 1960	+.064	n.s.	−.229	n.s.
3. Total commercial farms, 1960	+.344	$<$.05	+.473	$<$.01
4. Median house value, 1960	−.113	n.s.	−.216	n.s.
5. Retail sales, 1958	+.492	$<$.01	−.215	n.s.
6. Percent Negro, 1960	−.178	n.s.	−.130	n.s.
R^2 (percentage of variance explained) =	42.0%		40.2%	
R (multiple correlation) =	.65	$<$.01	.63	$<$.005

[a]Includes all Texas counties which had Negroes comprising one percent or more of their populations in 1960.
[b]As in Table 3, log transformations were first performed on variables 3, 4, and 5.
[c]As in Table 2 and 3, the probabilities are derived from two-tailed t tests.

and new industries, not in the more traditional, heavily Negro counties characterized by the "piney woods." These results reflect the powerful influence of
historically rooted norms of racial segregation in the unchanging parts of East
Texas that operate much as previous research has indicated: traditional areas are
the most resistant to desegregation.

Central Texas does not share the deep involvement in segregation and the
confederacy with East Texas. With Fort Worth, Dallas, Houston, Austin, and San
Antonio within its area, Central Texas is heavily urban. Yet these cities now face
so-called "*de facto*" residential segregation as a major barrier to the spread of
school desegregation. Hence, rapidly growing counties with commercial farming
have carried the process farthest.

Ecological relationships seldom satisfy by themselves, for they seem to be
cold statistical indicators distant from the practical process that they attempt to
predict, yet they provide the social context for our analyses of public opinion
data. It is to these less-distant analyses that we now turn.

ATTITUDE AND SCHOOL DESEGREGATION

Attitudes rarely have been employed to predict broad social processes. As an
individual concept, attitudes generally have been exploited to predict only
individual behavior, and these attitude-behavior studies often have failed to
consider the social context in which both are shaped. Yet the need is great to
place attitudes in social perspective and to use them in the aggregate to predict

broader processes. In social science the use of attitudes in this fashion seldom has been attempted for the practical reason of cost. Without a new aggregating technique, it was necessary to sample individually each ecological unit involved in the process under study. Such a procedure was prohibitively expensive. For example, working with the more than 180 Texas counties under scrutiny in this study, it would have required a seperate probability sample in each of the counties—a task approximately as expensive as 30 or more national surveys.

The methodological breakthrough which overcame this difficulty is comparatively new. It allows a simulation of an opinion climate for each smaller unit (for example, county) from survey data drawn only from a larger unit (for example, state).

The application of this opinion climate simulation technique to school desegregation in Texas is straightforward. Save for the following changes, the present simulation is almost identical in method to that of Pool *et al.* (1965).[4] Instead of the state, our unit of analysis is the county. Instead of predicting the presidential vote, we attempt to predict the extent of school desegregation throughout Texas and each of its regions. Instead of seven variables to define the demographic types, we use three highly relevant variables—education, age, and city size.

In August, 1963 and again in August, 1964, Joe Belden Associates of Dallas, Texas asked as a part of its regular quarterly state survey a series of questions concerning attitudes toward the desegregation of a variety of public facilities including schools. Responses to these questions were recorded on an 11-category scale, ranging from 1 (most unfavorable) to 6 (neutral or no opinion) to 11 (most unfavorable). For present purposes, it was sufficient to collapse this response scale down to three categories such that a 1-4 response was registered as favorable to racial desegregation 5-7 as neutral, and 8-11 as unfavorable. Each of the Belden surveys included over 800 white interviews.[5]

Three relevant background variables were selected with which to form the demographic types for the attitude simulation: *education, age* and *city size.* Each of these dimensions was split into three meaningful categories, forming a total of (3^3) 27 demographic types. Providing the percentage favorable to public school desegregation for all 27 demographic types, Table 5 shows college respondents to be the most favorable in 7 out of 9 comparisons, older respondents to be the least favorable in 7 out of 9 comparisons, and urban respondents to be the

[4]We initially had more ambitious plans. We had hoped to conduct separate white and black simulations and fuse them in the final model. Even with combining polls, however, enough relevant black survey data could not be amassed to allow an adequate simulation of black opinion climates.

[5]Pooling the two surveys to obtain a more adequate 1600 respondents requires at least that the distribution across demographic types are similarly rank-ordered in 1963 and 1964 according to their "percent favorable" toward school desegregation. Fortunately, this is the case; the Spearman rank-order rho correlation across the two years is +.81 ($p < .001$).

TABLE 5 WHITE TEXAN PERCENTAGE OF FAVORABLE TO SCHOOL DESEGREGATION BY EDUCATION, CITY SIZE, AND AGE, 1963-1964[a]

	City size								
	Metropolitan			Urban			Rural		
Education	Younger	Middleaged	Older	Younger	Middleaged	Older	Younger	Middleaged	Older
College	54.5 (68)	54.9 (51)	44.8 (29)	67.7 (93)	59.3 (46)	60.9 (46)	41.1 (73)	48.3 (58)	38.3 (47)
High school	48.3 (87)	45.6 (79)	29.1 (55)	39.7 (116)	52.5 (101)	39.0 (77)	36.9 (111)	30.6 (108)	28.7 (94)
Grade school	19.0 (21)	50.0 (16)	31.7 (41)	55.6 (27)	61.3 (31)	44.4 (54)	41.2 (17)	43.2 (37)	30.8 (52)

[a]Taken from the combined Belden surveys of August 1963 and August 1964. The numbers in parentheses refer to the number of respondents in each cell.

TABLE 6   CORRELATIONS BETWEEN SIMULATED
ATTITUDE CLIMATES AND EXTENT OF
TEXAS SCHOOL DESEGREGATION[a]

	Belden survey		
	1963	1964	1963-1964 combined
Percent favorable on school desegregation item alone	.312	.344	.332
Percent difference index on school desegregation item alone (favorable-unfavorable)	.318	.349	.352
Percent favorable on complete 8-item desegregation scale	.311	.336	.328

[a]All coefficients shown are Pearson product-moment correlations for 181 interracial Texas counties. All coefficients are significantly larger than zero at better than the .001 level of confidence.

most favorable in 8 out of 9 comparisons. Not surprisingly, then, the most favorable type (67.7%) is comprised of younger college educated white residents of urban areas. More surprising, however, is the next most favorable type (61.3%), middle aged grade school educated white residents of urban areas, and the least favorable type (19.0%), younger grade school educated white residents of metropolitan areas. Once the data of Table 5 are obtained, the simulated county white opinion climates are readily produced. One merely sums up the products of the cell entries of Table 5 with the appropriate white adult proportions of each demographic type for each of the Texas counties with 1% or more of its 1960 population nonwhite.

Attitude Results

Table 6 presents the basic correlational findings. While all of them are significantly larger than zero at better than the .001 level of confidence, these coefficients are relatively modest. They range between +.311 and +.352, thus accounting for roughly 12% of the variance. The most remarkable feature of Table 6 is the stability of the estimates. Observe the near identical relationships achieved by the two indices of measurement for the school desegregation item alone; nor does the full scale of eight desegregation questions do better than the single direct question on schools. Indeed, the scale does not perform quite as well in all three cases. As with Pool, Abelson, and Popkin's (1965) success with a single blatant item on anti-Catholicism, the single blatant item on public school desegregation provides satisfactory estimates of relevant intergroup opinion.

TABLE 7   CORRELATIONS BETWEEN SIMULATED
ATTITUDE CLIMATE AND EXTENT OF
TEXAS SCHOOL DESEGREGATION BY
REGION, CITY SIZE, AND PERCENTAGE
OF NONWHITE CONTROLLED
SIMULTANEOUSLY[a]

| | City size | | | | |
| | Rural | | | Urban | |
Nonwhites (%)	1-10	11-30	31+	1-10	11-30
No regional controls	.374[b]	.622[c]	.295	.084	−.064
East Texas	—	.622[c]	.167	—	.220
Central Texas	.190	.557[b]	—	.301	—
West Texas	.370[b]	—	—	.111	—

[a]The two Belden surveys for 1963 and 1964 are combined for these correlations; and only the percentage favorable to the single item on school desegregation is used as the indicator of attitude climate. The metropolitan category is omitted because of insufficient data; in addition, the 31%+ category of percentage of nonwhites for urban counties is omitted for the same reason. All correlations are based on a minimum of ten cases; blank cells had too few cases for stable results.

[b]The correlation is significantly different from zero at better than the .02 level of confidence.

[c]The correlation is significantly different from zero at better than the .001 level of confidence.

Finally, each of the surveys considered separately, as well as the combination of the two, produced extremely similar results. The tiny differences are in the expected directions; that is, the survey nearer to the 1965 data on the dependent variable yields consistently higher coefficients than the earlier survey.

The scarcity of relevant survey data for Texas near 1965 restrained us from using a larger number than 27 demographic types. Had we been able to have had a larger number, we would certainly have used region as an additional control variable. Recall the importance of region in the ecological analyses. At this point, however, we now at least can check to see how well the simulation predicts the school desegregation process within subsets of Texas counties, especially within the three diverse regions of the large state. The correlations are only +.24 for West Texas and +.41 for Central Texas, but it is +.60 for East Texas.[6] The major feature of these results is their diversity across region. Thus,

[6]These correlations are for the two surveys combined using the percentage of favorable measure on the single item on school desegregation as the indicator of the attitude climates. These coefficients are significantly different from zero at the .001 level of confidence for East Texas, .01 for Central Texas, and .05 for West Texas.

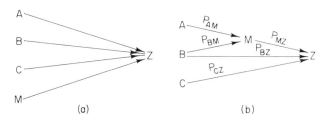

Figure 1   Contrasting analysis models: (1) regression analysis model, (b) path analysis
model.

the simulated attitude climate accounts for only 6% of the school desegregation
extent variance in West Texas, but 16% in Central Texas. In East Texas, the
Black Belt area where racial norms and attitudes are widely known to be the
most salient in the entire state, the extent of desegregation variance accounted
for by the simulated white attitude climate rises dramatically to 36%. The far
higher prediction in East Texas suggests that further controls, especially for the
percentage of nonwhites, should be applied to these relationships.

Table 7 follows up this lead by attempting to ascertain under what conditions the predictions of the simulated white attitude climate vary. The findings
are striking: white opinion climate predictions are highest in rural counties with
moderate nonwhite populations percentages. Hence, the largest correlation,
+.62, occurs for rural counties in East Texas with moderate nonwhite proportions, followed by similar counties in Central Texas.

ECOLOGY, ATTITUDES, AND
SOUTHERN DESEGREGATION

Contextual analysis, the central idea of this research and the particular focus of
this chapter, attempts to place independent variables of diverse levels into a
single meaningful model. As with figure-ground relationships in perception, such
intermediate factors as attitudes must be placed in the wider perspective furnish-
ed by such distal factors as ecological variables. Then the model must follow
logically on to the shaping of the dependent variable, the extent of public school
desegregation in Texas counties.

To achieve such a contextual model, we need both new conceptual and
methodological tools. First, we conceptually distinguish between a number of
logically possible forms of *mediation* with which climates might serve as the
intermediate links between distal ecological variables and the actual desegrega-

tion process. Furthermore, we must operationalize these types of mediation partly in terms of a relatively new methodological tool well suited for approaching such contextual problems—path analysis (Duncan, 1966; Wright, 1960).

In this section, then, we will present a brief discussion of path analysis and how we propose to utilize it for distinguishing between various types of mediation. Next we shall review the results. To anticipate these results, we shall find that each of our logical types of mediation is illustrated in the analysis and models for the entire state of Texas and its regions.

Path Analysis

Without considering its more technical aspects, let us review briefly the nature of the technique used in the analyses which follow. Path analysis is intimately related with the regression analyses which characterize the previous tables on ecological and attitude climate predictions of school desegregation. Indeed, it can be viewed as merely a new manner of interpreting the results of regression analyses. Like regression analysis, it assumes interval measures and linear effects and cannot easily handle interactions between variables. However, path analysis differs from routine regression analysis interpretations in a number of significant ways, and it has the great advantage of ordering a complex array of variables and teasing out the effects of intercorrelated independent variables.

The principal analytical distinction between the two methods involves how the effects of the independent variables are conceived to operate upon the dependent variable. In standard regression analysis, all independent variables are assumed to act simultaneously and relatively independently of each other on the dependent variable. By contrast, path analysis assumes asynchronous relationships with the effects of antecedent or distal variables operating through intermediate variables. Figure 1 shows the two models in simplest form. Note how regression analysis disregards all possible time sequences and forms of mediation, and observe how the path analysis model considers both. Thus, independent (or "distal") variable A has its effect on dependent variable Z through the intermediate variable M. Variable B has both mediated and direct effects upon dependent variable Z. Finally, distal independent variable C has only an unmediated direct effect upon dependent variable Z.

The evaluation of social psychological models with path analysis contributes greatly to the delineation of relationships that structure the overall correlations, for it provides a systematic and internal means to probe the various formulations of a problem. Since the strongest point of path analysis is the increase in understanding that it provides of a model's internal relationships rather than prediction *per se*, it is an especially useful tool for the social psychologist who prefers the data of the field to those of the laboratory.

The Assumptions of a Path Analytic Model of School Desegregation

Several assumptions underlie the models of school desegregation:

1. Ecological factors represent a set of exogenous variables.
2. An attitude climate represents an endogenous variable.[7] Both classes of variables affect the dependent variable, school desegregation, but ecological factors can exert their effects on desegregation either directly or indirectly through a county's attitude climate.
3. Attitude climates influence the dependent variable in a direct manner, that is, they cannot act in the reverse direction influencing ecological factors.
4. Attitude climates serve only as mediators: they mediate the effects of ecological factors specified in the model, or factors external to the model.

Assumptions 3 and 4 may seem extreme, but they are necessary simplifications to avoid feedback loops in the model and to account for the effects of unmeasured ecological factors or external factors, such as federal court decisions, that vary among counties and relate to the attitude climate of a county and the extent of its school desegregation. In general terms, such a view seems quite justified for this preliminary effort at contextual models.

This set of assumptions defines the limit of our inferences about the flow of causality and the specification of temporal sequences. Path analysis provides a useful tool for ordering variables and suggesting the relative importance of contextual factors in relation to school desegregation, so that our interpretation can be refined and our understanding heightened of the desegregation process beyond that possible with the one level analyses discussed earlier.

Contrasting Types of Mediation

Three logically distinct types of mediation can be specified in advance as possible ways for attitude climates to mediate ecological factors in shaping the extent of school desegregation in Texas.

First, attitude climates may act as *full mediators* by translating virtually all of the ecological effects upon the process. We know this is the case (*a*) when the ecological variables predict the attitude climate of the county more accurately than they do the extent of school desegregation; and (*b*) when a significant beta

---

[7]Simon (1957) terms variables exogenous which serve only as independent variables in a multistage causal model; in the model of Fig. 1, *A, B,* and *C* represent exogenous variables. He terms a variable endogenous when it serves as a dependent variable at one stage of a model and as an independent variable at another stage of the model. Variable *M* in Fig. 1 represents an endogenous variable.

weight exists between attitude climate and desegregation, even after the effects of the ecological variables have been removed.

In path analytic terms full mediation ideally requires that the direct paths of all the ecological variables be negligible; implicitly this assumes that the effect of cross-product terms on the decomposition of the attitude climate-school desegregation correlation will be substantial and that a large proportion of this correlation can be explained by this set of cross-product terms.

Second, *selective mediation* occurs when the attitude climate mediates the effects of some of the ecological variables but not others. In this case, the total battery of ecological variables will explain more of the variance of the extent of school desegregation than it does the variance of attitude climates. However, the standardized beta weights of a subset of ecological variables are larger in the prediction of attitude climates than they are in predicting racial change, and this directly confirms the operation of the attitude climate as a "selective mediator." Finally, a significant beta weight must exist between the attitude climate and the extent of school desegregation.

As defined by path analysis, selective mediation occurs when some direct effects to the extent of school desegregation and indirect effects through the attitude climate are meaningfully eliminated. After these deletions, it is assumed that the correlations between the demographic and attitude measures and the desegregation measures remain accurately estimated.

Third, *residual mediation* occurs when the attitude climate provides an especially strong prediction of educational desegregation, but the ecological factors individually yield weaker predictions of both the attitude climate and desegregation. In other words, attitude climate is adding a large unique contribution to the variance explained of the extent of interracial schools. In the terms of our general contextual model this implies that attitude climate is mediating a variety of residual factors important to the desegregation process but unmeasured by our particular array of census variables.

Residual mediation from the perspective of path analysis, like full mediation, relies on the decomposition of the attitude climate-school desegregation correlation for its definition. When only a small proportion of this correlation can be explained by the cross-product terms and a large proportion of this correlation results from the direct path coefficient of the attitude climate, we have a path analytic definition of residual mediation. Earlier we assumed that the attitude climate mediated factors either specified in the model or external to it. When the factors internal to the model fail to account for the attitude climate-school desegregation correlation, then the magnitude of this correlation must stem from the ability of the attitude climate to mediate a set of factors external to the model. A large direct path coefficient usually implies that this is the case. However, some exceptions to this conclusion drawn from the basis of the magnitude of the direct path coefficient will be discussed in a later section.

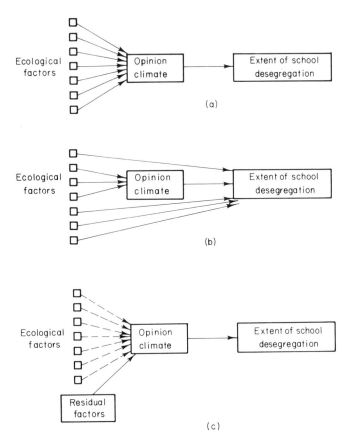

Figure 2   Contrasting types of opinion mediation: (a) full mediation, (b) selective mediation, (c) residual mediation.

Figure 2 gives in diagrammatic fashion each of the above three contrasting types of mediation.

School Desegregation Regression

Before employing path analysis to assess the importance of a county's attitude climate for the desegregation process, we must demonstrate the predictive ability of the attitude climate after the effects attributable to the ecological factors have been taken into account. A standard regression analysis reveals whether or not the attitude climate serves as a significant predictor of school desegregation, yet does not delineate clearly the intricate patterns of shared covariation. A large unique contribution of the attitude climate indicates the presence of residual mediation in school desegregation, while a significant beta weight points to the possibility of selective mediation, as well as its overall predictive importance.

In general, the addition of the attitude climate indicator to the model results in a moderate increase in the explained variance of the extent of school desegregation, manifests a significant beta weight, and fails to change dramatically any of the beta weights associated with the ecological factors (compare Tables 3 and 4 with Table 8).

For the entire state the attitude climate has a beta weight of +.196 and increases the explained variance from 34.5 to 36.9%. It is third in magnitude compared with the beta weights of the ecological variables.

In East Texas the attitude climate makes a significant difference. When entered into the regression of school desegregation as the last variable, it increases the explained variance by 6.1%. Moreover, it has a beta weight of +.382, larger than all others except that of retail sales. In fact, its entry into the model sharply decreases the beta weight of the retail sales indicator from +.492 to +.397.

The attitude climate's role in Central Texas tends to be more moderate. It adds only 3.3% to the explained variance in school desegregation and has a beta weight of +.222. Within this region, however, the attitude climate provides an elegant illustration of an error suppressor effect (Guilford, 1968). Upon its entry into the model, it reverses the sign of retail sales from negative to positive (−.215 to +.204).

Attitude Climate Regressions

The regressions of the ecological factors on the attitude climate are statistically significant and explain approximately 25% of the variance (see Table 8). Some of the demographic factors contribute more to the prediction of the attitude climate than the extent of school desegregation. This is especially true for population change, and at times for other ecological factors. Yet the significant prediction of the attitude climate by the ecological factors does not imply that the attitude climate fails to contribute independently to the prediction of the school desegregation. Indeed, the ecological factors appear predictive of the attitude climate in a manner relatively unrelated to their prediction of school desegregation. Thus, the contention that the attitude climate of a county serves as proxy for its demography lacks strong confirmation.

Mediation in Terms of Regression Analyses

Evaluated in terms of mediation, the attitude climate operates most frequently as a residual mediator, occasionally as a selective mediator, and not at all as a full mediator. The initial evaluation of the county's attitude climate as a

TABLE 8 COMBINED ECOLOGICAL AND ATTITUDE PREDICTIONS OF PUBLIC SCHOOL DESEGREGATION

	Total state		East Texas		Central Texas	
	Ecological prediction of attitude climate	Ecological and attitude prediction of desegregation	Ecological prediction of attitude climate	Ecological and attitude prediction of desegregation	Ecological prediction of attitude climate	Ecological and attitude prediction of desegregation
Population change	.336	-.020	-.198	.090	.317	.338
Median home value	.276	.133	-.136	-.148	.112	-.140
Retail sales	.291	.239	.196	.397	-.221	.204
Total commercial farms	.123	.346	.221	.298	.132	.445
Negro median education	.091	-.044	.229	.058	-.091	-.132
Percent Negro	.011	.037	-.071	.183	.176	-.072
Attitude climate		.196		.382		.222
R^2	27.2%	36.9%	28.2%	48.1%	16.7%	43.4%

mediator of factors internal and external to the model relies on our regression-based definition of the three types of mediation. A more detailed view of the mediative role of attitude climate in path analysis terms follows shortly.

Viewed in terms of the regression analysis for the entire state, the attitude climate selectively mediates a prosperous urban cluster: population change, median home value, and retail sales (see Table 8). At the same time, its unique contribution, an increase of 2.4% in the explained variance, points to the possibility of residual mediation. Its significant beta weight (+.196) and the moderately successful ecological prediction of the attitude climate suggest that residual and selective mediation occur simultaneously for the entire state.

The manner in which attitude climate mediates factors external to the model is clearly demonstrated with East Texas. Residual mediation relies on a large unique contribution of the attitude climate to the explained variance of school desegregation and a significant beta weight. Its unique contribution of 6.1% exceeds all other variables in the model except retail sales. Likewise, selective mediation occurs, as defined previously, from the regression perspective. Population change, total commercial farms, retail sales, and Negro median education appear to have a significant proportion of their effect on the extent of school desegregation mediated by the attitude climate indicator. Of the three models, residual mediation is most extensive in East Texas.

In Central Texas the attitude climate selectively mediates population change and to some extent Negro median education. But, more importantly, it mediates the effect of retail sales in an extreme manner. Once the attitude climate enters the model, it reverses the direction of the retail sales relationship with the extent of school desegregation. Its negative beta weight in the prediction of the attitude climate portends this reversal of signs. As a result, it appears that the covariation in retail sales that correlates negatively with attitude climate and negatively with school desegregation are one and the same. Thus, the entry of attitude climate into the regression takes into account that segment of covariation between retail sales and school desegregation that relates negatively. At the same time, another segment of covariation in retail sales relates positively to the extent of school desegregation and becomes free to operate with the inclusion of the attitude climate in the model.

Unexpectedly, then, attitude climate in Central Texas clarifies the nature of ecological relationships with desegregation. The liberation of suppressed variance represents another possible, but infrequent, form of selective mediation.

Path Analytic Models of School Desegregation

The results of these regression analyses demonstrate the predictive importance of a county's attitude climate for the extent of school desegregation, illustrate different forms of mediation on the part of the attitude climate, and

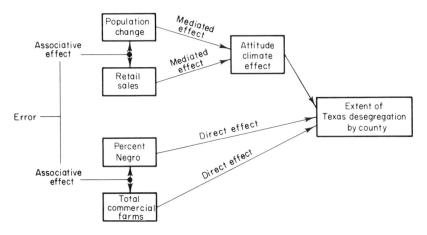

Figure 3   Types of effects in path analysis.

reveal that the prediction of a county's attitude climate and school desegregation
by the ecological factors are relatively independent of each other. However,
these regression analyses fail to delineate precisely the mediating role of the
attitude climate, especially in terms of providing an estimate of the extent to
which the climate serves as a residual and/or selective mediator.

Recall that regression analysis is equivalent to a path analysis with the
specification of all possible paths and the synchronous measurement of all
independent variables. The path analyses that follow attempt to specify in a
more precise manner the form and extent to which the attitude climate mediates
the effects of the ecological factors present in the model and factors external to
the model. Deleting a subset of paths within the various models provides a means
to investigate the types of indirect effects that the various ecological factors have
on the extent of school desegregation.

Indirect effects in path analysis represent that part of the correlation
between the independent variable and the dependent variable that can be
attributed to shared covariation. Conceptually, indirect effects can be separated
into at least two types depending on the temporal position of a variable in the
model. A *mediated* effect results from the common variance of two independent
variables shared with the dependent variable, but the variables appear in the
model in temporal sequence (for example, first population change, followed by
attitude climate). An *associative* effect results from the shared explanatory
variance of two variables measured at the same point in time (see Fig. 3).

As discussed previously, for the sum of all three of these effects to
necessarily equal the correlation, all relationships in the model must be specified;
however, for theoretical purposes as well as for parsimony it is convenient to
eliminate some relationships (paths) from the independent variables. The effect
of this elimination process can be evaluated by the discrepancy of the predicted

correlation (the sum of the effects obtained from a reduced model) and the actual correlation $(r_{ik} - r'_{ik})$. A small discrepancy indicates that the deleted relationships (paths) are of little significance in this model, but a large discrepancy indicates that much of the original correlation can be traced to the shared variance of the eliminated paths.

Furthermore, the direct effect of any variable can be broken down into its net and collinear components.[8] In the case of a mediating variable such as the attitude climate of a county, the net effect estimates the extent to which it mediates factors external to the model and the collinear effect represents error. The collinear effect results from an allocation of common variance shared by all the independent variables based upon the ability of the given variable to influence the others. We explicitly assumed, however, that the attitude climate of a county could not influence its past demography; thus, in this case the collinear effect must be considered to be error.

The extent to which the attitude climate serves as a mediator of external factors not specified in the model (residual mediation) can be easily estimated. It is merely the "net direct effect" of the attitude climate divided by the total correlation of the attitude climate and the extent of school desegregation. This ratio estimates the proportion of the attitude climate's correlation that can be attributed to factors external to the model.

The key question becomes: What is the effect of eliminating some possible ecological relationships? To simplify the presentation of the data, each relationship is separated into its direct, mediated, and associative effects. The only possible mediated effect in these models is through the attitude climate of the county, and in some cases this effect is eliminated. To estimate associative effects, only variables that are contained within the same subset of variables are considered to have an associative effect (see Fig. 3). For instance, if the population change and retail sales variables were postulated to have their effect only through the attitude climate variable and the percentage of Negroes and total commercial farms variables are assumed to have only direct effects with school desegregation, then only the shared variance within each group of synchronous independent variables is considered to be part of the associative effect (Fig. 3). The shared variance between, say, total commercial farms and population change is considered error variance as it contributes to the magnitude of the discrepancy between the observed and predicted correlations.

---

[8] A path coefficient or beta weight can be decomposed into two independent components: its net effect and its collinear effect. An independent variable's unique contribution to the variance explained of a dependent variable is not estimated by the square of the beta weight, rather it is this quantity adjusted for the independent variable's multicollinearity with the other independent variables in the model. The net effect of an independent variable refers to the square root of the unique contribution; the collinear effect of an independent variable refers to the beta weight minus the net effect. For a more detailed explanation, see Brownlee (1965), or Pettigrew, Riley and Ross (in press).

TABLE 9   PATH ANALYSIS OF PUBLIC SCHOOL DESEGREGATION IN TEXAS, 1965

		Direct effect to school desegregation	Mediated effect through attitude climate	Associative effect	Predicted correlation $(r'_{ik})^a$	Discrepancy $(r'_{ik} - r_{ik})$
Population change	Total State	N.p.[b]	.070	.092	.162	.022
	East Texas	N.p.	.042	.081	.123	-.016
	Central Texas	.384	.070	-.291	.163	.005
Median home value	Total State	N.p.	.041	.205	.246	-.015
	East Texas	.141	.090	.043	.274	.004
	Central Texas	-.202	.053	.341	.192	-.033
Retail sales	Total State	.135	N.p.	.271	.406	.024
	East Texas	.158	N.p.	.272	.430	-.016
	Central Texas	.204	-.071	.248	.381	-.051
Total commercial farms	Total State	.364	N.p.	.037	.401	-.045
	East Texas	.312	N.p.	.093	.405	.013
	Central Texas	.445	N.p.	.031	.476	-.015
Negro median education	Total State	.045	N.p.	.135	.180	.027
	East Texas	.062	.041	-.181	-.242	-.054
	Central Texas	-.092	.061	-.046	-.077	.010
Percent Negro	Total State	-.029	N.p.	-.010	-.039	.029
	East Texas	-.061	N.p.	.099	.202	-.027
	Central Texas	-.072	N.p.	.089	.017	-.017

		Net effect[c]	Mediated effects of ecological variables	Predicted correlation	Error
Attitude climate	Total State	.161	.111	.272	.048
	East Texas	.368	.173	.541	.022
	Central Texas	.168	.113	.281	.062

[a] r'_{ik} is the predicted correlation between each variable and the extent of school desegregation.
[b] N.p. indicates that no path was specified in the model.
[c] This is the path coefficient corrected for its collinear effect.

The Entire State of Texas

The path analysis for the entire state of Texas reveals the following:

1. The attitude climate of a county serves as a selective mediator for two variables: Population change and retail sales. (Deleting the paths of all other ecological factors to the attitude climate has little effect on the accuracy of this predicted correlation.)
2. For a majority of variables in the model, the attitude climate indicator is unimportant in explaining their overall relationships with the extent of school desegregation (that is, only direct paths are important).
3. Residual mediation occurs noticeably, as the net effect of the attitude climate represents over 50% of its overall correlation with the extent of school desegregation.

The results presented in Table 9 reveal small discrepancies between the observed and the predicted correlations of all variables in the model of the extent of school desegregation. Moreover, the results of Table 9 point out the importance of associative effects in explaining the correlations of retail sales, median home value (both greater than +.20), and Negro median education with the extent of school desegregation.

Another interesting aspect of the findings for the state of Texas stems from the relative independence of the attitude climate effect. A significant part of the relationship of the attitude climate to the extent of school desegregation derives from its ability to mediate factors external to the model, rather than to mediate selectively the effects of demographic factors present in the model. Thus, the relatively strong beta weights of retail sales and median home value when regressed on the attitude climate of the county (Table 8) appears to be the product of variance in the attitude climate indicator unrelated to the extent of school desegregation. Regression analyses of these data could lead to deceptive inferences about the role of the county's attitude climate. Here is a particular instance where a path analytic model clarifies the manner in which shared variance operates in the explanation of a dependent variable. It also delineates the way in which selective and residual mediation occur together.

East Texas

The path analysis in East Texas produces results similar to those for the entire state except that the coefficients tend to be larger. The results demonstrate that:

1. The attitude climate of the county selectively mediates the effects of population change, median home value, and Negro median education (the mediated effects of the other ecological factors are negligible).
2. Residual mediation is stronger in East Texas than in any other model.

Once again the discrepancies between the observed and predicted correlations prove to be small, indicating that the model provides an adequate fit for the data. However, the mediating effect of the county's attitude climate, in fact, is limited to median home value, as it has the only large mediated effect through the attitude climate indicator. Negro median education and population change have small mediated effects through the attitude climate of the county. The latter paths remain in the model because of the variance they share with the other demographic factors and to reduce the discrepancy between the observed and predicted correlation.

At the same time the importance of associative effects is apparent in explaining the overall correlations of the other independent variables with the extent of school desegregation. Population change, retail sales, median home value, and percentage of Negroes all have large associative effects, and especially retail sales, where it is +.272.

Residual mediation appears strongly, as the net effect of attitude climate is +.368 compared with a total mediated effect of +.173. Note that the independence of the attitude climate effect and its mediation of factors external to the model are striking. Recall that the regressions in Table 8 reveal large beta weights for several of the demographic variables when regressed on the attitude climate of the county. Once again, as with the entire state, demographic factors appear to explain variance in the attitude climate of a county not related to variation in the extent of school desegregation within East Texas, as indicated by the net effect of the attitude climate. The large associative effects in East Texas for retail sales, Negro median education change and percentage of Negroes also point to the complexity of the patterns of shared variance, while the strong direct and negligible indirect effects of total commercial farms on school desegregation maintain their unexpected importance.

In East Texas, then, the path analysis simplifies the results of the regression analysis by (a) eliminating a subset pf paths in a meaningful way, (b) illustrating the importance of residual mediation, and (c) pointing to the differential impact of the various indicators of urbanism on the school desegregation process. Most important, however, path analysis demonstrates the strong role of external factors in the prediction of school desegregation.

Central Texas

For Central Texas the results of the path analysis yield several interesting findings.

1. The attitude climate of the county mediates a cluster of urban factors selectively and factors external to the model residually. Over 45% of the attitude climate effect relies on factors not included in the basic demographic set.

2.   Large associative effects occur for all but one of the ecological factors.
      Often these associative effects are necessary to account for a difference
      in sign in a direct path coefficient of a variable and its zero-order
      correlation with school desegregation (median home value and Negro
      median education) or to account for a path coefficient larger than its
      respective zero-order correlation (population change).
3.   The discrepancy between the observed and predicted correlations are
      larger for the Central Texas model than for the two others, yet more
      paths remain in the Central Texas model than in the other models. This
      apparent contradiction derives from several strong and complex rela-
      tionships among the independent variables which are not present for
      East Texas or the entire state.

In Central Texas, we see three illustrations of the mediated effect of an
ecological factor opposite in sign from its direct effect (retail sales, median home
value, and Negro median education). Selective mediation of this type points to
the role of the attitude climate as a liberator of suppressed variance in other
independent variables. Yet this difference in sign underestimates the role of the
attitude climate as a mediator as estimated by our procedure. The negative
mediated effect of retail sales (−.071) literally cancels out the positive mediated
effect of the attitude climate for population change (+.070), thereby increasing
the discrepancy between the observed and predicted correlation for the attitude
climate to .062.

The associative effects of population change, median home value and
percentage of Negroes show signs opposite from their direct path coefficients.
Similar to the case of the mediated effects, these associative effects with
opposite signs reflect the ability of variables to have suppressed variance liberated. In particular, note how population change has an associative effect of −.291,
almost twice the magnitude of its correlation (+.158), a necessary condition to
produce its direct effect of .384. A closer exploration of this associative effect
reveals that the entry of the attitude climate into the model produces a
substantial reallocation of shared variance. Thus, population change draws much
of the variance from retail sales that produced its original negative direct effect
with the school desegregation process before the entry of the attitude climate
into the model.

This brief analysis of the associative and mediated effects of median home
value, retail sales and population change illustrates the types of conditions
necessary for (a) error suppression to occur, (b) a path coefficient or beta weight
to exceed its correlation, and (c) the discrepancies between the observed and
predicted correlations to be unexpectedly large.

This analysis of the intricate statistical relationships provides several insights
into the school desegregation process in Central Texas. First, the apparent and

reasonable relationship between median home value and school desegregation, as indicated by its zero-order correlation (+.226), proves to be spurious. After we consider population change, retail sales, and the attitude climate, it appears that the older, more stable, less commercial suburbs represent those most resistant to school desegregation. Second, commercial concentration in a county, agricultural or not, exerts a direct effect on the extent of school desegregation; but at the same time it exerts a slight negative effect through a county's attitude climate. This negative effect is more characteristic of the nonagricultural commercial counties and results from those counties that are moderate on retail sales, have a generally positive attitude climate, and are mainly suburban in their composition. Third, the median level of Negro education interacts with the attitude climate of a county such that it has a negative direct effect; but with school desegregation, a positive effect mediated through the attitude climate. This suggests that a positive racial climate is necessary for the Negro median education variable to have a positive effect on the extent of school desegregation. In fact, this positive effect stems from a set of counties high in Negro median level of education and moderate on retail sales and population change; these are the more recently developed, middle-sized cities of Central Texas.

SUMMARY AND IMPLICATIONS

We have attempted in this chapter to demonstrate the predictive value of attitude data in a contextual model of an on-going social process. Building on the relevant ecological studies of racial change, the chapter has shown how the extent of public school desegregation in 1965 across the counties of Texas can be accounted for first in terms of census variables alone, second in terms of aggregated attitude data alone, and, finally, in terms of both census and attitude data.

The utility of treating attitude results as an aggregate variable to predict social phenomena is relatively new in social psychology; we hope our work will stimulate further research efforts along these lines. Such a trend would serve as a useful reply to those critics of the attitude concept who view attitudes only in the context of potentially predicting the behavior of individuals.

Another general implication of the work reported here is the value of placing attitude results within a meaningful social structure context, in this case the critical census characteristics of each county unit. Research literature abounds with the failures of attitudes to predict behavior when attitudes have been ripped out of their social context and treated as if they operated in a social vacuum. For our purposes, the techniques of path analysis lend themselves well to the development of two-level contextual models that show the attitude climates of Texas counties as a mediator of ecological and residual influences.

We believe path analysis, as yet little used in social psychology, could prove to be a valuable methodological asset for contextual models with an individual focus as well as a societal focus.

The basic test of our results and our three crude models, however, must be whether or not they provide insights into the school desegregation process which we did not have previously. Did our findings and the path analytic models which grew out of them tell us anything new? We believe that a number of new social psychological implications for racial change emerge from: (*a*) the relationships found between the attitude climates of Texas counties and the extent of public school desegregation in 1965; and (*b*) the importance in East Texas of residual factors unmeasured by the census variables but mediated by attitude climate. The implications of each of these results deserve brief discussion.

a. Recall that the attitude climates of whites independently contributed to the prediction of school desegregation in the entire state of Texas, in Central Texas, and especially in East Texas. Yet in Table 7 we noted that it proves most important in rural counties with 11-30% of their populations Negro. Combining these and other results with general balance theory considerations. (McGuire, 1969), we can formulate the following interlocking series of assumptions and assertions:

1. The simulated climates of Texas counties reflect reasonably accurately the actual white attitude climates.
2. Variations in attitude climates across counties reflect in part structural characteristics of the counties.
3. Decision-makers, such as school board members, will reflect to some degree the white attitude climate of their county in their own attitudes.
4. Decision-makers will reach school desegregation decisions in varying degrees consistent with both their own views and their perceptions of their county's attitude climate.
5. Sharp inconsistencies between the decision-makers' actions and beliefs lead to intense strains to change their actions, their beliefs, or simply "to leave the field," for example, by resigning from the school board. Indeed, all three of these possibilities are common phenomena among white Southern officials. Thus, quietly slipping back toward racially separate patterns once federal pressure eases is widespread; Hyman and Sheatsley (1964) have noted considerable shifts among white Southerners favoring racial desegregation *after* it has already taken place in a given area; and resignations from county office have become commonplace in the Deep South.
6. Fear can upset balance predictions, leading to a relatively liberal official in a Black Belt county resisting racial change for fear of local pressure

and a relatively conservative official assenting to racial change for fear of federal power.

7. The relationship between the actions of decision-makers on educational change and white attitude climates are highest for counties: close to the traditional racial norms of the Deep South, with a relatively homogeneous white population, and where racial attitudes are particularly salient for both white and Negro residents. Rural counties in East Texas, where attitude climate is most strongly associated with school desegregation, meet the first two of these conditions. The importance of the salience of racial attitudes is suggested by the higher correlations between attitude climate and school desegregation in counties with moderate Negro population percentages rather than those with high percentages of Negroes. A number of studies have demonstrated that white racial attitudes in Southern counties with less than 30% Negro population are more positive and flexible, and that racial discrimination is, in fact, more variable and less harsh in such counties (Pettigrew, 1957, 1958, 1959). This variability makes racial attitudes and practices more salient as well as more open to alteration. By contrast, the racial norms of solid segregation are so fixed and pervasive in the counties with heavily Negro populations that racial attitudes count for less in determining school policy. It has been noted that Southern counties with large percentages of Negroes tended to have *smaller* lynching rates when the size of the Negro community is held constant. In short, racial discrimination in Black Belt counties becomes such a culturally sanctioned "given" that it neither needs lynching nor saliently expressed racial attitudes to support it. Negro insistence is less likely in such areas, and consequently white resistance, while potentially massive, is less likely to be invoked. As suggested by the lynching data, the price of "racial peace" in such counties is an effective system of racial oppression and denial of basic rights.

b. The importance of residual factors, mediated by attitude climate, in accounting for the school desegregation process in East Texas tempts speculation as to just what these unmeasured factors might be. The most obvious possibilities involve external pressures that would influence both racial opinion and policies—such as court orders and federal cutoffs of educational funds under Title VI of the 1964 Civil Rights Act. Indeed, such outside pressures were brought to bear more sharply on East Texas than on any other part of the state. The region did initiate the school desegregation process relatively early under these pressures, but, not suprisingly, was comparatively slow in extending the process throughout its public schools.

This suggests an additional and less obvious residual factor: namely, the actual initiation of the process which leads to attitude change. Contrary to conventional wisdom, social psychological research in race relations has shown repeatedly that the racial attitudes of white Americans typically follow rather than precede actual institutional alterations (Pettigrew, 1966, 1971). Laws can and do change "the hearts and minds of men"; they do so by first changing behavior which for reasons of consistency and public commitment leads in time to changed attitudes. As applied to East Texas, we can speculate that the early initiation of school desegregation in the region triggered intracounty and intraindividual processes that led to altered racial attitudes and practices which in time became functionally autonomous from the external pressures that induced the beginning of the process.

The popular misconception is that governmental pressure applied to highly resistant areas will only prove counterproductive and retard racial progress. Yet our findings point to the opposite view: *external pressures for racial change are likely to be most important and influential in areas most resistant initially to the change.* This hypothesis should hold best when, as cognitive dissonance theory specifies (Aronson & Carlsmith, 1963), the external pressure applied is the *minimal* needed to induce the new policies and behavior. The reciprocal hypothesis also seems tenable: *any significant and perceived lessening of external pressures for racial change is likely to lead to the most retrogression in racial attitudes and practices in areas most resistant initially to the change.*

REFERENCES

Aronson, E., & Carlsmith, J. M. Effect of the severity of threat on the devaluation of forbidden behavior. *Journal of Abnormal and Social Psychology*, 1963, 66, 584-588.

Blalock, H. M., Jr. Per cent non-white and discrimination in the South. *American Sociological Review*, 1957, 22, 109-121.

Bogue, D. J., & Beale, C. L. *Economic areas of the United States.* New York: Free Press, 1961.

Brownlee, K. A. *Statistical theory and methodology in science and engineering,* (2nd Ed.). New York: Wiley, 1965.

Duncan, O. D. Path analysis: Sociological examples. *American Journal of Sociology,* 1966, 72, 1-16.

Guilford, J. P. *Fundamental statistics in psychology and education,* (4th Ed.). New York: McGraw-Hill, 1968.

Hyman, H. H., & Sheatsley, P. B. Attitudes toward desegregation. *Scientific American,* July 1964, 211, 16-23.

McGuire, W. J. The nature of attitudes and attitude change. In G. Lindzey and E. Aronson (Eds.), *The handbook of social psychology* (2nd Ed.) Vol. 3. Reading, Massachusetts: Addison-Wesley, 1969. Pp. 136-314.

Pettigrew, T. F. Desegregation and its chances for success: Northern and Southern views. *Social Forces,* 1957, 35, 339-344.

Pettigrew, T. F. Personality and socio-cultural factors in intergroup attitudes: A cross-national comparison. *Journal of Conflict Resolution,* 1958, 2, 29-42.

Pettigrew, T. F. Regional differences in anti-Negro prejudice. *Journal of Abnormal and Social Psychology*, 1959, 59, 28-36.

Pettigrew, T. F. Parallel and distinctive changes in anti-Semitic and anti-Negro attitudes. In C. H. Stember (Ed.). *Jews in the mind of America.* New York: Basic Books, 1966. Pp. 377-403.

Pettigrew, T. F. *Racially separate or together?* New York: McGraw-Hill, 1971.

Pettigrew, T. F., Riley, R. T., & Ross, J. M. *Understanding racial change: Research in American race relations.* Cambridge, Massachusetts: Harvard University Press, 1972.

Pool, I., Abelson, R. P., & Popkin, S. *Candidates, issues, and strategies* (Rev. ed.). Cambridge, Massachusetts: M.I.T. Press, 1965.

Simon, H. A. *Models of man.* New York: Wiley, 1957.

Wright, S. Path coefficients and path regressions: Alternative or complementary concepts? *Biometrics,* 1960, 16, 189-202.

Part Four
Attitudes and International Social Change

The final research area—that of international attitudes and social change—shares much in common with that of racial attitudes and change which we considered above. Here, too, one encounters critical problems of communication between different racial groups, and also runs into additional complications attributable to nationalism and differences in language, culture, and standard of living. Additionally, one is struck by the role of social and technological change which, in disturbing the *status quo* between cultures, between races, between nations, between regions of the world, and between the haves and have-nots, has given rise to pervasive changes in attitudes, opinion, perceptions, expectations, and values.

In the 19 years following World War II, 380 international conflicts occurred involving underdeveloped countries (Orlansky, 1970), about which there is considerably less information than that on western, industrialized nations. In trying to understand present international conflict, and find desirable resolutions of particular disputes, one must consider whether the assumptions one is willing to make about attitudes, opinions, values, and motivation of western populations make as much sense for cultures in other parts of the world. To the extent that such assumptions correspond to reality, one can expect success in international activities.

What, then, can be said about the adequacy of the present state of knowledge concerning attitudes and related variables in the underdeveloped parts of the world?

Orlansky (1970), who recently reviewed the relevant literature on internal war finds a great deficiency here:

Most explanations of internal war include factors such as disappointment due to disparities between expectations and achievements, conflict among significant segments of the population, and reduced effectiveness of the elite. These factors center upon how members of a society view each other and their future, that is, their perceptions of the world in which they live. Yet, there is a marked absence of attitudinal data for these factors in present analyses of internal war. Thus, there is a great need for the systematic collection of attitudinal data in societies undergoing conflict. Such data must be collected in series over time to detect changes in the attitudes of adequately sampled, representative segments of populations. Then, the relations among attitudinal data and various demographic and economic indicators must also be examined [pp. 3-4].

In the history of research on other cultures and on international perceptions, two streams of effort that relate highly to our present concerns are discerned: (*a*) the case study of a single culture or society; and (*b*) comparative or transactional research on communications, opinions, and attitudes involving more than one culture. The "single-culture, case study" approach often involves participant observation in which the researcher actually lives among his subjects, observing them in the course of their daily activities, and gradually forming impressions of their attitudes, motives, and values. The chapter by Guthrie is based on this observational approach, which typically is used by anthropologists and, more recently, by social psychologists and clinical psychologists. One should note, parenthetically, that his chapter represents only a fragment of the very large interdisciplinary research program that he directed in the Philippines, which included anthropologists, sociologists, and even a nutritionist.

Guthrie analyzes one of the resistances to the adoption of modern ways, namely, the persistence of certain attitudes ("subsistence attitudes"), opinions, and habits that were adaptive in a traditional economy of scarcity but which must change if a modern technologically oriented society is to emerge. As a psychologist, Guthrie introduces into this anthropological context the psychological concepts of reinforcement contingencies, behavior, motives, and attitudes and opinions. Contiguous to these concepts, sociological and anthropological concepts like *ethos,* social change, modernization, and the revolution of rising expectations are found in his contribution.

Implicit here is an issue that pervades this entire volume. What are the relationships among "attitudes" and "behavior"? Related to this central issue is the question of how one can change attitudes and behavior most effectively. To what degree should efforts be concentrated on the classical strategy of changing attitudes by directing persuasive communications at relatively passive, essentially unrewarded, and often unmotivated audiences? Rather, should the alternative approach of arranging the social environment be adopted so that revised schedules of reinforcement will bring about desired behavioral changes, which, in turn, may give rise to consonant attitudes and opinions? Both Abelson and Triandis raised this same question in earlier chapters.

The second contribution in the area of international social change and attitudes was written by Ralph White, who has spent a substantial portion of the last several decades analyzing attitudes, opinions, and behavior in the context of international social change and conflict. Whereas Guthrie's contribution concerned intrasocietal attitudes abroad, the chapter by White deals with perceptions, images, beliefs, and attitudes with respect to other nations and populations. While he does not, here, explicitly stress the concept of social change, it should be emphasized. The cases involving attitudes, opinions, images, and perceptions with which White is concerned—the "cold war," the Vietnam conflict, the Bay of Pigs (White, 1969)—all have involved national groups undergoing rapid social and political change growing out of the 20th-century breakup of the old colonial order. All of his cases involve international conflict and all involve a set of psychological concepts referring to processes that occur within the individual: images, perceptions, attitudes, opinions, values, and ideologies.

With respect to the attitudinal focus of this volume, let us point to White's use of data from opinion and attitude surveys conducted in Vietnam in his analyses. Professor White makes a cogent case for the importance of utilizing data from such attitude and opinion surveys in international decision-making. He points out that, if adequate attention had been paid by high level decision-makers to available data (thereby avoiding "illusions"), the Bay of Pigs episode and the involvement of the United States in Vietnam might not have occurred. In each case, White states that no reliable data existed which showed sufficiently widespread support in the country in question for United States involvement, and one of the premises of such international actions would seem to be the likelihood of finding majority local support for the outside forces.

REFERENCES

Orlansky, J. The state of research on internal war. Research Paper P-565. Institute for Defense Analyses, Arlington, Virginia, August, 1970.

White, R. K. Three not-so-obvious contributions of psychology to peace. *Journal of Social Issues*, 1969, **25** (4), 23-39.

10

The Shuttle Box of Subsistence Attitudes[1]

George M. Guthrie
The Pennsylvania State University

Although they make up more than 50% of the world's people, peasants have received relatively little attention from social scientists. Because they live in large villages and towns and have commercial and social contact with cities, peasants are bypassed by many anthropologists who prefer an isolated group so that they can have a clearer idea of the total pattern of social interaction of their subject population. Psychologists and sociologists have given little attention to peasants because peasant groups are usually too far from the classroom, and are often unable to fill out questionnaires even in their own dialect, or respond to interviews in the interviewer's language. Neither governments nor social scientists can continue to ignore them, however, since peasants are in the forefront of the population explosion, the revolution of rising expectations and, so to speak, the expectation of rising revolutions. This contribution will be concerned with those aspects of peasant behavior which function in ways to maintain their poverty-ridden status and which restrict the extent to which peasants are able to gain the better things in life which they see in the cities.

In contrast to preliterate or primitive peoples, peasants are usually participants in one of the world's major religions: Hinduism, Islam, Buddhism, or in the case of Latin America and the Philippines, Christianity. Furthermore, they have given up tribal costumes, usually manage a couple years of school, and carry on their transactions for money rather than by barter. A western visitor is reminded of the extremely poor in his society and is tempted to think of peasants with the same concepts and expectations. In many cases, however,

[1] The research upon which this paper was based was supported by the Advanced Research Projects Agency and monitored by the Office of Naval Research under contract Nonr656(37). I wish to acknowledge also the helpful comments of my colleagues David Szanton and Howard Hoffman.

peasants are not like the extremely poor in the United States. They are not excluded from the larger society because of racial or ethnic factors; they speak like and look like the industrialized citizens of the cities. When they move to the city, as many do, they often succeed in making a transition to an industrial style of life. Their family structure is strong and intact so that there is little of the alienation, anomie, and lack of social control which may appear in extremely poor groups in industrialized countries. In the case of Filipinos who migrate to the United States, even those from peasant backgrounds make a remarkably satisfactory adjustment to an urban, industrial pattern of living. Americans entrust themselves to their care when they enter a hospital in the United States, a sure indication that someone is convinced that they have entered the modern world.

In this contribution I would like to describe a constellation of attitudes associated with a subsistence style of life and propose an *egalitarian motive* that has many of the properties of avoidance learning and which may bring some order out of contradictory observations. From this, one may be able to deduce some steps which might increase the effectiveness of action programs calculated to bring about social and economic development. The research on which this paper is based was done in the Philippines.

THE PHILIPPINE SETTING

The Philippines shares a great many similarities, economic and historic, with many other developing countries. It is located in the tropics; the majority of the citizens are engaged in food production in agriculture or fishing; the average income is low, with a distribution skewed so that a few are wealthy and the rest are very poor; industries are small and oriented to processing or assembling for the immediate local market. The Philippines was governed by Spain for 300 years and by the United States for 50 years. As is the case with many new nations, the Filipinos achieved political independence after World War II. Some remarkable changes occurred in the 1960s with the arrival of transistor radios and television and the development of air travel. Rural communities, where three-quarters of the nation lives, were brought into much closer contact with cities, particularly Manila, the source of modern ideas and manufactured goods, and much that embodied or symbolized a better life.

Americans helped to establish a nation-wide system of schools, beginning shortly after they conquered the islands at the turn of the century. As a result of this policy, more than half of adult Filipinos are literate and the use of one of the world's major languages, English, is widespread. The infrastructure of human resources in the Philippines is developed better than in most emerging nations. In spite of human resources, the Philippines is not developing as rapidly as Filipinos or outsiders would like. With conditions of education and communication satisfied, with a central government in control of the whole nation, and with at least modest agricultural and other resources, the country should be progressing more rapidly than appears to be the case. There are many reasons for this slow development: the extensive damage of World War II, a population growing at 3.5% per year, the island structure which makes communications difficult and costly, and the history of foreign occupation during which the economy developed as a supplier of raw materials. Even with these handicaps, however, there is much that could be done at the village level which would improve the level of living for all, steps which would not require outside capital. Because we in the United States debate foreign assistance expenditures so much we come to believe that development is dependent on outside funds, we lose sight of the fact that development can be influenced by decisions and actions taken within the community. Individuals and families can take steps which will enhance or deplete their resources and these individual decisions are frequently determined by social psychological factors within the group.

I would like to outline some of these processes as we have observed them in the rural Philippines. Similar processes probably operate in other developing countries as well. It appears that a set of attitudes—a readiness to respond in certain ways and a direction of behavior—characterizes many of the social interactions of rural Filipinos. Behavior seems to be motivated to reduce inequalities, to maintain good feelings between neighbors, and to make sure that no one perishes from hunger or lack of other basic necessities. This constellation of attitudes functions in a way to inhibit the economic development of the community since it restricts the increase of the total supply of goods which the group might produce.

OBSERVED BEHAVIOR PATTERNS

I would like to describe a series of observations which prompted my formulation since these are the data I have. In contrast to most presentations on attitudes, this presentation is not based on scales nor evidence of change on scales, but on behavior.

A number of us have just completed a series of studies of modernization in the Philippines. In addition to my own material, I shall rely heavily on that of David and Cristina Szanton, anthropologists who studied the fishing industry and the public market in a town in the central Philippines. My own work was directed at four communities in the Tagalog-speaking area near Manila. The communities selected were 50, 100, 200, and 400 km. from Manila since a major independent variable in this study was exposure to modernizing influences.

For example, the most distant town was on the coast of an island south of Manila. The island had a north-south ridge of mountains reaching up to 6000 ft.

which effectively isolated the narrow eastern and western coastal plains. Until the 1920s the population had remained small, but it grew quickly after malaria was controlled. Logging provided the first livelihood, and after the forests were removed, the people tried to grow bananas on a commercial basis. Defeated by recurrent typhoons, they turned to raising coconuts. As the forests up the slopes of the mountains have been cut, a few entrepreneurs have begun to raise cattle at the higher altitudes. I also studied people in a *barrio*, or rural cluster of houses, outside the town but still on the plain, using a standard interview and participant observation techniques. The community was located on rolling land which was planted in coconuts which had reached the bearing age. The people also grew corn, and some rice where the land was level enough to collect water during the rainy season. Although much of the land was owned by one family, the tenancy situation was relatively benevolent; neither tenant nor landlord was making enough to prompt one to try to grasp a greater share.

In this research I was concerned with differences in attitudes associated with access to modernizing influences (distance from Manila), sex, and social class. A serious problem of response bias was encountered in the preliminary work— peasants are even more eager to please than are sophomores. We coped with this problem by posing alternatives equated for desirability. The results of this $4 \times 2 \times 2$ analysis showed no differences associated with sex, virtually none with distance from Manila, but considerable differences associated with social and economic factors (Guthrie, 1970). It was not a case, however, where landowners held modern attitudes and peasants traditional; both tended to choose the modern alternatives.

It was this considerable disparity between the modernity of attitudes espoused and the current style of living and technology which prompted the present analysis. What factors prevent rural Filipinos from achieving a level of living commensurate with their knowledge and attitudes?

Here are some of the observations on which I base my inferences:

1. A school teacher and his family began to grow vegetables at their home and to establish vegetable plots at the school, plots which the children tended. Neighbors came, or sent their youngsters, to ask for help—a share of the vegetables—as soon as they were ready for harvest. Other neighborhood children helped themselves. As soon as the school year was over, people who lived near the school destroyed the fence so that pigs could eat the vegetables from the school plots. The teacher reduced his own garden plot and continued the plots at the school only because the government required schools to do so.

2. A woman kept three native hens under her house, feeding them scraps of food from the house and permitting them to forage in the vicinity of the house. The hens laid a couple dozen eggs a year, most of which were

hatched to supply fighting cocks and chickens to eat on special occasions. She was fully aware that improved breeds would lay 5-10 times as many eggs but she kept her present flock because, "They are as many as I can watch. They roost high in the trees where no one can reach them at night. If I had purebreds, people would ask for them in the day and steal them at night. This way they can see that I have none to spare."

3. In another community an ambitious farmer purchased a pedigreed boar in order to improve the quality of his hogs. One morning, shortly after he brought it to his piggery, he found it with its throat slashed from ear to ear.

4. A particularly perceptive Peace Corps volunteer, Albert Bradford, pointed out a Filipino expression which was used quite commonly in his place: "He will be brought down." Whenever anyone prospered or appeared to be progressing more rapidly than his neighbors, this folk saying was heard. When President Kennedy was assassinated, the townspeople grieved but explained the catastrophe by referring to the principle that anyone who goes up will surely be reduced. In the face of this outlook, individuals felt obliged to deny their own effort, insisting that their economic achievements were a matter of luck and that their successes were undeserved.

5. In one of our communities a man wished to open a savings account at a recently established bank. At great inconvenience, however, he opened his account in another town in order to avoid the problems which he anticipated if others learned that he had some savings. The demand for help would be based on the supplicant's need and the other's surplus. To fail to lend under these circumstances would be to brand oneself as proud and callous, and would lay oneself open to active resentment expressed in gossip, theft, and even the threat of physical damage.

6. A sentence completion technique developed by Phillips for use in Thailand during 1966 yielded many interesting insights with a Philippine population (Guthrie & Azores, 1969). Of particular interest here was the emphasis on *pakikisama*, or skill in getting along with people: One is expected to be sensitive to the feelings of both peers and subordinates. One must never behave in a proud way, implying that one is superior to others. Even the most menial of employees demands consideration by virtue of his own humanity. Supervision then becomes the art of gentle persuasion in which the manager avoids drawing attention to differences in status and is especially careful not to humiliate when he points out mistakes. Furthermore, a good employer is concerned for the personal welfare of his worker and that of the worker's family in a blend of paternalism and sharing. Power relationships, in general, are hazardous since the exercise of power yields

pleasure, but there may be a great deal of resentment from those upon whom the power falls. In many situations, relationships are personalized, the individual using the power of his office as though it were his own and the subordinate interpreting all directions as personal rather than as expressions of a duty of the office holder.

7. In her study of markets Cristina Szanton (in press) observed that a fish vendor who bought a good supply at a good price was expected to share his merchandise with other vendors who did not buy enough to support a day's sales. In this way a reasonably profitable supply might be divided into three or four parts and each vendor would make only enough to stay in business. While individual vendors acknowledged that this sometimes provided protection against losses, they were quite aware that good profits were lost when they sold half of their day's supply at their cost. Fist fights might break out where male vendors refused help to other vendors who had been less enterprising or fortunate. Female vendors of vegetables and corn shared in much the same way. Any woman who refused to share was the object of righteous indignation and angry comments.

8. In his study of commercial fishing, David Szanton (1971) found that small enterpreneurs set out early each morning to meet the returning fishermen to buy a couple of cases of fish directly from the boat crew. In doing so they deprived the boat owner of his share if he was not on the boat to protect his own interests. Even if the owner was there, the small boat owner would plead the need to make a living, the right to survive, and would often succeed in making a transaction with the boat owner. The owner, or the crew, could not resist the expectation that they share their catch with another who also "has the right to live."

    Meanwhile, the crew and the operator of the fishing outfit show a similar process of dividing the catch into so many portions that no one has a surplus. The crew is larger than necessary; the fishermen take some of the catch as their payment and additional fish without the owner's knowledge. The captain and the owner pad the expenses and understate the value of the fish so that there is little apparent profit to share with the fishermen. The fishermen make only enough to survive from one day to the next to the extent of reducing the amount they eat when the full moon makes night fishing poor or impossible.

9. A Filipino acquaintance returned from the United States where she had been studying for three years. In the course of her time abroad she had picked up colloquial American English and had become much more fluent than she was when she left. This, incidentally, was one of the purposes of her going abroad. Upon her return she was teased for her new speech patterns and called various humiliating or embarrassing

names until she reverted to her former style of speaking with its limited vocabulary, errors of construction, and local intonation pattern. Only then was she acceptable because she was not getting ahead of the others.

10.   There are a number of expressions one hears among rural or fishing people which express the idea that one is getting by. *Dilihensiya* and *remedios na lang* express the idea that one is succeeding each day in making it to the next and that this is what one might expect. Occurring with this low margin of safety is a pattern of extensive hospitality to strangers. I was, for example, very uncomfortable when a rural tenant farmer killed his only hen to feed me, a visitor. To have failed to feed me would have been considered inhospitable; to save the chicken would have been an act of greed. He will not starve, of course, because he can ask a neighbor for a hen to start a new flock, continuing his relationship of sharing with his neighbor. One gets by not by accumulating material resources and savings but by maintaining and enhancing one's status in the community through sharing any surplus that exists. Security lies in having a good reputation as one who helps others when he has more than he needs.

So much for observations. What one finds is a situation in which the vast majority of people live from one day to the next with no savings, even with an insufficient supply of food for the next meal. Children gather "food for the day" in the shallow water along the shore, or dig for clams on the sandy beach. Children are stunted in growth and adults experience recurrent periods of hunger. There has been sufficient exposure to education and to media of mass communication so that the people know that life is different for others, including other Filipinos. One is forced to raise the visitor's question, "Why don't they . . . ?"

These observations were selected to illustrate facets of a social process which might be called the "subsistence attitude" or the "egalitarian motive." The subsistence attitude, in which one plans ahead but provides only enough for the day, is maintained, I believe, by the fact that any surplus is surrendered more or less immediately to acquaintances who claim a greater need. The egalitarian motive persists because sharing reduces the intensity of anger and resentment which arise when one person gets more than others and refuses to share it.

How, one may ask, is this pattern of life experienced by those who participate in it. Since peasants produce few social scientists or philosophers, one can hardly expect an elaborate philosophy. They did, however, tell a good deal when they were asked about their town, especially what was good or bad about it in comparison with other towns. A town was good if it offered an opportunity to earn a living. It was good if there was law and order and if the mayor required the police to protect the people. A town was good where all the people are equal and where no person or family feels proud and superior to others, even if they do have more money. A town could be proud of a son who has been industrious and has prospered, provided that he had not forgotten his roots.

Not only is goodwill necessary for him but so is political power or influence to protect achievements and possessions. All important families hold public office or sponsor candidates in order to protect themselves against laws or regulations which discriminate against them. Even the formal apparatus of government is brought into the struggle between families and factions. When the balance of power is tilted, the winners are not content merely to win but they seek to demolish their competitors. The vanquished survive by joining the victors. An oligarchy in each town or village is not maintained, however, because factions spring up within the victorious group, reconstituting competing factions with a slightly different membership. Therefore, one sees at the political level many processes which parallel those I have described between individuals.

The picture projected is of a society where individuals behave toward one another in ways such that the total supply of goods and services generated is barely enough to keep people alive. There is little incentive for individual members to increase their own contributions even though as individuals they know how, and they would enjoy having more than they have at the present time.

PEASANTS AND POVERTY

When one thinks about peasants in developing countries one is reminded of the poor in the cities of the United States and the pioneers one reads about as school children. Unlike many of the urban poor, peasants are not members of ethnic or racial minority groups. They constitute the overwhelming majority of the population, and they are not excluded for reasons of color, religion or ancestry, as is often the case in the United States. In contrast to pioneers, peasants do not have expanses of land waiting for them; the little available land is "grabbed" by those who know the right procedure and the right people. Although many pioneers almost certainly were peasants in their homeland, they broke out of the peasant bind when they left Europe and prospered to a degree that had not been possible before. Notice that, in the transition, they did not obtain additional education; no one provided the infrastructure; communication probably got worse rather than better; and the government administrative structure under which they lived was probably no more sophisticated in America than it had been in Europe. They did not have the conditions for development which one has been told are essential for developing countries. The same is true of many who migrate from one country to another within the developing world, including the Chinese. For a century Cantonese and other South Chinese have migrated to Southeast Asia, making the transition from peasants to merchants quickly and completely without any outside assistance or special training. Peasants, pioneers, and the urban poor share a number of characteristics but cannot be equated beyond the fact that all may be exceedingly poor.

PEASANT ATTITUDES

As indicated at the beginning, although they are the most numerous social group on earth, peasants have received attention from only a relatively small number of social scientists. Since peasants produce, or at least retain, few poets or novelists in their number, one is also denied a contribution to their understanding from the humanities. Fortunately, experienced anthropologists such as Redfield (1960), Lewis (1951), Foster (1967), Nash (1966), and Wolf (1966) have moved the locus of their research from exotic hill tribes to the heavily populated peasant lowlands. In addition, other social scientists, including Inkeles (1966), Lerner (1968), Banfield (1958), and Rogers (1969) have inspected aspects of peasant social and economic organizations with particular attention to factors which might affect change. Much of their work has been summarized by Wolf (1966) and by Rogers (1969). According to Rogers (1969, pp. 19-41), the subculture of peasantry has ten central elements:

1. Mutual distrust in interpersonal relations.
2. Perceived limited good—there is only so much to go around and the total supply cannot be increased.
3. Dependence on and hostility toward government authority.
4. Familism.
5. Lack of innovativeness.
6. Fatalism.
7. Limited aspiration.
8. Lack of deferred gratification.
9. Limited view of the world—little knowledge of the world beyond the confines of their village or neighborhood.
10. Low empathy—inability to imagine themselves in some other role.

I have observed that many of these qualities are present to various degrees in Philippine rural people. The problem with such a list, however, is that one is tempted to equate description with explanation. Peasants do not try new ways to make a living because they lack innovativeness; they use up any gain immediately since they are unable to defer gratification. It is clear that this list was prepared by an outsider concerned that peasants functioned in a way to keep themselves in poverty. This analysis, however, does not suggest steps which might be taken to modify the culture of peasants so that social and economic development could be promoted. The remedy most commonly offered for this bill of complaints against peasants is education, apparently in the belief that educated people would be smart enough not to treat one another as peasants do. The unfortunate fact, however, in the Philippines at least, is that virtually the same pattern of jealousy, lack of cooperation, and resulting low productivity occurs even in the education establishment, and among rural people who have obtained an education and returned to the rural areas. Many of these qualities beset the highest levels of government in the developing countries. Even the wealthy are rich peasants.

The most significant attempt to analyze this constellation of attitudes and behavior is that of Foster (1965), who begins by observing:

> The members of every society share a common cognitive orientation which is, in effect, an unverbalized, implicit expression of their understanding of the "rules of the game" of living imposed by their social, natural and supernatural universe . . . basic premises and sets of assumptions normally neither recognized nor questioned which structure and guide behavior in much the same way grammatical rules unrecognized by most people structure and guide their linguistic forms [p. 293] .

Foster continues that peasant behavior can be understood in terms of the "image of limited good." This cognitive orientation, or basic unverbalized view of the world, leads peasants to act and feel in certain consistent and predictable ways:

> . . . broad areas of peasant behavior are patterned in such fashion as to suggest that peasants view their social, economic, and natural universes— their total environment—as one in which all of the desired things in life such as land, wealth, health, friendship and love, manliness and honor, respect and status, power and influence, security and safety, *exist in finite quantity* and *are always in short supply*, as far as the peasant is concerned. Not only do these and all other "good things" exist in finite and limited quantities, but in addition *there is no way directly within peasant power to increase the available quantities* (Foster, 1965, p. 296, Foster's italics).

Foster follows with many examples of the operation of the implicit belief that not only are physical goods in a fixed, limited supply but so are love and honor as well. This belief is not as fixed, however, as the above quotations might imply, because Foster states at the end of his paper, "Show the peasant that initiative is profitable, and that it will not be met by negative sanctions, and he acquires it in short order [p. 310] ."

SOME ATTITUDES OF RURAL FILIPINOS

When we asked peasants about themselves, however, we got a somewhat different answer, different than Rogers' list of ten characteristics and with no mention of an "idea of limited good." My Filipino respondents had some rather clear ideas about the qualities of a good community; understanding these qualities enables us to see some of the processes which may contribute to the retardation of development. A good community is one in which (Guthrie, 1970, pp. 35-41):

1. The citizens have *pakikisama*. This virtue among Filipinos refers to positive skills in interpersonal behavior—charm, hospitality, awareness of the others' feelings, and ability to make the other person feel important and worthwhile.
2. People are respectful toward older family members and neighbors, and aware of their obligations.
3. There is a good mayor who is able to maintain law and order by driving out lawless elements, and who is able to obtain "pork barrel" expenditures for the town from the national government.
4. There are opportunities to make a living through such activities as buy-and-sell in the local market.
5. There is entertainment in the town in the form of a movie theater and possibly some cabarets; but gambling joints and prostitutes are bad for the town.

When asked for the characteristics of a good person, my respondents mentioned helpfulness more frequently than any other characteristics. Where the majority are very poor, and where there are virtually no formally organized sources of help, each family must count on its neighbors and friends when needs arise due to sickness, unemployment, or a pressing ceremonial function such as a wedding or a funeral. The most undesirable characteristic was snobbishness, looking down on those with less money. The best models for children were men who were hard-working, sincere, gentlemanly, courteous to older people, obedient to parents, and intelligent; and women who were hard-working, industrious, modest, religious, courteous, obedient, and home-loving.

Peasants have ideals too, although not much attention has been paid to them, and their ideals and their day-to-day behavior often do not coincide. Many of their behavior patterns are a realistic adjustment to their social and material environment. There is not much point in accumulating a great deal of food in a tropical environment. Food spoils; friendships keep. One's goods can be stolen but not one's good name or one's favors due. With no security in old age one is obligated to have many children and to raise them with a strong sense of family obligation. With the ever-present danger of hunger one also must get along with his neighbors.

There are now three perspectives on peasants: (*a*) the social scientists' characterization, which is calculated to account for their backwardness; (*b*) the peasants' own view, which points out the satisfactions of their way of life; and (*c*) at the beginning of this paper, some observations of behavior patterns which suggest that peasants frequently behave toward one another in ways that keep them at an extremely low level of material possessions. Many actions which would increase the overall supply of goods and services in a community arouse reactions in others which are aversive to the actor, while other activities are reinforced which act as restraints on increased productivity. The reasons peasants or social scientists offer for these restraints to development do not matter for the moment. The importance of the practices that function as reinforcement contingencies can be assessed only if they are changed.

CHANGES IN ATTITUDES

Fortunately, such changed situations can be found and, when contingencies are altered, peasant behavior is replaced by that typical of industrial peoples. The changes are dramatic and quick because peasants have been exposed through various media to the industrial style of life; they know how it works. Filipinos who move to Manila and, with an education, enter the business or industrial life of the city are able to function very effectively. They often succeed in carrying on two styles of life if they retain land and ties in the provinces, even to the extent of conducting the affairs of city life in English while transactions with tenants are in a dialect. Even more complete is the transition of a Filipino who comes to the United States in a professional role such as physician, nurse, or engineer. They may become very homesick but encounter little difficulty in coping with most phases of American society in a way which is typical of members of an industrial society. One may say that their education has made a difference; but their classmates who returned to the *barrios* and provincial towns functioned equally well in those traditional settings.

The peasants' way of life is established and maintained by its consequences; if those consequences, or the factors that control them, are changed, their behavior will change. The persistence of peasant traits is due to the persistence of pervasive, environmental factors such as the threats of hunger, crop failure, epidemics, or powerful landlords. In the face of such threats, sharing of meager possessions was essential to survival. This *ethos* has been preserved, and by continuing to act as though an emergency were present, peasants maintain a state of shortage, a low-grade emergency which keeps behavior appropriate to an emergency at a high state of strength. Furthermore, as is the case with other avoidance behavior, peasant behaviors are difficult to extinguish when alternative behaviors cannot be elicited. Once elicited, however, the alternative behaviors increase rapidly and avoidance activities extinguish quickly. Having moved to the city, peasants find it impossible to return to the countryside. They say it is sad or boring. In this analysis I would say they can no longer continue the avoidance behavior of peasant life.

Those who continue to live in rural areas, however, do not change because their social or material environment has remained constant. They continue the pattern of mutual distrust, dependence on the family, fatalism, low innovativeness, and limited aspiration. They act in many ways as though the total supply of goods available to them were limited and that another's prosperity caused their deprivation. Within this pattern of attitudes there develops a set of interpersonal activities which can be called *leveling*. To make clear that this is not merely a deficiency in the achievement motive, let us refer to this strongly motivated, enforced sharing as the *egalitarian motive*. This motive operates so that an individual feels threatened when another person is successful and ashamed when he himself is more successful than others. Since he has learned that he has little control over his fate, the peasant denies that his success could be due to his own efforts, insisting that it is a matter of luck. In doing so, he may deflect somewhat the envy of others.

Discussing Filipino values, Lynch (1964) pointed out that associated with this view of the world is the belief that any success should be shared. There is also an intense reaction against anyone who declines to share or who acts as though he were superior to others because he has more than they do. Furthermore, as he is not willing to accept full responsibility for his successes or failures, the peasant is willing to take poorly calculated risks because he sees outcomes as beyond his control. Finally, a neighbor who has a good crop, or a good catch of fish, or some extra chickens is under strong obligation to share his luck rather than hoard his surplus as though he felt superior to other people.

It is within this cognitive-emotional configuration that the leveling activities occur which were described earlier. Peasants act toward one another in ways which work against the overall improvement of their condition. Lynch (1961) labeled this process a *sociostat* when he observed it among Filipino college students in Manila. Nash (1966), from whom I have taken the term *leveling*, has described in his report on peasant and primitive economies processes which protect the values and norms of a society:

> Leveling mechanisms are a way of forcing the expenditure of accumulated resources or capital into channels that are not necessarily economic or productive. Every society has some form of leveling mechanism, but in primitive and peasant economies leveling mechanisms play a crucial role in

inhibiting aggrandizement by individuals or by special social groups. Leveling mechanisms may take various forms: forced loans to relatives or
co-residents; a large feast following economic success; a rivalry of expendi-
ture like the potlatch of the Northwest Coast Indians in which large
amounts of valuable goods were destroyed; the ritual levies consequent on
holding office in civil and religious hierarchies in Meso-America; or the
giveaways of horses and goods on the Plains Indians. Most small-scale
economies have a way of scrambling wealth to inhibit reinvestment in
technical advance, and this prevents crystallization of class lines on an
economic base [pp. 35-36].

The emphasis by Nash, however, is on processes that go on between larger
social groups and on the disposal of surpluses, rather than on factors which
inhibit the production of a surplus by an individual or a family.

AN INTERPRETATION

One cannot help asking how this apparently self-defeating behavior came about
and what processes maintain it in the face of apparent opportunities to change.
Many observers have pointed out that much peasant conservatism is a fundamentally sound strategy for people who have few reserves. The old agricultural
practices usually yield enough to get by; a new crop or cultivation technique
might increase the harvest, but it might fail completely. In the latter event,
which is frequent enough to be widely feared, the peasant cultivator is in dire
straits with no reserves to see him through to the next season when he can go
back to the reliable way of doing things. His margin of safety is so close that he
cannot risk unproven, unfamiliar ventures.

The leveling activities, or the egalitarian motive, described here is another
matter. I believe that leveling can be understood as a form of avoidance
behavior. The people of the rural Philippines, and peasant groups the world over,
have been subject throughout history to events which have seriously threatened
their existence. They have survived only because their meagre resources have
been shared. What little food there was took care of everyone. In this circum-
stance the image was literal; to the extent that some members hoarded, others
starved.

Every year in many parts of the Philippines there is a period of weeks or
months when food is scarce. In rice-growing areas this occurs in the interval
before the harvest when the last stores of rice have been depleted. In fishing
communities there are months when fish migrate to other waters, and the full
moon every month takes away a week of fishing because the boats' lights cannot
compete with the light of the moon. In addition to these predictable events

typhoons sweep in from the Pacific inundating the rice and destroying the coconut and banana harvest for many months. These storms also flatten their houses, destroy the roads and boats, and loosen slides which take away houses, terraces, and lives. In the period which follows, people must help one another, sharing whatever may be left. Anyone who holds back in such an emergency is a most despicable person.

Finally, until recently, epidemics have ravaged the countryside. Up to the beginning of this century cholera, small pox, and malaria were well known and feared. Even today a form of cholera strikes the more vulnerable. When resistance is lowered by poor nutrition, both children and adults fall victim to tuberculosis. The plea for money to pay for treatment goes to relatives, landlords, and government officials, anyone who may have means or influence to get help for the one who is in danger. In short, there are frequent emergencies in which a man looks to his neighbors for help and makes it the greatest virtue to be helpful. In these circumstances it is not shameful to ask of another, because each has a right to survive. The needy one avoids disaster by asking, and the fortunate person avoids the anger of the supplicant and the scorn of his friends by giving. Because each individual has a right to live, a person in great need is justified in stealing if no other course is open. One form of sharing or another enables an individual or a family to avoid the consequences of the frequent and severe emergencies they face. The perseveration of sharing after the outside danger is gone is to be expected from research on avoidance responses under controlled experimental conditions.

AVOIDANCE LEARNING

A set of persistent behavior patterns which restrict or eliminate an increase in the gross municipal product has been outlined above, in which leveling activity, or enforced sharing, is widely accepted as proper and is enacted under many different circumstances. Leveling frequently disappears when an individual or a family moves to a different living environment. I believe that an understanding of leveling can be increased, and possibly some methods of altering its more antidevelopment manifestations be developed, by examining some of the psychological research on avoidance learning, particularly that of Solomon and his students (Solomon and Wynne, 1954).

Briefly, it has been found that an animal such as a dog or a rat can be trained to move from one end to the other end of a box when he hears a sound which precedes the onset of a shock administered through the wires in the floor of the end where he is standing. Having moved to the other end, he must return to the first end to avoid the shock when he hears the sound again. Appropriately named a *shuttle box*, the apparatus enables an experimenter to study the behavior changes of an animal as it learns to shuttle back and forth. This learning presents a few problems for learning theorists who want to avoid the anthropomorphism of saying that the animal knows a shock is coming and moves in order to avoid it. However, such problems are minute when compared with the problem which arises when the shock is discontinued and the animal continues to shuttle back and forth at the sound without any sign of extinction. For example, dogs that had received a few intense shocks during the acquisition trials, went on jumping when the shock was turned off, giving as many as 600 avoidances without any indication of extinction. The experimenters gave up before the animals quit! Furthermore, with occasional reinforcements avoidance reactions remained at maximum strength.

Speculating about the significance of the age at which traumatic events have occurred Solomon and Wynne (1954) suggest:

> . . . early, severe traumata are likely to produce classically conditioned emotional responses of a lasting sort. Later severe traumata are more likely to produce a variety of instrumental acts of a high strength [p. 380].

The traumatic experiences, to which I have referred, occur at the later stage since infants, as a rule, are protected and unaware of the danger which adults face. Concerning threatening experiences after infancy, Solomon and Wynne (1954) suggest:

> Later traumata will have somewhat different consequences. Here we can expect quick instrumental action, so that the repetition of CS-US pairings would be greatly cut down. We would expect a lot of conditioned avoidance reactions of a fairly discrete nature to develop, but no extremely strong classically conditioned anxiety reactions *in most cases* [p. 380].

This description fits the behavior we have been observing very closely: threatening experiences in later childhood and adulthood, which are reduced by the instrumental acts of sharing, persist after the danger has passed without manifestations of marked anxiety. In the experimental setting and in the countryside they become more stereotyped with the passage of time; in the laboratory the latencies of avoidance responses reduce over time, and in the field people's leveling activities appear as quickly as anyone gets just a little ahead of his peers.

Solomon, Kamin, and Wynne (1953) explored the efficacy of various extinction procedures when extinction did not appear after hundreds of trials, at the rate of 10 trials each day, in which no shock has been administered. The experimenters raised the barriers between the halves of the shuttle box so that the dog had to exert considerable effort to jump from one section to the other. After 490 trials of this sort they electrified the opposite compartment so that the dog jumped into shock from a compartment in which he would not be shocked if he would only stay. After 100 additional trials the dog still jumped regularly. They continue:

> As he jumped on each trial, he gave a sharp anticipatory yip which turned into a yelp when he landed on the electrified grid in the opposite compartment of the shuttlebox. We then increased the duration of the shock to 10 seconds and ran the dog for 50 more trials. Latencies and behavior did not change. Evidently punishment for jumping was ineffective in extinguishing the jumping responses (Solomon et al., 1953, p. 291).

Proceeding with the same dog, they placed a glass barrier on trials 4-7 so that the dog bumped his nose if he tried to leave the compartment. As before, he was shocked on trials 1-3 and 8-10 if he jumped into the other compartment. On trials 8-10 of the first day the glass barrier was used the dog did not attempt to jump when the conditioned stimulus was presented:

> At long last, after 647 extinction trials, the dog failed to jump in the presence of the CS alone. On the following day, the dog jumped into shock with short latencies on the first three trials, thus showing complete spontaneous recovery. He did not jump on trials 8-10 (Solomon et al., 1953, p. 292).

On five subsequent days with no glass barrier he jumped only once. Extinction was, as the authors observed, an all-or-none affair.

The results obtained with this dog were replicated with others. Of 23 dogs, trained to a criterion of 10 avoidances on 10 trials, 13 showed no extinction after 200 ordinary extinction trials and the other 10 dogs who were carried to only 10 extinctions continued to jump without fail. The glass barrier brought about extinction in only 2 of 9 dogs over 10 days or 100 trials. The shock procedure resulted in extinction in only 3 of 13 dogs over a similar 10-day period. Combining shock and barrier, however, eliminated jumping for 14 of 16 dogs.

In later research (Maier, Seligman, & Solomon 1969), Solomon and his colleagues found that if a dog was given a number of shocks from which he could not escape, and then placed in the shuttle box within 24 hr. he would not learn to avoid by jumping to the other half of the box when the sound was presented prior to the onset of shock in the floor of the half in which he happened to be. Maier et al. (1969) report:

. . . a dog which has experienced inescapable shocks prior to avoidance training soon stops running and howling and remains silent until shock terminates. The dog does not cross the barrier and escape from shock. Rather it seems to give up and passively accept the shock. On succeeding trials, the dog continues to fail to make escape movements [pp. 319-320].

If several days had elapsed between the inescapable shock and the shuttle box experience, the dog learned to escape as rapidly as did unshocked controls. Apparently the inescapable shock leads to the development of *learned helplessness* only if the dog is called upon to learn to escape immediately after he has had the experience of stress from which he could do nothing to escape. As in the earlier experiments Maier *et al.* (1969) sought to modify the persistent behavior.

[They] reasoned that forceably dragging the dog from side to side in the shuttle box, in such a way that the dog's changing compartments terminated shock, might effectively expose the dog to the response-reinforcement contingency. This was the case. The experimenter pulled three chronically helpless dogs back and forth across the shuttle box with long leashes. This was done during CS and shock, while the barrier was absent. After being pulled across the center of the shuttle box (and thus terminating shock and CS) 20, 35, and 50 times, respectively, each dog began to respond on his own. Then the barrier was replaced, and the subject continued to escape and avoid. The recovery from helplessness was complete and lasting.

The behavior of animals during "leash pulling" was interesting. At the beginning of the procedure, a great deal of force had to be exerted to pull the dog across the center of the shuttle box. Less and less force was needed as training progressed. A stage was typically reached in which only a slight nudge of the leash was required to impel the dog into action. Finally, the subject initiated its own response, and thereafter failure to escape was very rare. The initial problem seemed to be one of "getting the dog going" [pp. 329-330].

Other techniques, such as calling to the dog from the safe side of the box, dropping food on the safe side, kicking the dangerous side of the box were of no avail. The dogs did not learn to escape until they had been tugged into the correct response and reinforced (by escaping the shock) for doing so.

Solomon's research may help toward an understanding of peasants who, caught in a social shuttle box, continue to behave as though the shock was still on. The persistence of their behavior is inherent in the circumstances in which it was acquired. Modification of their behavior requires that they have the opportunity to acquire other avoidance strategies and that they become desensitized to the situations which prompt the jumping so insistently. These conditions apparently are met when the peasant experiences a physical and social move to an industrial setting. Much more study is needed to devise means of changing his behavior in his home community. The first step is to get a clearer picture of why it continues in spite of its obvious self-defeating results.

There are two qualities of avoidance responses which bear especially on the behavior we seek to understand: Avoidance responses extinguish very slowly and a single reinforcement restores the response to a high strength after it has been partially extinguished. A period of severe deprivation and threatened extinction is highly disturbing, possibly leading to a condition akin to the dog's learned helplessness. Sharing activities not only reduce the danger for many individuals in the physical sense of making food available, but also reduce the panic. Sharing removes the necessity of developing responses which cope with the recurrent sources of danger. Since the emergency took place within the family and the home territory, there are many cues wherever the peasant turns which have been associated with anxiety-ridden intervals. Under these circumstances anxiety-avoidance responses—forced sharing, and suspicion of anyone who may be getting more than he needs—are likely to occur. Activities which prevent an aversive stimulus are remarkably resistant to extinction. Furthermore, when avoidant responses have been extinguished, they can be reinstated readily at high strength by a recurrence of the original aversive experience.

Human beings, with their symbolic activities, demonstrate all of these phenomena. In addition, they learn a good deal by imitation, a process that leads to some of the homogeneity and stereotyped patterns of peasant behavior. It seems likely also that they can reinstate symbolically or vicariously aversive experiences by seeing or hearing about others who are undergoing threat or deprivation. Once avoidance behavior has been acquired, its mere execution is reinforcing; it extinguishes very slowly in the absence of repeated aversive experiences and remains at a very high level with the help of occasional aversive episodes. Once a peasant's defence is adopted, it takes only an occasional crop failure or typhoon, or maybe just the news of such a disaster to keep him behaving like a peasant.

REFERENCES

Banfield, E. C. *The moral basis of a backward society.* New York: Free Press, 1958.

Foster, G. M. Peasant society and the image of limited good. *American Anthropologist*, 1965, **67**, 293-315.

Foster, G. M. *Tzintzuntzan: Mexican peasants in a changing world.* Boston: Little, Brown, 1967.

Guthrie, G. M. *The psychology of modernization in the rural Philippines.* Manila: Ateneo de Manila University Press, IPC Papers, No. 8, 1970.

Guthrie, G. M., & Azores, F. M. *Philippine interpersonal behavior patterns.* Manila: Ateneo de Manila University Press, IPC Papers No. 6, 1969.

Inkeles, A. The modernization of man. In M. Weiner (Ed.), *Modernization: The dynamics of growth.* New York: Basic Books, 1966.

Lerner, D. *The passing of traditional society: Modernizing the Middle East.* New York: Free Press, 1968.

Lewis, O. *Life in a Mexican village.* Urbana: University of Illinois Press, 1951.

Lynch, F. Social acceptance. In *Four readings on Philippine values.* Manila: Ateneo de Manila University Press, IPC Papers No. 2, 1964.

Lynch, F., & Hollnsteiner, M. R. *Understanding the Philippines and America* (Lecture 14). Manila: Ateneo de Manila, Institute of Philippine Culture, 1961 (mimeo).

Maier, S. F., Seligman, M. E. P., & Solomon, R. L. Pavlovian fear conditioning and learned helplessness. In B. A. Campbell and R. M. Church (Eds.), *Punishment and aversive behavior.* New York: Appleton, 1969. Pp. 299-342.

Nash, M. *Primitive and peasant economic systems.* San Francisco, California: Chandler, 1966.

Redfield, R. *The little community and peasant society and culture.* Chicago, Illinois: University of Chicago Press, 1960.

Rogers, E. M. *Modernization among peasants.* New York: Holt, 1969.

Solomon, R. L., & Wynne, L. C. Traumatic avoidance learning: The principles of anxiety conservation and partial irreversibility. *Psychological Review*, 1954, 61, 353-385.

Solomon, R. L., Kamin, L. J., & Wynne, L. C. Traumatic avoidance learning: The outcome of several extinction procedures with dogs. *Journal of Abnormal and Social Psychology*, 1953, 48, 291-302.

Szanton, D. L. *Estancia in transition: Economic growth in a rural Philippine Community.* Manila: Ateneo de Manila University Press, IPC Papers No. 9. 1971.

Szanton, M. C. A right to survive: Subsistence marketing in a lowland Philippine town. University Park: Pennsylvania State University Press, 1972.

Wolf, E. R. *Peasants.* Englewood Cliffs, New Jersey: Prentice Hall, 1966.

11

The Pro-Us Illusion and the Black-Top Image

Ralph K. White
George Washington University

There is a type of cognitive distortion that does not seem to have been systematically studied; yet in my judgment it has contributed much to the likelihood of war. It is *the tendency to see the people in another country as more friendly to one's own side than they actually are.* It can be conveniently called "the pro-us illusion." Three recent, close-to-home examples[1] may serve to illustrate its nature and its war-promoting potential:

AMERICAN PERCEPTION OF THE SOVIET PEOPLE

There is for example the long-lasting, hard-dying delusion of many Americans that most of the people in the Soviet Union are against their present rulers and on the American side of the East-West conflict. From 1917, when the Communists first came to power, until perhaps the middle 1950s, this was a very widespread belief in the United States, and it contributed much to the rigidity of the militant anti-Communist policy of American policy makers such as John Foster Dulles.[2] The picture of millions of "secret allies" of the United States inside the Soviet Union sustained many in the belief that we would be "betraying" these allies if we were not implacably hostile to their rulers.[3] The research by Bauer, Inkeles, Kluckhohn and others (1956) at Harvard did much to put an end to this delusion among the well-informed, but it lingers on, especially among the ill-informed. Not so very long ago a prominent United States senator declared

---

[1] More briefly discussed by White (1969).

[2] For a brilliant discussion of the psychology of Secretary Dulles, see Holsti (1967). According to him, Dulles, "never rejected his long-standing theory that the Soviet regime was wholly without support by the Russian people [p. 34]."

[3] For an eloquent but one-sided defense of this thesis, see Lyons (1954).

that the Soviet Union is "seething with discontent" and hostility to its present rulers.

That this belief has contributed to the hardness of the American anti-Communist line is hardly open to question. A more controversial proposition is that this general hardness of the American line has contributed to the danger of war. Many hard-liners would deny it. In my judgment, however, and in the judgment of many other non-hard-liners such hardness has been excessive and its excessiveness has contributed mightily to the danger of a catastrophic culmination of the "cold war."

OUR PERCEPTION OF THE CUBAN PEOPLE

Another example was the belief of many Americans, at the time of the Bay of Pigs adventure, that most of the Cuban people were hostile to Castro in much the same way we were, and perhaps almost ready to rise up against him. It is hard to tell just what was in the minds of our policy makers at the time, but it looks as if they thought there was a good chance of some kind of uprising if we could provide the spark to ignite it.

The sad thing is that they could have known better. They had easy access to the research of Lloyd Free, a good solid piece of public-opinion survey work indicating that most of the Cuban people, less than a year earlier, were quite favorable to Castro (Cantril, 1968). But Free's evidence was ignored. According to Hilsman, the policy makers just did not try to find out what real evidence existed on the attitudes of the Cuban people—either quantitative evidence of the sort Lloyd Free had, or the more traditional kinds gathered by the intelligence service of the State Department (Hilsman, 1968). They made no genuine effort to get evidence that was free from obvious bias. (The testimony of refugees in Miami, which they apparently did get, was obviously biased.)

That much seems clear: their curiosity was inhibited. As to the reasons why it was inhibited, one can speculate along various lines. Perhaps it was a defense against dissonance. Festinger might say that they were embarked on an enterprise, and any doubts about the wisdom of that enterprise would have been cognitively dissonant. Or perhaps it was a defense of their black-and-white picture. They may have sensed that the information into which they did not inquire would have impaired their all-black image of Castro's diabolical tyranny over the Cuban people, and their all-white image of themselves as liberating the Cuban people from a diabolical tyrant. Heider might say that they were preserving psychological harmony or balance. In any case, it looks as if they shut their eyes because they were unconsciously or half-consciously afraid of what they might see. They cherished too fondly the pro-us illusion—and we know the fiasco that resulted.

OUR PERCEPTION OF THE SOUTH VIETNAMESE PEOPLE

Now, more disastrously, there is the case of Vietnam. There too we more or less kidded ourselves into believing that the people were on our side. In some ways it has been very much like the case of Cuba. In both cases there has been a great overestimation of the extent to which the people were pro-us, and consequently a gross overestimate of the possibility of achieving a quick military victory without exorbitant cost. In both cases too there has been a striking lack of interest, on the part of the top policy-making officials, in the best evidence that informed observers could provide.

The irony has been increased by our solemn official dedication to the great objective of enabling the people of South Vietnam to determine their own destiny. President Johnson, McNamara, Rusk, President Nixon, and others have continually talked about helping "the Vietnamese" (not some of them, or most of them, but "the Vietnamese") to defend themselves against the Viet Cong and invaders from the North—as if the Viet Cong were not Vietnamese, and as if it were self-evident that most of the people in the South were gallantly resisting these attacks from within and without, and eager for our help in doing so.

Actually that was always far from self-evident. More than three years ago I wrote an article (White, 1966) in which 25 pages were devoted to a rather intensive effort to cover the evidence on both sides of that question and to find out how the people of South Vietnam really felt about the war. The upshot of that analysis was that probably there were at that time a good many more South Vietnamese leaning in the direction of the Viet Cong than leaning in our direction.

Since then I have updated the analysis, on the basis of three more years of accumulating evidence, during which some shift away from the Viet Cong seems to have occurred. The new information includes all that I was able to glean during two months on the spot in Vietnam, where I had an unusual opportunity to interview well-informed Vietnamese. It includes the Columbia Broadcasting System-Opinion Research Corporation survey, in which more than 1500 South Vietnamese respondents were interviewed (1967), the writings of Douglas Pike, the outstanding authority on the Viet Cong (1966, 1969), and a good deal of other miscellaneous evidence. None of this information is conclusive. For instance, the CBS-ORC survey obviously never solved the problem of getting peasants to speak frankly with middle-class, city-bred interviewers. However, by putting together all of the various sorts of information, which is what I did in the book *Nobody Wanted War* (1970, pp. 37-103), we can, I think, make some fairly educated guesses.

The general upshot of the revised analysis differed from the earlier one chiefly in giving more emphasis to sheer indifference or ambivalence on the part of a great many of the South Vietnamese. It looks as if a large majority now feel so disillusioned with both sides that their main preoccupations are simply the effort to survive, physically and economically, and a fervent hope that peace will come soon, regardless of which side wins. They have "a plague on both your houses" attitude. However, the results of the earlier analysis did seem to be confirmed in that it still looks as if, among those who do care intensely about which side wins, the Viet Cong has the edge. My own very rough and tentative estimates, representing the situation in 1967, were these: about 20% really dedicated on the side of the Viet Cong, something like 10% equally dedicated on the anti-Viet Cong side, and the remainder, something like 70%, relatively indifferent or ambivalent. Since in any political conflict the people who count are the people who care, what matters here is the estimate that, among those who *are* dedicated to one side or the other, more have been against the position of the United States than for it. The upshot still seems to be that the psychological balance tips *against* the Saigon government and the intervening Americans. That is probably true even in 1970, and in previous years it was apparently much more true. For instance, my estimate is that in early 1965, when the United States first became heavily involved, it was closer to 40 to 10, not 20 to 10, in favor of the Viet Cong.

Suppose our policy makers had known that most of the emotionally involved people were against us, and had known it clearly, at the time they were making those fateful commitments and staking American prestige on the outcome. Suppose that in 1961-1962, when Kennedy decided to make his major commitment, and in 1964-1965, when Johnson decided to make his, they had said to themselves: "Of course we know that if we fight in Vietnam we will be supporting a small minority against a much larger minority." Would they have done it? Would we then have had all the tragedy of the Vietnam War?—all the blood, all the guilt, all the moral ignominy in the eyes of most of the rest of the world, all the sensitive intelligent young people here at home estranged from their own country? I doubt it. The American superego—*if* well-informed—is too genuinely on the side of national self-determination, too genuinely against any clear, naked form of American domination over little countries on the other side of the world, even in the name of anti-Communism. Furthermore, the United States' sense of realistic self-interest is too much against squandering thousands of lives and billions of dollars in a long, uphill struggle—which is necessarily a long and uphill struggle if most of the people who care are against us. So the question is: if Kennedy and Johnson (and the many millions of other Americans who saw the situation essentially as they did) had clearly realised that the people were more anti-us than pro-us, would the whole Vietnam mess have been avoided? I think so.

In this sense Vietnam was avoidable, just as the Bay of Pigs was avoidable. The one essential factor in avoiding both of these tragedies would have been to look hard and honestly at the best available evidence (not social science data, in the case of Vietnam, but the testimony of the best-informed area experts such as

Joseph Buttinger). Our policy makers in 1962 and 1965 did not look hard and honestly at the best available evidence, and the chief reason for this, it seems to me, was that they were clinging to an image of the United States as helping a beleaguered and grateful South Vietnam—not intervening in a nasty civil war in which most of those who were emotionally involved would be against us. Like the adventurers who planned the Bay of Pigs they were not really curious, because they half knew what the answer would be if they did look honestly at the facts. They too shut their eyes and put their hands over their ears because they were cherishing too fondly the pro-us illusion. We know now the disaster that resulted.

REASONS FOR THE PRO-US ILLUSION

What, now, can we as psychologists say about the pro-us illusion?

Most obviously, it is a form of wishful thinking. Like many other human beings, Americans like to be liked, and like to believe that they are liked. It is unpleasant to feel hated, and the evidence that one is actually hated can be glossed over for that reason.

However, this explanation seems only partial, at best. In international affairs, as in relationships between individuals, there is such a thing as "paranoid" exaggeration of the hostility of others, as well as wishful ignorance or minimization of it. We have by no means ignored the hostility to us in the minds of Stalin, or Mao, or Castro. It therefore is worth while to consider some other factors that may reinforce simple wishful thinking in particular cases.

One such factor is the moral self-image. We do not like to see ourselves as haters. We like to see ourselves as having neighborly, friendly feelings toward all our international neighbors except when those neighbors make such friendliness impossible. This is especially true in the present-day world in which the shadow of nuclear war hangs over everyone; we know that hatred can lead to war and resist thinking of ourselves as contributing in any way to the horror of a possible nuclear holocaust. Since seeing others as hating us does to some extent imply fearing and therefore hating them, we resist both.

Another is the tendency to universalize one's own reality world. Piaget and many others have noted the tendency of human beings, especially children, to assume that the world as they perceive it is the world as others perceive it. To the naive perceiver the world is simply the world, obvious to everyone; it takes some sophistication to realize that others may sincerely, honestly fail to recognize certain facts that seem obvious to oneself. If, then, we regard it as obvious that the United States is peaceful and seeks only to help others to live in peace and independence, it is difficult to believe that any others could honestly regard us as diabolical imperialists and aggressors.

Still another factor, probably, is a wishful tendency to believe that success in some enterprise (such as the Bay of Pigs or the preservation of a non-Communist South Vietnam) will be possible, or possible without exorbitant cost. Doubts about the possibility of victory are cognitively dissonant, once the enterprise has been embarked upon, and damaging to group morale; they tend to be denied, therefore, both for unconscious psychological reasons and consciously, by those who are leading the enterprise and feel they must have a united group behind them. Since the belief that "the people are on our side" is an important element in the belief that victory is possible, or possible without exorbitant cost, there is a strong tendency to cherish and sustain it.

THE BLACK-TOP IMAGE

Now comes the great paradox. In spite of everything that has just been said about the pro-us illusion, there is a seemingly contrary type of cognitive distortion that also, in my judgment, has contributed greatly to war and the likelihood of war. It is *the tendency to see the "rulers" of an antagonistic country as more implacably hostile to one's own side—and more generally diabolical—than they actually are.* Let us call it "the black-top image" of an enemy.

Perhaps its most obvious form is the Communists' black-top image of the capitalist West in general and the United States in particular. The orthodox Communist view is not that the United States itself is evil but that the "ruling circles" in the United States—Wall Street and the Pentagon—are evil in every imaginable way: they exploit the common people, rule the country behind a facade of democracy, deliberately whip up the arms race and war hysteria, and engage in aggression against "the peoples" of many developing countries such as Vietnam. Even if we grant a sizable kernel of truth in their picture of the "military-industrial complex" in the United States (as I think we must), this conception of a radical dichotomy between good "people" and evil "ruling circles" is surely, to say the least, an exaggeration.[4] The excessiveness of it has surely done a great deal to create the "cold war" that still threatens the peace of the world. It operated perhaps most potently during the years 1945-1950 when Stalin's diabolical image of the capitalist-ruled west contributed much to his apparently genuine fear of the West and his belief that he had to have physical power throughout Eastern Europe, in Berlin, in Korea, and elsewhere, in order to be safe. It is a major factor now in the Soviet Union's accelerated pursuit of

---

[4] For a summary of the evidence as to the war-promoting role of the "military-industrial complex" (properly defined) and also of the evidence that the entire "Establishment" in the United States cannot be fairly accused of promoting war, see White (1970, pp. 252-261).

the arms race. It increases the readiness of the Soviet Union and Communist China to support "wars of liberation" even in countries in which a Communist-led anti-American movement is not (as I think it was in Vietnam) supported by a majority of the politically involved citizens. For all of these reasons it is a major factor, and perhaps the most important single factor, increasing the likelihood of World War III.

Then there is its mirror image in the United States. Americans too have a black-top image of their most dangerous opponents. Right or wrong, or half-right and half-wrong, Americans tend to see both the USSR and Communist China as ruled by single dictators or small oligarchies of tyrannical, power-hungry fanatics, while the exploited common people are either hostile to their rulers or indifferent and apathetic. In my judgment this black-top image of our Communist enemies contains a much larger element of truth than their black-top image of us. Both Russia and China *are*, in a sense, totalitarian countries, in which a small group at the top does almost all of the actual ruling.[5] At the same time, there are strong reasons to believe that these rulers are far from being as diabolical as most Americans think they are. Probably they are trying, as sincerely as the leaders of most other countries are, to serve the welfare of their own people as they conceive of that welfare (with an emphasis in their case on the very long-run welfare of the people, as they conceive it), with a desire for peace (in the Soviet Union, and perhaps in Communist China) that is at least as strong as ours in the United States, and with a foreign policy influenced by cognitive distortions that, in general, greatly affect the thinking of the common people as well as the leaders. The Soviet and Chinese leaders, like the Soviet and Chinese people, are human beings; both are "good" as well as "evil," and both share the kinds of misperception that lead to war.

There are many other examples. In World War I the great devil in the eyes of most of the American people was not the German people but the German Kaiser (who has been shown by post-war scholarship to have been a flamboyant, vacillating weakling, obsessed by paranoid ideas about the British, but not a war-plotting criminal). In the case of Cuba most Americans have seen Castro as a full-fledged devil, and there is much evidence that he is not actually that bad. In the case of Vietnam the prevailing image among militant Americans is that Ho Chi Minh was a ruthless dictator, a ruthless aggressor, and not much else. Actually there is reason to believe he was a great deal else. As for the role of the Viet Cong in South Vietnamese villages, the prevailing view of militant Americans is that they have acquired domination of thousands of villages by sheer terror, assassinating and kidnapping village leaders, health workers, teachers, and anyone else who opposed their power. Certainly they have used terror on a large

[5] For a more detailed analysis of probable psychological differences between the Soviet people and their Communist leaders, see White (1965):

scale, but this picture ignores both the terror and torture on the government side and the genuine dedication of the Viet Cong to the welfare of the common people. There is much reason to regard the Viet Cong as more self-sacrificing and idealistic than most of their peasant followers, as well as more ruthless, and there is much reason to think that their basically anti-government orientation has been different in degree but not essentially different in kind from that of most of their followers (see White, 1970, especially pp. 42-66).

There is abundant evidence, then, that when nations are in conflict, the enemy image on each side tends to be not a simple blackening of the enemy nation as a whole, but a diabolical picture of its leaders or rulers. It is a black-*top* image. At the same time the common people usually are pictured as innocent dupes of their leaders, if not actually hating those leaders and longing for liberation by "us."

REASONS FOR THE COMBINATION

Why is there so often an exaggeration of the evilness and hostility of the leaders, combined with an exaggeration of the friendliness of the common people? Why do the black-top image and the pro-us illusion so often coexist?

One answer could be that there is a "need to hate someone" (as a result of various familiar psychological mechanisms, including projection and displacement of domestically generated hostility onto foreign scapegoats), and that picturing the enemy's rulers as diabolical is more whole hearted when they also can be pictured as tyrants oppressing and exploiting their own people. When this has occurred, it becomes easy to picture the common people in the opposing nation as resenting this tyranny, and hoping for "liberation," more than is actually the case. Or, to put it briefly, there is an impulse of aggression, and then a need to rationalize that aggression by picturing the hate object as a tyrant.

Related to this is a moral self-image that tends to picture the self always as helping, not hurting, an underdog. The self-esteem of the Communists greatly depends on picturing themselves as engaged in long-term liberation of the exploited masses in capitalist countries; mirror-image-wise, the self-esteem of Americans depends to a fair degree on "defending the Free World," especially the poorer and more helpless parts of it, from Communist aggression and dictatorship. This is not to say that such thoughts can compare with national self-interest as major motivating forces in foreign policy. It is to say that the self-image of any nation is almost sure to include some belief that that nation is for, not against, the poor and the downtrodden everywhere. This belief promotes two further beliefs: that the downtrodden must be grateful for one's own actual or potential help, and that the tyrants who tread them down must be resentful of it.

If a war is going on, the melodrama is heightened. When St. George is locked in battle with a dragon, it is only fitting to have a maiden in distress who needs to be saved from the dragon's claws, and the people within the enemy nation constitute one maiden that is always available for the role. (Another consists of the other nations, preferably small and helpless ones, that are presumably being conquered by the dragon in his role as "the aggressor.") This does not mean that tyranny and aggression do not exist, or that the role of St. George is not sometimes necessary, but it does mean that there is a more or less predictable tendency to exaggerate both the "dragon-ness" of the enemy nation's leaders and the "innocent-maiden-ness" of those they are leading.

Another psychological approach is by way of the concept of ambivalence and dissonance. It often happens that there are both positive and negative feelings toward the same nation. A great many Russians, for instance, clearly have strong positive, friendly, admiring feelings toward the United States, along with the negative feelings that have been continually fostered by their official propaganda and by events such as the arms race, the U-2 episode, the Vietnam war, and so forth. The positive feelings also stem from many sources: the image, established during Czarist days, of America as a great and successful democracy, the image of America as economically efficient and therefore as a model that Russia should imitate, our common struggle against Hitler, and so forth (White, 1965, pp. 256-257). If we make the reasonable assumption that there is something inherently unstable in ambivalence, since positive and negative feelings are in a sense opposite and incompatible when directed to the same object, then it is not surprising that the typical Russian perception of the United States clarifies the matter by fastening all guilt upon our leaders and all innocence upon our "common people." In a word, their image of America is differentiated or dichotomized (like their image of the world as a whole) into two parts: the good guys and the bad guys.

Freud, presumably, would here go along with Heider (1958) and Festinger (1957). Festinger might perhaps say that it is cognitively dissonant to see the very same individuals as good and bad at the same time, and that consonance can be restored only if the enemy image is differentiated into two parts, with one part (the leaders in this case) seen as all bad and the other as all good. Heider perhaps would speak of the imbalance that exists when a group perceived as generally bad (the enemy nation's leaders) has to be credited with doing any good thing, or when a group perceived as generally good (the common people in the enemy nation) has to be regarded as doing a bad one. The resulting tendency to an all-good or all-bad image at least would help to account for the momentum of any black-and-white picture after the general positive or negative character of each half of the picture has been established (though it would not in itself account for the picture being initially established in this way). It would also help to account for the typical sharpness of the perceived contrast between leaders and people. Suppose P dislikes O (the leaders of the other country) and likes X (the common people in that country). There is imbalance as long as O is assumed by P to be somehow united with X. Balance can be restored, however, if O and X are seen as separate and antagonistic to each other. And once they are perceived as separate and antagonistic, it becomes easier to see O as hostile and X as friendly to oneself.

In any case it seems clear that these two typical distortions, the pro-us illusion and the black-top image, are complementary and interdependent. They are two sides of the same coin. Or, in terms closer to those of "systems theory," the causal relations between them are more or less circular. We have to see the enemy's leaders as evil in every way, including oppression of their own people, in order to hate them wholeheartedly; we have to see the common people as innocent in order to sympathize with them wholeheartedly (which feeds our hate) and also in order to see ourselves as peaceful men of good will rather than as haters who cause wars.

REFERENCES

Bauer, R., Inkeles, A., & Kluckhohn, C. *How the Soviet system works*. Cambridge, Massachusetts: Harvard University Press, 1956.

Cantril, H. *The human dimension*. New Brunswick, New Jersey: Rutgers University Press, 1968.

Columbia Broadcasting System. *The people of South Vietnam: How they feel about the war*. Private publication, March 13, 1967.

Festinger, L. *A theory of cognitive dissonance*. New York: Harper, 1957.

Heider, F. *The psychology of interpersonal relations*. New York: Wiley, 1958.

Hilsman, R. *To move a nation*. New York: Delta, 1968.

Holsti, O. R. Cognitive dynamics and images of the enemy. *Journal of International Affairs*, 1967, 21, 16-39.

Lyons, E. *Our secret allies: The peoples of Russia*. New York: Duell, Sloan, & Pearce, 1954.

Pike, D. *Viet Cong*. Cambridge, Massachusetts: MIT Press, 1966.

Pike, D. *War, peace, and the Viet Cong*. Cambridge, Massachusetts: MIT Press, 1969.

White, R. K. Images in the context of international conflict: Soviet perceptions of the U.S. and the USSR. In Kelman H. C. (Ed.), *International behavior*. New York: Holt, 1965.

White, R. K. Misperception and the Vietnam War. *Journal of Social Issues*, 1966, **22**(3), 1-167.

White, R. K. Three not-so-obvious contributions of psychology to peace. (Kurt Lewin Memorial Address, 1969) *Journal of Social Issues*, 1969, **25**(4), 23-39.

White, R. K. *Nobody wanted war: Misperception in Vietnam and other wars.* New York: Doubleday, paperback, 1970. Pp. 386. Rev. and expanded ed. of a 1968 hardcover ed. of the same book.

Author Index

Numbers in italics refer to the page on which the complete references are listed.

Subject Index